Theology of Money

NEW SLANT: RELIGION, POLITICS, ONTOLOGY

A series edited by Creston Davis, Philip Goodchild, and Kenneth Surin

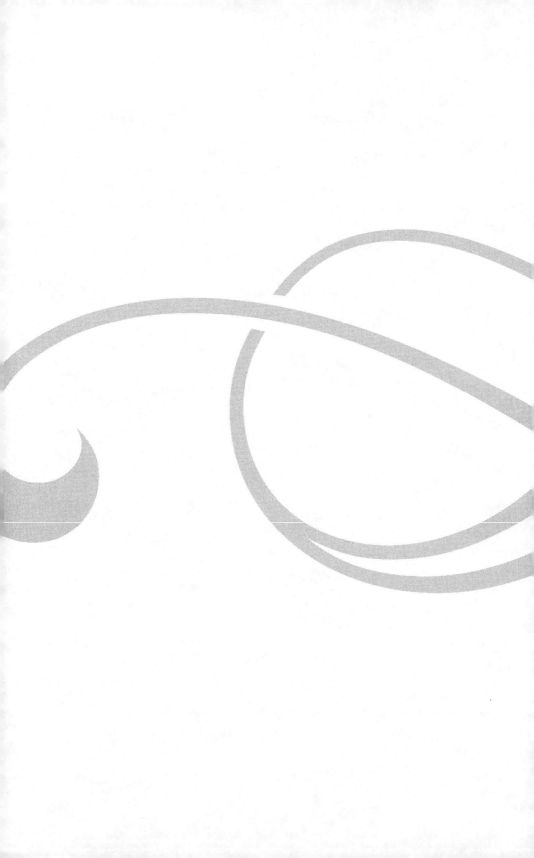

THEOLOGY

OF

MONEY

Philip Goodchild

DUKE UNIVERSITY PRESS
Durham & London 2009

© 2009 Duke University Press
All rights reserved.
Printed in the United States of America on acid-free paper ∞
Designed by Jennifer Hill
Typeset in Arno Pro by Tseng Information Systems, Inc.

Library of Congress Cataloging-in-Publication Data
appear on the last printed page of this book.

Money, which represents the prose of life, and which is hardly spoken of in parlors without an apology, is, in its effects and laws, as beautiful as roses.

RALPH WALDO EMERSON, 1844

Would you know what money is, go borrow some.

GEORGE HERBERT, 1640

CONTENTS

A PARABLE—
ON THE WISH TO BE IMMORTAL

If one were only rich, in a luxury mansion, surrounded by gardens and servants, enjoying the finest of foods, the most subtle of wines, the warmest of friends, the most generous of lovers, freed from care over maintenance of property, for all could be instantly replaced, freed from work, there being no need to work, freed from obligations, there being no need to seek favor, until one dismissed the servants, for there needed no servants, sold the mansion, for there needed no mansion, abandoned friends and lovers, for there needed no friends and lovers, and renounced even the knowledge that one was a homeless wanderer before one's last penny had already gone.

ALL HUMAN LIFE and endeavor aims at some form of human flourishing, welfare, or wealth. A distinctive feature of religious life is that flourishing is normally attained by means of a renunciation: time spent on productive activity or enjoyment is interrupted by ritual or sacred activity. Spiritual bonds and goals take precedence over worldly bonds and goals. Duty takes precedence over desire, or love of God takes precedence over love of self and others. Indeed, in religious life it is believed that flourishing does not lie within human power alone. It is achieved through the aid of some special divine grace, ancestral blessing, or sacred power. This detour in the path toward wealth opens up a realm for the transcendent, conceived perhaps in terms of grace, mystery, the sacred, special insight, authority, spiritual presence, or another world. Flourishing has a transcendent source that is activated only through a prior renunciation.

The distinctive feature of a secular age, as Charles Taylor has recently pointed out (in *A Secular Age*), would appear to be the removal of any collectively agreed on goals beyond human flourishing. Enlightenment would appear to be the liberation of human activity from superstitious observances and regulations. There is only work, enjoyment, and recuperation, all in the service of flourishing. What most concerns humanity are the conditions under which flourishing may take place, and if there is any postponement of pleasure, this is merely to ensure that these conditions can be preserved and enhanced. The religious detour is replaced by an economic detour. Attention is turned from the divine to the mundane. Human fulfillment, moral practice, and social cohesion are no longer founded on divine authority and grace. They are founded on human endeavor and agreement.

This is a familiar story. Whether religious or not, we now all live in a secular age insofar as the practical conditions for our wealth are purely mundane. This story can be explained in terms of a series of contrasts: between spiritual authority and natural law, between transcendent order and immanent system, between duty and freedom, between hierarchy and democracy, between faith and science, between spiritual and material progress. Historical progress from the first term of the contrast to the second may be narrated in two ways: either as the removal of old illusions or as the construction of new knowledge and institutions. In either case, it is a story of the self-liberation of humanity.

There is something unconvincing about these narratives of emancipation. Most lives remain preoccupied with material needs and social obligations. Perhaps these are obligations to clients, employers, landlords, or creditors. Emancipation is not yet complete in practice, and it never will be in a society of mutual dependence. Moreover, emancipation itself requires faith. The self-liberation of humanity presupposes that the natural order behaves in a stable way, that human decision has the power to manipulate this order to its will, and that the authority ensuring social cohesion and cooperation can be decided by human contract. In premodern society, there was insufficient evidence for such faith: the stability of nature, the power to shape the world, and confidence in human cooperation were all too fragile, subject to the dangers of accident, disease, aggression, or curse. Only religious faith provided the hope of security. Whence, then, came the confidence for humanity to venture out of the protective order of religious faith that was the only source of stability and authority? Was it merely a matter of sifting, through experience, the true conditions of stability and prosperity from the false? Was it purely a matter of turning attention from ideas to real interactions within the world? Or was the rise of modernity a transformation rather than a rejection of faith? If there is no purely immanent system, then are the dichotomies that structure narratives of progress and emancipation anything more than illusory?

One may question the dichotomy between the religious and the economic. Of course, the great preoccupation of human life and endeavor has been with procuring its own survival and flourishing, and the basic categories through which the world is experienced are furnished daily by these habits and practices. Yet this preoccupation cannot simply be contrasted with religious preoccupations. When the greatest contributor as well as the greatest threat to human welfare is humanity itself, then the conditions that enable collective welfare must include those observances which regulate human conduct. An economy that ensures effective distribution is the source of human flourishing, and a religious life that authorizes the obligations and regulations through which this distribution occurs is the guarantor of economic life. Religious preoccupations have been, in past societies, a major part of the conservation of economic life and practice, for human flourishing is not obtained simply by material means. Human welfare is dependent on cooperation and material distribution, and in most societies the authority that lends credit to such practices has ultimately been religious. Those who renounce the world in favor of the transcendent are in practice just as concerned with the source of material welfare as those who labor in the fields, for they are concerned with the conditions of trust and authority. A religious age is no less concerned with the conditions of its existence than a secular age.

The great transformation of modernity, then, involves a change that is at once both religious and economic and should be conceived under both registers simultaneously. The effective basis for trust and authority that daily ensures material and economic cooperation is no longer local custom or authoritative religious prescription. Distribution has to be effected by its own immanent, independent, or self-regulating order — the market. The story of modernity has been narrated by the economic historian Karl Polanyi (in *The Great Transformation*) as the reorganization of society according to the ideal of the self-regulating market. Indeed, the separation of the economic sphere of life from the political and religious spheres is what the notion of a self-regulating market means. Just as the independent order of nature is the basis for science separate from faith, and so the theoretical condition for atheism, the independent sphere of the market is the practical condition for atheism. While it is possible to imagine a godless universe in theory, it is impossible to live without effective distribution. Therefore, it is only when a self-ordering system of distribution is achieved that atheism becomes a live option. Only under these conditions are religious observances made redundant in economic life.

Several historical impulses came together to create the conditions for a secular age. One impulse was the industrial development of mechanical inventions and the use of fossil fuels. This increased the productive power of humanity so that it could make the natural order stable and manipulable. Yet the motive for increasing production was not for the individual producer's use but, rather, for exchange: industrialization could not have occurred without a commercial society organized for trade. A second impulse, then, was the promotion of market relations, developed primarily for long-distance trade, as the principal means of distribution within a society. This was achieved by deregulation—the active intervention of sovereign authority against prior customs and observances. Yet the question remains as to whether a market, once liberated and promoted by state power, will itself grow to infiltrate and regulate the other spheres of social interaction. While there may be no limits to the desire for gain and pleasure that drives growth, production and consumption remain restricted by effective demand. Desire has no economic power in a market without money or credit. Indeed, a market that regulates production and distribution through prices exists only on the basis of money as the common commodity against which values are compared and through which exchanges are enacted.

There is, therefore, a third impulse alongside production and consumption that drives the transformation of economic life: the authority of money. Nevertheless, a market is not simply grown by more money, since demand becomes less effective resulting in inflation. Similarly, a society as a whole cannot increase in wealth through increased production if there is insufficient demand, expressed in the form of money, for additional products. The third impulse is the invention of a new kind of money, one that is created as a debt. A debt is an obligation, a commitment to economic activity, and a commitment to repay in money. It is a promise, and money holds its value as long as this promise is trusted. Once debt becomes a medium of exchange, a widely circulating form of money, then the entire nature of the market changes with it. A market based on debt money is an immanent system of credits and liabilities, of debts and obligations, and it is capable of unlimited growth. It ensures participation and cohesion, with promises of wealth and threats of exclusion, through a system of social obligations. Debt takes over the role of religion in economic life.

Money is the condition for liberty and prosperity. Without money, one is dependent on others; with money, one can demand their service. Money calls forth increased production by opening the possibility of unlimited accumulation, by enabling investment in the means of production, and by giving an effective authority to demand. Yet money does not provide a source for social cohesion until it brings with it an obligation: the obligation of debt. If in religious life people renounce enjoyment to achieve spiritual goals, then in modern economic life people renounce their property, labor, and time in the pursuit of money. Modern secular life is ascetic like religious life, even if it has its moments of hedonism. Human flourishing is still ensured by a detour. A preoccupation with the conditions of one's life is now a preoccupation with money. Through its use in structuring everyday life and practice, money lends its shape to the categories of modern life and thought.

Local cult, transcendent God, or mobile debt: each may function as the basis of authority and the source of sustenance in daily life. There is, however, a decisive difference between traditional religions and the use of money. While the transcendent remains shrouded in mystery, a source of power and authority that is not subject to human manipulation, money remains rather mundane. If one thinks of money at all, it is as an object of human control, a tool expressing human will. One does not consider the nature of its power. While the goal of spiritual life is to attain consciousness of the divine order and meaning of things, the goal of economic life is merely wealth and enjoyment. Money is regarded as the means, human flourishing as the end. It is in modern life that alienation is complete and the consciousness of humanity departs entirely from the conditions of its existence. It is in modern life, rather than religious life, where ideology is most fully instantiated. If modern economic life differs essentially from religious life, it does so not because it possesses a truer understanding of its conditions of existence or of practical efficacy. The essential difference lies in its lack of consciousness. There is no need to venerate or even consider money, the source of the modern age. There is merely a practical need to make money. The economic detour is seen as purely a detour. At the same time, the quest for profit and the growth of debt are unlimited. The only end for human life, which in practice is the making of money, is misperceived as human flourishing.

This book, on the theology of money, is therefore an anachronism: it is written to bring our collective faith back to consciousness. This is not a task for economists, for there is no practical economic need for it. Such an understanding is itself an interruption of practical life, for it is not the case that by raising our consciousness we can simply choose to be different. We are dependent on a complex web of needs and obligations, mediated by money, over which no one is master—evident from the numerous financial crises that afflict us all. Instead, the quest to understand the power of the beliefs enshrined in money is an attempt to pursue a traditional theological quest, to understand the conditions of existence within our contemporary age. In so doing, the aim is to show how human life and endeavor are shaped by practices of contracting, accounting, and evaluating. The purpose is to expose such practices in all their contingency, irrationality, arbitrariness, and violence; to enable us to ridicule their pretensions, marvel over their powers, and weep over their ultimate consequences. For the dangers of chaos, instability, and possessive spectral forces have not departed from the modern world. The aim is to show what devotions, sacrifices, and convictions lie at the basis of contemporary existence, and to call for a new effort of devotion, sacrifice, and conviction that may evoke another social order.

The global order of credit capitalism found its birthplace in England and this book has been written within the economic context of a contemporary English university. Among other things this has necessitated an early publication in England to meet the requirements of the national Research Assessment Exercise, and so to contribute to the economic viability of my institution, department, and position. In the contemporary English university, thought is regulated by its price in the form of the funding it can attract. Yet the global order of credit capitalism has been propagated most forthrightly by the United States, and I am therefore delighted to commend the book's publication and distribution to a global audience through Duke University Press. My thanks are due to the conscientious readers for the Press, to Reynolds Smith and his editorial team, and to all who have shown and will show patience with this book and with the future of its ideas.

PHILIP GOODCHILD
Nottingham, February 2008

Introduction

A PARABLE

And the Spirit immediately drove Jesus out into the wilderness. He was in the wilderness forty days, and he was with the wild beasts, and the angels waited on him. He fasted forty days and forty nights, and afterwards he was famished. Money came and said to him, "If you are the Son of God, command these stones to become bread. For I would do as much for the least of masters whom I serve." But he answered, "It is written, 'One does not live by bread alone, but by every word that comes from the mouth of God.'"

Then Money took him to the holy city and placed him on the pinnacle of the temple, saying to him, "If you are the Son of God, throw yourself down, for you can command your angels to bear you up, so that you do not dash your foot against a stone. For I would do this much for the greatest of masters whom I serve." Jesus said to him, "Again it is written, 'Do not put the Lord your God to the test.'"

Again, Money took him to a very high mountain and showed him all the kingdoms of the world and their splendor, and said to him, "To you I will give their glory and all this authority, for it has been given over to me, and I give it to anyone I please. If you, then, choose to master me, it will all be yours." Jesus said to him, "Be gone, Money! For it is written, 'Worship the Lord your God, and serve only him.' One cannot serve God and Mammon."

As Money departed, he replied, "If the owner is unwilling to sell, one may always pay someone to remove him. I will go seek out Judas Iscariot. For though some seek bread, some seek power, some seek the world, and some seek to leave it, most will accept money instead."

And suddenly the earth was opened, and the fire of the infernal mint was seen rising up to touch Money so that his face shone like the sun, and the voice of Mammon came from the depths, saying, "This is my son, my beloved, upon whom my fire rests. Whosoever eats of his flesh and blood will have life in all its fullness."

JESUS OF NAZARETH

THE TEACHINGS OF Jesus of Nazareth on wealth stand out as distinct within the history of religions. Many others have taught and practiced asceticism, the renunciation of worldly ways and pleasures. Jesus, by contrast, warned against wealth while feasting and drinking himself. The kingdom of God was a feast promised for those without wealth. Such teachings on wealth make sense within the tradition of Hebrew prophets who protested against theft, exploitation, and the appropriation of property. The warnings against riches are economic: the true meaning of corruption of the soul through avarice is the debasement of the lives of others. This economic meaning of Jesus's sayings may be evaded if they are interpreted individually; when surveyed together, however, the meaning is both radical and transparent.

Jesus announced a gospel of good news to the poor (Luke 4.18).[1] Woes were proclaimed to the rich and blessings to the poor (Luke 6.20–26). Jesus's followers were enjoined to sell their possessions and give to the poor (Luke 12.33). Keeping the Ten Commandments was insufficient for a landowner; selling possessions and giving to the poor were also required (Mark 10.21). It was impossible for the rich to enter the kingdom of God (Mark 10.25). Jesus sent out his followers to travel without money (Mark 6.8). He did not habitually carry spare money (Matt. 17.27, 22.19), and his disciples had a common purse carried by the traitor Judas Iscariot, who was accused of stealing from it (John 12.6). Wealth was described as "unrighteous" (Luke 16.9). Prudent economic behavior such as planning and accumulation were rejected (Luke 12.13–21, 13.22–31). The use of wealth was regarded as minor in contrast to the ways of God (Luke 16.11). The extraction of taxes, the fundamental activity that maintained the political power of the Roman Empire and the Herodians, belonged to a different sphere from the service of God (Mark 12.17). Similarly, the children of God were regarded as free from paying the temple tax (Matt. 17.26). When Jesus attacked the center of religious power in his society, it was the tables of the moneychangers that he overthrew (Mark 11.15). All debts were to be forgiven (Matt. 6.12); hence, even the principle of contract, the fundamental political power of civil society, was to be laid aside. In declaring that one cannot serve God and wealth (Matt. 6.24), Jesus set the divine power of the Kingdom of God in the starkest opposition to one of the most fundamental principles of both worldly and religious power—the power of money. Such is the radical significance of his teaching. Jesus's betrayal by Judas for the sake of money (Matt. 26.15) was a poignant rejection of the heart of his teaching.

Jesus may therefore be regarded as among the most radical of religious political thinkers. The fifth-century British heretic Pelagius explained such teaching with the observation that the chief sources of wealth in the ancient world were extortion, robbery, and the inheritance of the benefits of extortion and robbery.[2] Jesus's protest was at once political, moral, and religious. In a precapitalist economy, it was evident to all that inequalities in wealth largely arose from the accumulation of the products of others' labor, whether through theft, slavery, tribute, patronage, taxation, or debt. Accumulated wealth was stored and exchanged in the form of money; without money, there is less scope for such unequal accumulation. Christian theology has attempted to evade the uncomfortable legacy of the social significance of money by internalizing Jesus's message: it is love of money, not money itself, that has been regarded as the root of all evil (1 Tim. 6.10). Christian theology has preferred to concentrate on the opposition of the world to Jesus, expressed in his execution as a criminal or in the scandal of proclaiming a crucified itinerant preacher as the son of God. In doing so, it has tended to overlook the radical opposition of God to the world, or divine judgment, proclaimed by Jesus himself: "Woe to you who are rich" (Luke 6.24). The proclamation of a new savior belonged well within the hopes, desires, and political norms of the ancient world, even if the specific choice of a humble and crucified savior gave offence. By contrast, a proclamation against the most fundamental and pervasive ways of the world was nothing less than a claim to reveal a different underlying principle or power: the rule or kingdom of God. Jesus opposed the power of God to the power of money. Every time Christianity has worshiped Christ enthroned as a heavenly Caesar, it has repeated Iscariot's betrayal of Jesus.

Theology cannot be neutral here. As Saint Paul well understood, the central question of theology is that of the essence of the power to be used in final judgment (e.g., 1 Cor. 15.24). If theology is to judge the ways of the world by the power of truth and goodness, then it must explain truth and goodness in accordance with their own specific power. Theology, concerned with the ultimate criteria of life, is the most fundamental and radical inquiry. It attempts to discern how truth, goodness, and life come to be constituted. It offers to the world a vision of life interpreted according to the richest categories of meaning. It has the duty to invest life with the deepest layers of spiritual wealth—that is, it has to determine what is the nature of true wealth. This is the vocation for theology, whether Christian or not, and it is the most fundamental inquiry, whether pursued by believers, nonbelievers, or no one at all. Worldly wealth, which can only measure exchange value in terms of money, is to be judged against a new revelation of divine power.

Such a judgment is inevitably surprising: divine power is an eschatological replacement of all fundamental principles. In this life, material wealth is the source of all benefits, all delights, all investments, all sustenance, all welfare, and all charity. Few ascetics have questioned its necessity for those who remain in the world. To question its benefits risks charges of insanity. The quest for wealth is the one practical activity that unites the diverse people of the contemporary world. It is the means or precondition for undertaking all subsequent worthy ventures or enjoying all pleasures. As George Bernard Shaw put it, "Money is indeed the most important thing in the world; and all sound and successful personal and national morality should have this fact for its basis. Every teacher or twaddler who denies it or suppresses it, is an enemy of life. Money controls morality."[3] In a capitalist economy, where accumulation occurs through the use of money, the moral and political relations from which wealth derives are no longer directly evident. The equitable relation of voluntary trade appears to embody justice. To oppose money as the fundamental principle of the social order is therefore deeply immoral and unjust from the perspective of that order. This opposition is hostile to just standards of measure and hinders opportunities for accumulation. To question the pursuit of wealth is to set oneself against all common sense, all agreement, all political power, and all practicality. Moreover, since wealth gives access to power, to question the pursuit of wealth is to abandon all power, dooming oneself to a futile quest. It is little wonder that Christian theologians have sought to accommodate themselves to the world rather than risk their entire heritage by abandoning all power.

Nevertheless, the strategy of internalization to accommodate oneself to wealth betrays an infidelity. Jesus appears to have been quite content to enjoy the hospitality of the wealthy, to allow others to provide for him out of their wealth, and to consume to the extent that he and his followers were accused of gluttony (Matt. 9.10–11; Luke 8.3; Matt. 11.19). Feasting provides the paradigmatic symbol for the arrival of the Kingdom of God. It was not, however, the subjective enjoyment of wealth that was his target; it was wealth as a principle of power or judgment. Jesus's opposition to the service of wealth marked the greatest differentiation from the ways of the world. In this difference lies an opportunity to explore how the value of values may be determined. Jesus's announcements raise the most fundamental of theological problems: what is the value of values? Do our scales of evaluation express true values? The true nature of theological inquiry perhaps only became clear after Friedrich Nietzsche, the self-proclaimed Antichrist, raised the problem of the revaluation of all values.

It is nothing less than a revaluation of all values that Jesus himself proclaimed. Money, as the measure against which all things are priced, is the contemporary principle of the value of values. A revaluation of all values may start by exploring money. It need be a question not of deciding in advance for or against money, or for or against Jesus, but of noting the significance of money in the determination of the value of values and inquiring into its true nature. Money, above all else, has seemed to be indispensable: while Jesus's following was initially formed as a community of shared possessions, voluntary poverty, and gift exchange, it has repeatedly abandoned this central practical ideal. Perhaps his followers were right to do so. A theology of money must determine the principles, the value of values, through which judgments of economic behavior can be formulated. For this, Jesus did more than proclaim an opposition; he also illuminated some of its principles:

Do not store up for yourselves treasures on earth, where moth and rust consume and where thieves break in and steal; but store up for yourselves treasures in heaven, where neither moth nor rust consumes and where thieves do not break in and steal. For where your treasure is, there your heart will be also.

The eye is the lamp of the body. So, if your eye is healthy, your whole body will be full of light; but if your eye is unhealthy, your whole body will be full of darkness. If then the light in you is darkness, how great is the darkness!

No one can serve two masters; for a slave will either hate the one and love the other, or be devoted to the one and despise the other. You cannot serve God and wealth. (Matt. 6.19–24)

God and wealth are set in competition; for time, in terms of "storing up treasure"; for attention, in terms of the health of the eye; and for devotion, in terms of service. Our evaluations are primarily expressed not by what we say or simply by what we do, but by how we pray—the determination of our time, attention, and devotion.[4] This is where the power of money is to be sought: not simply in the worship or accumulation of wealth for its own sake, but in the way time, attention, and devotion are shaped by the demands of the social institution of money.

All religions, in essence, direct and distribute time, attention, and devotion. Religions enrich life by establishing patterns for living. If there is an opposition between God and money, then fundamentally it comes down to this: wealth contains its own principles according to which time, attention, and devotion are allocated. In a society organized primarily for the pursuit of wealth, nothing could seem more evident and unquestionable than that time, attention, and devotion should be allocated to the pursuit of wealth. It is the very obligation to do so that constitutes the spiritual power of money. It is the very obligation to do so that is the object of a theology of money.

The human sciences of wealth do not study how time is spent; they merely observe the effects of allocations of time, attention, and devotion. While they study the outcome of economic activity, the investigation of the powers and principles by which time, attention, and devotion are distributed should belong, by contrast, to the discipline of theology. A theology of money is an exploration of the nature and effects of money's mysterious power.

The problem that lies before us is whether there is something intrinsic to the nature of money that directly opposes God, justice, or nature. "God" may be invoked here as a symbol for the order of nature—the ultimate criteria of power, truth, and goodness; the source of the value of values. Theists and atheists may disagree over the unity, logic, and metaphysics of such a symbol, and over the value of values itself. However, they rarely disagree that something plays the role of the source of the value of values, whether or not the symbol "God" is used. Once it is discovered that money does indeed veil the source of the value of values, a second problem results: how may the value of values become manifest in human life? These two problems form the agenda for this study.

THE BANK OF ENGLAND

In 1694, when printed tracts declaring the content of true belief were circulating throughout England, a new gospel was announced. It was a gospel of such significance that its tracts are even now carried on a daily basis by most English (and Welsh) subjects: "I promise to pay the bearer on demand the sum of twenty pounds." The Bank of England, formed by an act of Parliament at the instigation of William Paterson, provided a permanent loan of 1.2 million pounds at 8 percent interest to King William III for his religious wars. At the same time, the Bank also provided a note issue, in units of 20 pounds, of the same amount, guaranteed by the security of the government's promise to pay through taxation. Such notes were issued as loans to worthy private borrowers. The original subscribers to the Bank would receive interest on these loans, as well as on the loan to the king. Money was effectively created in excess of the original deposit.

The establishment of the Bank of England inaugurated the period when credit effectively functioned as money. Since metal coins had always been tokens of value, the creation of money as credit does not so much change as reveal the essence of money. The credit theory of money, propounded by Mitchell Innes at the beginning of the twentieth century, states that "a sale and purchase is the exchange of a commodity for a credit. From this main theory springs the sub-theory that the value of credit or money does not depend on the value of any metal or metals, but on the right which the creditor acquires to 'payment,' that is to say, to the satisfaction of credit, and on the obligation of the debtor to 'pay' his debt, and conversely on the right of the debtor to release himself from his debt by the tender of an equivalent debt owed by the creditor, and the obligation of the creditor to accept this tender in satisfaction of credit."[5]

The creation of money has been notably explained, in the context of Holland rather than England, by the economist John Kenneth Galbraith:

The process by which banks create money is so simple that the mind is repelled. Where something so important is involved, a deeper mystery seems only decent. The deposits of the Bank of Amsterdam . . . were, according to the instruction of the owner, subject to transfer to others in settlement of accounts. (This had long been a convenience provided by the Bank's private precursors.) The coin on deposit served no less as money by being in a bank and being subject to transfer by the stroke of a pen.

Inevitably it was discovered — as it was by the conservative burghers of Amsterdam as they reflected incestuously on their own needs as directors of the Dutch East India Company — that another stroke of the pen would give a borrower from the bank, as distinct from a creditor of the original depositor, a loan from the original and idle deposit. It was not a detail that the bank would have the interest on the loan so made. The original depositor could be told that his deposit was subject to such use — and perhaps be paid for it. The original deposit still stood to the credit of the original depositor. But there was now also a new deposit from the proceeds of the loan. Both deposits could be used to make payments, be used as money. Money had thus been created. The discovery that the banks could so create money came very early in the development of banking. There was that interest to be earned. Where such reward is waiting, men have a natural instinct for innovation.

There was an alternative opportunity involving bank notes, one that was to be wonderfully exploited in the eventual American Republic. That was to give the borrower not a deposit but a note redeemable in the hard currency that had been placed in the bank as capital or as a sedentary deposit. With this note the borrower could make his payment: the recipient of such payment might, instead of redeeming the note for cash, use it for his payments, and so on ad infinitum. Meanwhile back at the bank interest was being received on the original loan. One day, perhaps, the note would be returned and redeemed for the hard cash of the original deposit. But by then the borrower would have repaid his loan, also in hard money. All would be well, and interest would have been earned. There was a chance also that the note would continue its passage from hand to hand and never be returned for collection. The loan which led to its emission would earn interest and in due course be repaid. The note meanwhile would continue its rounds. Against the original coin that allowed of the original loan, no claim would ever be entered.[6]

Such banking practices emerged in Florence, Genoa, Venice, and Amsterdam. They were inevitably the cause of cycles of euphoria and panic, dependent on the fluctuations of confidence in the bank. The Bank of England was exceptional in providing monetary stability.[7] The value of money was underwritten by the power of the state to raise taxes, and since the Bank's notes were readily and promptly redeemed in hard coin, they were not presented for redemption. Credit came to occupy the secure monetary space formerly occupied by coinage alone.[8] The Bank gradually took over the money supply and the responsibility to stabilize the value of money. In the words of Galbraith, the Bank of England is, "in all respects, to money as St. Peter's is to the Faith."[9] It became the model on which all other central banks were based and was pivotal in Great Britain's rise to global dominance during the eighteenth century and nineteenth century, just as the U.S. Federal Reserve became pivotal in the twentieth century.

Note the confluence of counterbalancing and cooperating forces in such a system. First, there is the demand for unproductive government expenditure in forms such as warfare, which open up new regions for profit and exploitation. Destruction and excessive consumption become preconditions for the creation of wealth by contributing to demand. Second, in warfare there is the comparative strategic advantage of having a secure source of funding to pay for soldiers, equipment, and invention. Transportable and convertible wealth, in the form of a currency whose value extends beyond the political territory of issue, is the "sinews of war." Government expenditure, then, may be balanced by the greater profits enabled by strategic advantage recovered through taxation. Such growth in the public-sector economy may also be balanced by growth in the private sector. Third, there is the ongoing demand for capital to engage in productive investment. Such demand is present wherever opportunities for profit emerge. Fourth, there is the payment of interest on capital as a result of increased profitability due to new opportunities created. While assets and liabilities cancel themselves out in such a system, the absolute size of the economy grows. In short, both supply and demand increase in the public and private sectors in such a system. The original investors in the Bank of England lent the same money to the state and to civil society. The security of the loan to civil society was guaranteed by the state in the form of future taxation; the security of the loan to the state was guaranteed by economic growth in civil society. It was a brilliant, self-confirming system of mutual dependence and benefit.

The public creation of money is the source of prosperity, stimulating growth. Indeed, the creation of new money is regarded by some commentators as one of the principal causes of the industrial revolution and the emergence of modernity.[10] Joseph Schumpeter has explained what is essential here: the entrepreneur is not necessarily a possessor of wealth. Indeed, the entrepreneur is the typical debtor in capitalist society.[11] Schumpeter goes so far as to say that credit is such a central part of the capitalist engine that the rest of the system cannot be understood without it.[12] Moreover:

The practically unlimited demand for credit is matched by a practically unlimited supply of credit. . . . The banks can always grant further loans, since the larger amounts going out are then matched by larger amounts coming in. The demand for credit makes possible not only itself, but also a corresponding supply; and every supply makes possible a corresponding demand, so that supply and demand in this case do not confront each other as independent forces. . . . The productive demand for any commodity, e.g. wool, is limited, at constant quantity of money, by the falling probability of processing continually increasing quantities; by contrast, demand for credit is self-propagating, in that the consequences of its expansion and increasing satisfaction go on creating the economic conditions for even more credit demand.[13]

Capital growth begins with borrowing for investment, for all economic activity is limited by the supply of money. There is always so much more that could be done if only more money were available. As Samuel Butler put it, "It has been said that the love of money is the root of all evil. The want of money is so quite as truly."[14] If money can be created in the form of loans for the purpose of profitable activity, then effective limits to economic growth are removed. There is no shortage of money when it can be replaced by credit and repaid at a profit. The consequence was nothing less than Karl Polanyi's "great transformation."[15] Production for the sake of profit rather than use became the dominant motivation for social activity and interaction. Capitalism — its growth and its globalization — is explained by banking. Economic activity, formerly a limited segment of social life, came to predominate over all other aspects of social life, including religion. The preachers' declamations against the evils of usury and the love of money were unheeded by those who saw the evidence of prosperity brought about through profit.[16] As William Cobbett was to observe in 1829:

Time has taught me that public credit means the contracting of debts which a nation never can pay; and I have lived to see this goddess produce effects, in my country, which Satan himself never could have produced. It is a very bewitching goddess; and not less fatal for her influence in private than in public affairs. It has been carried in this latter respect to such a pitch, that scarcely any transaction, however low and inconsiderable, takes place in any other way.[17]

Prior to the modern world, the economic sphere was bounded by the limits of the production of value by human labor, on the one hand, and the finite amount of money in circulation, on the other. In the modern world, however, the limits of production have been partially overcome by harnessing the energy stored in fossil fuels and the elements. At the same time, the finitude of currency has been overcome by treating signs of monetary value as themselves valuable, ensuring the value of newly created money by issuing it in the form of loans, attached to debts. Rates of production and rates of interest escape finitude by compound growth. Production for the sake of profit replaces production for the sake of use.

It is easy to observe how this shift naturally leads to secularization and a direct opposition between God and money. Where God promises eternity, money promises the world. Where God offers a delayed reward, money offers a reward in advance. Where God offers himself as grace, money offers itself as a loan. Where God offers spiritual benefits, money offers tangible benefits. Where God accepts all repentant sinners who truly believe, money may be accepted by all who are willing to trust in its value. Where God requires conversion of the soul, money empowers the existing desires and plans of the soul. Money has the advantages of immediacy, universality, tangibility, and utility. Money promises freedom and gives a down payment on the promise of prosperity.

Money exercises a spectral power that exceeds all merely human powers. Adapting itself to any desire, it also shapes desire. First, the value of money is transcendent. It is a promise, taken on faith, and only realized to the extent that this faith is acted out in exchange. One cannot hold the value of money in one's hand, even if one can use that value to pay for things. "The eye has never seen, nor the hand touched a dollar. All that we can touch or see is a promise to pay or satisfy a debt due for an amount called a dollar."[18]

Second, money is both a means of payment and a measure of prices. As a measure of prices, money endows all things with a universal value: the price is the same, whoever is the buyer. Yet as a means of payment, money grants the power of effective demand only to those with money. To achieve what one values, one must value money first as the means of access to what one desires. Since it is the means by which all other social values may be realized, it posits itself as the supreme value. Nothing is more liquid, more exchangeable, or more valuable than money. Whatever one's own values, one must value money first as the means of access to all other values.[19]

Third, money is only "value in motion." One cannot achieve profitability without investing one's money. The value of assets is determined not by their intrinsic worth but by their expected yield, their anticipated rate of return. The value of assets is determined by speculative projections. Moreover, even if these anticipations prove misguided, at every stage the value of assets is determined by the next wave of anticipations about the future. Thus, the future never ultimately arrives: it is purely ideal. Financial value is essentially a degree of hope, expectation, trust, or credibility. Just as paper currency is never cashed in, so the value of assets is never realized. It is future or transcendent. Being transcendent to material and social reality, yet also being the pivot around which material and social reality is continually reconstructed, financial value is essentially religious.[20]

Fourth, wealth brings access to power: extrinsically through military superiority, access to information, sway over public consciousness, political influence, and selective funding; and intrinsically through investments, profits, growth, favorably negotiated contracts, and liberation from the constraints of the natural necessity and social responsibility that limit the economic freedom of those without wealth. As a result, the power of wealth grows exponentially in a cycle of profitability. Yet since wealth can grow only if it devotes itself to making profits and paying back debts, it necessarily depletes the resources required to meet natural necessities and social responsibilities — in particular, the needs of subsistence and sustainability. As the condition for all social activity, the imperative of sustaining the money system and creating wealth take priority over the need for sustaining the environment, population, or religion.

Fifth, speculative profits can be made only on the basis of profits extracted from production and consumption, and to achieve this, an increasing quantity of the world's physical resources must be appropriated for production, exchange, and consumption through the colonization and commodification of the world.

Sixth, increased production and profits require increased investment and debt. While production is of commodities, debts and interest are repaid in the form of money. Increased production can lead to the repayment of debts only if there is more money to pay for them; yet money can be created only in the form of further loans or else it is inflationary. As a result, the global economy, since the founding of the Bank of England, has been progressively enslaved to an increasing spiral of debt. The global economy is driven by a spiral of debt, constrained to seek further profits and always dependent on future expansion. The spectral power of money lies ultimately in its nature as debt.

An anthropologist's judgment on the nature of modernity would identify the value of money as the modern religion, the transcendent principle of the social order.[21] As Mary Douglas explains, money is ritual activity:

The metaphor of money admirably sums up what we want to assert of ritual. Money provides a fixed, external, recognisable sign for what would be confused, contradictable operations; ritual makes visible external signs of internal states. Money mediates transactions; ritual mediates experience, including social experience. Money provides a standard for measuring worth; ritual standardizes situations, and so helps to evaluate them. Money makes a link between the present and the future, so does ritual. The more we reflect on the richness of the metaphor, the more it becomes clear that this is no metaphor. Money is only an extreme and specialised type of ritual.[22]

Since the value of money is a purely ideal construct, the religion of money has its own theology. Its principles are fourfold: money is the promise of value on which actual value may be advanced; money is the supreme value against which all other values may be measured; money is a speculative value whose intrinsic worth waits to be demonstrated; and money is a debt or social obligation that requires that social activity be continually reordered around increasing profit and the repayment of debt, while also continually expanding the debt and the obligation. Economic globalization is the universalization of this religion through its drive for growth and power, its progressive colonization of all dimensions of life, and its commitment to growing debt. A theology of money is required to explain the distinctive nature of this spectral power in the modern world.

A THEOLOGY OF MONEY

A true theology of money, a systematic inquiry into the force of money as a system for universal evaluation, has perhaps never before been undertaken. The history of Christian reflection on money is of limited service insofar as it concentrates on subjective attitudes toward wealth;[23] the history of economic science is of limited service insofar as it concentrates on an objective science of money as a functional instrument. Money as a source of evaluation transcends distinctions between subject and object, and problematizes what we have come to expect from science. Our method must be philosophical, and a philosophical digression on the nature of modern reason is required to orient our image of thought so that it may become capable of disclosing the theology of money.

Modern thought established a threefold division between objects, subjects, and knowledge. Material reality, including functional instruments, is considered to be independent of human agency, with its desires and projects. Object and subject, however, may be mediated by a third independent term, a science that guides human agents to a more effective realization of their projects through the use of functional instruments. Nothing reinforces this threefold division between instrument, agent, and science more than the everyday use of money. Money is a passive instrument, held in one's hand, subject entirely to the use of the free human agent, yet money is easily lost unless it is used wisely, and the science of the use of money determines the most effective means to realize desires and projects. The person with money to spend enjoys a liberty and mastery over the material world. The separation of instrument, agent, and science depends on the experience of freedom of those with access to wealth and physical power. At the same time, nothing calls this threefold division into question more than the everyday struggle to acquire money, where choices are driven by material necessity and evaluations are formed on the basis of opinions about ways to acquire money. Material need and social dependence express themselves through human agency. The subject does not stand apart from matter and culture; the subject is formed and guided through matter and culture.

The mystery of how subject relates to object, how personal preference affects material reality, and how knowledge facilitates and mediates their interaction provides endless labor for philosophers. Beneath this modern division between instrument, agent, and science lie some ancient philosophical assumptions. The science of money does not claim to present money itself; it claims to present the truth about money. An Epicurean assumption is that truth consists of discrete atomic facts, rather like commodities available in a market. Truth is assumed to be individual, objective, egalitarian, passive, and relatively permanent. It is presented through independent units of evidence or data. Evidence is repeatable, public, and exchangeable; it remains the same, whoever considers it. There are, however, two striking paradoxes concerning such an assumption about truth. First, the objectivity of truth is not itself objective, for such truths are never exhibited in their individuality and permanence. No truth can be demonstrated independently of a system of thinking enacted at a particular time. The properties of individuality, objectivity, and permanence attributed to truths by induction can never be known, for truth cannot be known independently of thought. The objectivity of truth is thus a subjective presupposition. Second, the independence of truth and value imposes an evaluation. Truths based on evidence are potentially universal because they can be acknowledged at all times and in all places. Truths are for anyone or about anything. They are entirely neutral in relation to value — or, more precisely, they are independent of value or without value. Such truths, then, hold neither objectivity nor value in themselves but must be attributed objectivity and value by the thinking subject. While the objectivity, universality, and value of truth are never presented in themselves, they can be inferred by induction when evidence is repeatable, public, and exchangeable. Science, as a social practice, repeats and exchanges thought in order to lend such thoughts an exchange value. Potential truths that cannot be repeated or exchanged are devalued. Only public truths are valuable.

These paradoxes reach an acute form when one considers the science of wealth. The science of wealth concerns itself with the effects of money on value, and yet value itself is only measured in terms of money. Far from being objective, the science of wealth is constructed from the perspective of those who use money for the sake of making more money. While the science of wealth would appear to be a neutral discourse on value, it selects for an object of study only that which is exchangeable, imposing exchangeability as a value as well as a form of evaluation. Far from being neutral in relation to value, it imposes an evaluation of the benefits of exchangeability.

A Cartesian assumption underlying modern thought is that thinking the truth is independent of being true. Immanuel Kant remarked, in regard to the ontological argument for the existence of God, that his financial position was affected very differently by a hundred real dollars than by the mere concept of them.[24] Truth is meant to be grounded in evidence, not speculation. The paradox here, however, is that money itself can be created through speculation, out of pure thought. A bank may create money as a loan to a speculative investor; speculation in general raises the prices of assets; the investor can then sell his assets, repay the loan, and keep the difference in money. Thinking is no longer independent from being when both take time. When it comes to money, then, the Cartesian assumption no longer holds true. Money seems to have a dual nature. On the one hand, at any particular time it holds a determinate value; on the other hand, when invested for a period of time it may gain or lose value. It is both fixed and in motion. Similarly, in practice the construction of knowledge takes place over time. Where thinking takes time, the truth of things is proposed by projecting a time when the work of thinking is complete and truth is known. The truth is represented as an atemporal symbol that substitutes for the temporal work of thought. In practice, this symbolization of the completed work of thinking is economic. It is formed in order to save time. The essence of modern reason is saving time. Yet since the work of thought is never completed, the future in which truth is given remains a speculative projection. Where thinking takes time, this model of truth is timeless. Since such truth is independent of time and thought, it is thoughtless. It cannot express the movement of thought or the movement of money.

A Parmenidean assumption concerning the truth of things is that the truth of things is true. This is a tautology, and like all tautologies it identifies a subject with a predicate. Nevertheless, subject and predicate differ precisely as subject and predicate; for them to be identical, there would have to be a third term to which they both refer. The same thing is then for thinking and for being. We return to the problem of the mediation between thought and reality. The truth of money is that which is the same in thought and in reality. If we locate this truth on the side of reality, then the truth of this truth can never be given within thought. If we locate this truth on the side of thought, then the truth of this truth can never be given within reality. In the case of money, if we understand it as essentially a commodity, then we cannot explain its appearance within thought, both as a measure of values and as an object of creation. If, by contrast, we take money to be essentially a standard of measure or comparison, then we cannot explain its real force and value. Money is a promise or sign of value, and as such the truth of money is not self-identically true. The value of a promise is not the same as the promised value.

In the case of money, then, the neat division between instrument, agent, and science is disrupted.[25] Money circulates between and participates in all three dimensions. It is an instrument of exchange, a promise of value, and a measure of value. Moreover, while money is a symptom that exposes the artificiality of such a division, it is not the only one. Truth itself is a reality, a thought, and a promise of value. One could perhaps say the same of time, or even of God. The modern metaphysical division between material reality, subjective desire, and knowledge cannot be maintained on philosophical grounds without invoking a deus ex machina to coordinate the separate domains. Awaiting the appearance of such a deus ex machina — since in the meantime, reality, thought, and knowledge do indeed interact — one can rely on money to effect their interaction.

The purpose of this sketch of the problematics of modern notions of truth is to explain why the normal procedures for the scientific construction of knowledge do not form a part of the theology of money.[26] The Epicurean, Cartesian, and Parmenidean assumptions will not be adopted here, since they veil what is most interesting about money. Moreover, precisely the reverse assumptions will be explored. First, instead of assuming that the truth about money can be composed from a series of discrete, atomic facts—or that the truth about money is itself a fact—it will be assumed that what are of most interest about money are the concrete relations it forms and mediates within specific contexts. In particular, money takes on significance in relation to the accumulated means of production, or capital; the social institutions of market and contract in which it is used; and frameworks of credit out of which it is constructed. In relation to money, one must always ask about the concrete relations it participates in. It is necessary to construct an ecology of money.

Second, instead of assuming that the truth about money is independent of thought and time, it will be assumed that what is of most interest about money is interest and speculation itself: its temporal nature. In relation to money, one must always ask about the tendencies, processes, and orientations that are under way. Such tendencies are veritable social forces. It is necessary to construct a politics of money.

Third, instead of assuming that the truth disclosed about money is already true, it will be assumed that what is of most interest about money is what is promised by the truth of money. The essence of money will be explored as credit or debt. It belongs within an objective social sphere of obligation and belief, the sphere of religion. It is necessary to construct a theology of money.

The truth of money to be disclosed will consist not in a linear chain of inferences on the basis of evidence, but in a resolution and condensation of a multiplicity of heterogeneous considerations into a point of view. The aim is to imagine the nature of money in such a way that what matters, the truth that drives thinking, becomes perceptible. The truth of money to be disclosed will not consist in a series of propositions so much as in a series of promises—promises that, like money itself, do not merely ask to be taken on faith but express their own active potency to reorient thinking. Instead of using reason to master reality, the aim is to allow truth to determine reason as a quality of vision or awareness that shapes time, attention, and devotion. Truth has a triple orientation in a theology of money: it is a relation with what is outside thought, or that which matters; it is an orientation toward the future, or what is potential; and it is an expression of a vision and awareness.[27] These are the methodological ambitions of this study. If this practice of thought seems unclear at this stage, it may become more concrete in the study that follows. Only at the end will the reader be able to assess whether such methodological ambitions have been achieved.

The current global economic system did not derive from the founding of the Bank of England alone. The actual causes are so varied as to call into question notions of linear causality. However, the original invention of money itself was an indispensable condition. The Bank's immediate political condition was the seizure of the state by a class of English agrarian capitalists in the Glorious Revolution of 1688. The values of this class became enshrined in political concepts of the right to own property, the liberty to form contracts, and the separation of social and economic life from religious control. The work of the English philosopher John Locke was crucial in articulating and preserving these values in a number of respects. His work in epistemology established empiricism as the basis for the pursuit of a purely technical reason; his work on political philosophy provided the theory and theological legitimation for the modern capitalist state; and his work on toleration separated the commonwealth, and the sphere of political economy, from the residual theological influence of the church.[28] Locke also contributed significantly to the emergence of economics through the study of money.[29] Even though he opposed the establishment of the Bank of England on political grounds, he was one of the original subscribers, with an investment of 500 pounds. While much of Locke's work has been criticized from a number of perspectives, the conceptual framework that he established for considering knowledge, right, liberty, and money has remained dominant precisely because it has successfully lent itself to the making of money. The value of a philosophy becomes reduced to its price.

Not only is this history written into the concepts of a philosopher such as John Locke; it is also written into money itself. Inscribed on each note issued by a central bank or deposit issued as a loan is a trace of the chaos of England in the fifteenth century, sixteenth century, and seventeenth century: of warfare between nobles within and beyond England's borders; of enclosures, rack-renting, and "sheep devouring men";[30] of peasant uprisings against taxation and enclosure; of religious dissent, conflict, and martyrdom; of dissolved monasteries and stripped altars; of seafaring,

trade, piracy, and slavery; of renaissance learning and stinging social criti-
cism; of the agrarian capitalist triangle of landowners, tenant farmers, and
wage laborers; of the rising urban classes of merchants and craftspeople,
with their mutual obligations; of the ferment of radical religious and political ideas. In the case of money, such a history is encoded not as information
but as a set of spectral forces. Each time money is used, an epistemology,
a metaphysics, a politics, an ethics, and even a theology is evoked. Money
condenses the spirit of capitalism. Money did not create capitalism—the
early factories and mills were rarely funded by bank loans—yet money
transmits, propagates, and vivifies it.

The present work bears the imprint of England at the opening of the
twenty-first century. Regarding modernity with hindsight rather than anticipation, it endeavors to challenge the legacy of John Locke by means
of a reintegration of epistemology, politics, religion, and economics, the
very disciplines he succeeded in separating. While there is currently no political institution to embody and safeguard the concepts established here,
the imminent collapse of the global economic order will create a demand
for new concepts and evaluations. The only authority accompanying such
concepts and evaluations will be the credit they attract by means of the
potential they offer. The exploration of the nature of money that follows is
purely philosophical: it endeavors to remove false problems by establishing
concepts and differentiations.[31] Since the aim is to condense, crystallize,
unfold, and perceive—rather than to argue on the basis of authority and
evidence—the final result will not always indicate where influence and engagement with other writers have taken place. In particular, the intellectual
giants on the subject of money who stand over this work are Adam Smith
and Karl Marx. It is the philosophical nature of their work, their capacity
to explore implications and unfold tendencies, that has set them apart from
pure economists, as well as from more empiricist philosophers, such as
John Maynard Keynes and Amartya Sen.[32] At appropriate points, I have
sought to indicate my differences from Smith and Marx. I find neither the
model of money as "the great wheel of circulation" nor the structural analysis of money as "the general equivalent" at all convincing. Since the aim of
this inquiry is to construct a theological understanding of money, rather
than to infer from or debate with authorities, I do not feel it appropriate
to force the presentation of this work into the hegemonic modern model

of reason. It is not a question of working dialectically toward a correct point of view by means of critical engagement with the works of others. This book is not written to advise political or economic subjects as to the opinions they should hold about money. It is written to criticize established opinions, to create new concepts and values, and to lend credit to future institutions that might embody these new concepts and values.

The range of my reading while working on this project is indicated in the bibliography. Important influences that I feel should be mentioned include theoretical and sociological studies involving money, such as those of Michel Aglietta and André Orléan, Elmar Altvater, Geoffrey Ingham, Maria Mies, and Georg Simmel.[33] In addition, a variety of more radical and popular thinkers and writers on money and its contemporary implications have also stimulated my thought, including Peter Challen, Clifford Hugh Douglas, Richard Douthwaite, Silvio Gesell, Frances Hutchinson, John McMurtry, Kamran Mofid, and Michael Rowbotham. A more theological example of such radical work, focusing on property rather than money, is given by Ulrich Duchrow and Franz Hinkelammert.[34] In addition, I recall benefiting from conversations with Angus Cameron, Peter Challen, Frances Hutchinson, Lars Iyer, Karen Kilby, Will Large, David Loy, Lissa McCullough, John Milbank, Michael Northcott, Kathryn Tanner, Neil Turnbull, and Jessica Wiskus, among the many others who have responded to presentations of aspects of this argument on numerous occasions over the past ten years. None of these was presented with the full argument of the book, so none can be blamed for failing to counsel restraint.

The book is divided into three parts. Part I, "Of Politics," is introductory. It explores the context for contemporary reflection to give the discussion concrete relevance; introduces the theory of money that follows by explaining its significance for political life; and argues that the modern conception of politics, concerned primarily with the power of agency—whether in the form of the state, the individual, or the corporation—has outlived its usefulness. Drawing on Carl Schmitt's analysis of the political, it proposes that there is an overlooked element of "political energy," supplementary to human decision and physical force, that determines any actual distribution of power. This element may be filled by religious or moral motivations, or by money. Material reality has brought modernity to a state of imminent collapse due to the ecological crisis in the form of abrupt climate change and the exhaustion of supplies of fossil fuels. Part I also argues a strong form of the "end of politics" thesis—the supersession of the autonomy of the state by finance capital. This argument locates money, credit, and debt as the principal incarnations of power in the contemporary world. What is at stake here is the nature of political theory as such, which, when written to advise a democratic subject, implicitly appeals to the illusion of subjective sovereignty. Political theology, by contrast, aims to describe or modify the authority or political energy that makes decisions effective. Once political energy has been subsumed into the power of money, then an emancipatory politics can proceed only by modifying the institution of money.

Part II, "A Treatise on Money," forms the body of the book and is a philosophical investigation into the nature, function, and promise of money in relation to the means of production or capital, the social institutions of market and contract, and the formation of knowledge through accounting. It proceeds systematically by the elucidation of concepts, explicating the reasoning that underlies the theory of money presented here. Its purpose is twofold: to diagnose the errors and illusions that are the source of the most significant threats humanity faces and to illuminate the principles necessary for reforming money as a social institution.

In Chapter 3, money is explored in relation to productive capital, which is the source of all wealth. Capital, defined as the means of production that has itself been produced, includes natural as well as human-produced capital. Since money measures value in exchange rather than productive capacity, and rates of profit may be enhanced in the short term by consumption of productive capacity as well as by its accumulation, and because economic growth, survival, and victory over competitors is achieved solely through rates of profit, then an economic system based on profit and debt will necessarily deplete its own conditions of survival. This is clear from the contrast between compound rates of growth, interest, and debt; the finitude of efficiency gains; and the finite possibilities of a single planet. Economy and ecology are mathematically incompatible. Moreover, money is a form of social or constructive capital that facilitates exchange and substitution. It therefore necessarily replaces preceding social orders that facilitated and stabilized production, thereby eroding society alongside ecology. Money flows in the opposite direction to produced value in market exchange. Adam Smith's metaphor of the "great wheel of circulation," on which modern economics is largely based, is erroneous since prices have no absolute value. The conditions of the production and consumption of goods differ from the conditions of the creation and cancellation of money as debt. The money economy parasitically inhabits the "real" economy of produced goods, determining its growth and flow. The global economy is driven by the cooperation of differing drives: a drive for survival that demands the necessities of life; a drive for pleasure that seeks the benefits of produced wealth; a will to power that seeks profits alone; and the obligation of debt that enforces an increase in production and profits. Yet money, as the principle of mediation of all demands, ensures that priority is given to the creation, acquisition, maintenance, and investment of money.

In Chapter 4, money is explored in relation to the institutions of the market, private property, and contract—from which it is inseparable and which it makes possible. The market is often regarded as a paradigmatic social scene of peace, equity, balance, justice, and freedom, and yet it is dependent on the sovereign threat of the use of force to ensure that contracts are honored. Since contracts represent only the demands of those with money, sovereign force is enacted via the market against all interests not explicitly represented within contracts. The market is therefore an agent of exclusion, exploitation, and destruction. All social formations that do not honor the rights of property and contract enshrined within the market are necessarily regarded as a threat to property, peace, and justice, and so the sovereign force associated with market society must necessarily be in a state of total war against all other social forces that resist its expansionary claims. The illusions of private property, right, and exchange value derive from treating exchange atemporally instead of in the social and temporal terms of contract. It produces the illusion that a market could operate in the absence of some state, religious, or other force that ensures the honoring of contracts.

Money, regarded as an implicit contract rather than as an object of private property, is no longer analyzed purely in terms of exchange value. It is analyzed, instead, in terms of the demand for nutritional value as well as an objective social evaluation that inheres within each contract. The formal economy of exchange is understood more fully against the background of an informal economy of nutrition and time, provision and care. The result is a reconsideration of economic class, no longer in terms of relations of production, but of diverse modes of appropriation of relations of provision and time. Householders, merchants, capitalists, bankers, and speculators emerge as fundamentally different economic classes. While all classes ultimately depend on bankers for the creation of credit, bankers themselves depend on speculators who take risks on the basis of non-measurable economic opportunities. In credit capitalism, therefore, the speculators are the only truly free class who are absolved from the demands of economic necessity.

The distribution of credit and absolution from social obligation are religious matters. An economic system that only distributes credit to opportunities for profit is bound for destruction. The distribution of credit, however, is the one free activity through which the social order can be transformed. Political emancipation from the power of money can come only when institutions are created to distribute credit along lines of socially accepted evaluations rather than purely according to the demands of money. Liberation may occur through the subordination of money to credit — and credit to evaluation — through the emergence of a new kind of social institution that expresses effective evaluations.

In Chapter 5, money is explored through the institution of accounting that gives it substance. It is demonstrated, through a version of transcendental argument, that exchange value does not pre-exist its recording by means of accounts but is itself a product of such accounting. Accounting, then, may best be regarded as a moral self-discipline that demonstrates that one is capable of paying debts and fulfilling obligations and so makes one worthy of the trust enshrined in contracts. It is the basis for credibility and credit. Accounting is essentially a system for saving time and directing attention. Nevertheless, economic opportunities and externalities have no agreed price. They cannot be properly counted. The paradox of accounting is that it directs attention to what is counted rather than to what matters. It propagates a morality of self-mastery and the pursuit of self-interest that is incompatible with the physical and spiritual realities of most people's lives.

Accounting produces a fundamental misrepresentation insofar as it counts only what can be exchanged instead of the conditions of exchange as such. In practice, it fails to effectively count land, labor, and capital because it only treats these as objects of exchange rather than as conditions of production. A revaluation of all values must begin with a reversal of the moral assumptions embodied in accounting. What is truly valuable always escapes representation and counting. It cannot be manipulated according to the sovereignty of human self-mastery but must be accorded a religious respect. The evaluation of values and the distribution of credit must come to take priority over accounting.

Part III, "Of Theology," is a conclusion. It recapitulates the theory of money presented earlier to unfold the spectral force present in money. It explores the nature and significance of a political theology of money. The theological problem overlooked by much modern thought is that perspectives on true wealth and true power are formed by commitments enacted through practices of attention. Perspectives presuppose a metaphysics, and the currency of any given metaphysics depends on its acceptability in daily life. Far from being the abstract concern of philosophers alone, solutions to the metaphysical problem of the nature of being—whether in the form of God, truth, or money—have in practice functioned as supreme political forces in history as well as in the contemporary world. Conversely, money becomes the pivotal object for the consideration of both the philosopher and the theologian.[35] Credit is the indispensable source of the creation of wealth, and the source of all political authority. Emancipation from the power of money can be achieved only by inventing a new institution for the distribution of credit that evokes a different metaphysics, politics, ethics, and theology. Such an institution may be formed by subordinating credit to evaluation. The task is to develop an institution that enables credit to be given to what is worthy of credit. Yet true credit can arise only from the commitment of flesh and blood, from the gift of time, attention, and devotion. The divorce between the religious and the secular can be overcome by a consideration of how attention, credit, and evaluation are to be ordered. The book concludes with some tentative recommendations of how principles designed to emancipate evaluation from the power of debt could be embodied in concrete institutions.

I

OF POLITICS

A PARABLE

Imagine — if one were only out of debt, owing nothing to anyone, free to do as one pleased, wishing this blessing upon all
others, so that one could cancel all debts owing to oneself, so
that one's debtors could in turn cancel all debts owing to themselves, until all debts were cleared, nothing more was owed, all
people were free, with no employment, no money, no society,
no religion, no life. Imagine. Just imagine.

One

POWER

MODERN THOUGHT, with its Cartesian heritage, has distinguished two kinds of power. There is the purely physical power deriving from gravity, solar radiation, and chemical and atomic bonds. It is released through combustion and muscular exertion and is found in power stations and military hardware. Then there is the purely human power of the will. It is expressed in speech and in action and is found in markets and in nation-states. Modern understandings of politics normally require both conceptions of power. Human will may act on human will through the image or threat of physical power. This is evident above all in Carl Schmitt's definition of the political, which is concerned with the distinction between friend and enemy. For Schmitt, war is the most extreme political means, and as such, it discloses the conceptual distinction that underlies every political idea: the possibility of distinguishing between friend and enemy.[1] Political concepts have a polemical character because they ultimately refer to the real possibility of physical killing.[2] The decisive political power is the authority to make war and so to publicly dispose of the lives of people, whether of the lives of the enemy or of one's own people, in sacrifice.[3] The authority of will over will here derives from no other foundation than the exercise of physical power.

It is necessary to complicate this duality with a third kind of power. War involves the concentrated disposal of physical power and its outcome is generally determined by an accurate distribution or restriction of such power. As General Erwin Rommel remarked in North Africa in 1942: "The first essential condition for an army to stand the strain of battle is an adequate stock of weapons, petrol and ammunition. In fact, the battle is fought and decided by the quartermasters before the shooting begins. The bravest men can do nothing without guns, the guns nothing without plenty of ammunition; and neither guns nor ammunition are of much use in mobile warfare unless there are vehicles with sufficient petrol to haul them around."[4] War may be regarded as a particular case of the power to distribute and exercise physical force. Such a distribution is at once physical and ideal in that it concerns the location and orientation of force. The political, more broadly, may take as its foundation the determination of the use of resources. While war enables the possibility of an enemy, sharing resources enables the possibility of a friend. While economics concerns the most profitable distribution of scarce resources, political economy concerns just distribution. Politics, as the exercise of human will on human will, is grounded on political economy through which the other is determined as a member of a class or as a friend or enemy. Collective physical force depends on a prior appeal to "right" that unites friends against enemies. Prior to the distinction between friend and enemy, political economy must also appeal to principles through which distribution will be ordered and limited, perhaps principles of ownership, right, or justice. Beneath the strength of physical force lie customs, traditions, and markets that determine concentrations of resources. Privileged distributions may occur through kinship, regions, language groups, currency areas, or nation-states, for example. The political, as Schmitt concedes, can derive its energy from the most varied human endeavors, including religious, economic, and moral dimensions.[5] Here we have a third kind of power, the intangible "energy" of the political, irreducible to physical force. It is the authority that guides and authorizes the action of will on will.[6] It is this energy that is the subject matter of a political theology.

Such energy, as a supplement to the will, cannot be encompassed within modernity's conception of humanity as universal political subjects. As soon as the will is given priority, any claims of the "authority" that energizes the will must be dismissed by the will.[7] Schmitt himself exposed the consequences of such universalism: in its effort to include all, it remains an exclusive category. He argued that the political entity cannot by its very nature be universal in the sense of embracing all of humanity and the entire world, for the political entity presupposes the real existence of an enemy and thus of another political entity. As a consequence, "To confiscate the word humanity, to invoke and monopolize such a term probably has certain incalculable effects, such as denying the enemy the quality of being human and declaring him to be an outlaw of humanity; and a war can therefore be driven to the most extreme inhumanity."[8] In a similar way, modern political thought, when it makes the political subject the universal category, excludes consideration of the energy of the political. While appealing to such energy in the name of universality, peace, justice, progress, civilization, democracy, or humanity, it deploys such energy purely in the name of the will. It becomes both arbitrary and totalitarian. Excluding deference to the authority or energy that lends validity to the democratic subject, it becomes a totalitarian denunciation of all authoritarianisms, drawing on its own repressed reservoir of ideological energy. It neglects the bases of the political in the influence over the human will of both physical power and the energy of the political. Authority, far from being abolished by democracy, recurs in a disguised form where its power is unlimited. The nature of such power in the contemporary world remains a theological-political problem.

MODERN HUMANISM

Modern political thought has been humanistic in three related senses. First, the human is constituted as independent of the divine. True power is not to be absorbed from sacred places, persons, objects, or rituals. The claims of theocracies or mythical cosmologies to embody the good are rejected as superstition. Spectral and occult powers are regarded as illusion. The will must be liberated from beliefs concerning participation in the good in nature just as it is liberated from the need to ward off spectral powers. In a secular polity, the good is something that must be willed. Such an emancipation or enlightenment occurs through the second sense of humanism: the human subject is constituted as such through rational self-reflection as a self-determining agent. The human at once distinguishes itself from the animal and liberates itself from superstitious hopes and fears through its reason. By means of reason, it represents the order in nature and imposes order on nature. The power of the will is exercised through representation. Yet the power of the will may only be confirmed as a power through the third sense of humanism: the human subject demonstrates its mastery over an external nature. The subject becomes a subject by exercising itself on an object, and the success of humanism depends on the continuation of this power of mastery. The fate of modern political thought rests on demonstrations of its effectiveness; it rests on a conception of power as mastery; it rests on the nonexistence of invisible powers beyond those of physics and the will.

Three key elements have characterized the modern Western attempt to dominate the unruly forces of nature. The scientific revolution aimed at extracting the ideal form of physical law from the behavior of matter to subject matter to abstract prediction and control; the technological-industrial revolution aimed at subjecting production to the force of the combustion of preserved organic power, together with management by rational recording, calculation, and communication, to maximize efficiency and output; and the capitalist and free-market revolutions aimed at liberating human choice from subordination to traditional or natural ends. The natural world has been mastered by science, technology, and economics. Should this mastery come to an end, one would have to inquire whether modern man is truly reasonable or truly secular.

At the turn of the millennium, the progress of humanism has run up against insuperable limits in each of these domains. The new sciences of chaos and complexity demonstrate how the behavior of matter frequently exceeds all powers of prediction. Science no longer gives mastery. The ecological crisis demonstrates how economic production is dependent on a broader framework of ecological cycles to supply its resources and absorb its waste, cycles that can easily become unstable. Technology no longer gives mastery. The globalization of the capitalist free-market economy demonstrates how social and personal choices are governed by autonomous processes driven by debt, profit, and the control of consumer desire rather than ordered by humane values and a substantive rationality. Economics no longer gives mastery.

Such practical impotence exposes the limits of modern political theory. Committed to a notion of power as mastery—humanity exerting its own intrinsic force rather than appealing to authority—it confines its own operation to representation. As pure theory or reflective knowledge, it aims to represent faithfully the actual or desired political constitution of reality so that a sovereign will may exercise its judgments. Theory is written on behalf of a judging will, whether this is the governing agent of a nation-state, the private will of a democratic subject within civil society, or the collective force of a revolutionary organization.[9] Theory informs sovereign speech and action. But it is doubtful whether this notion of power should constitute the norm for politics. As Pierre Manent points out, the deliberate and rational constitution of the modern liberal state has been exceptional in the history of politics.[10] It is by no means clear that the primary vectors of power continue to pass through sovereign human agency. There are many other thoughtful modes of exercising power in human relations apart from the alliance between representation and sovereignty found in judgment — to name just a few, provision, production, reproduction, possession, association, legislation, normalization, violence, promise, threat, selection, suggestion, persuasion, information, funding, moralizing, praying, or even simply giving attention. Yet power cannot be restricted to human relations. Beyond human agency, human life is also shaped by the agency of nonhuman powers, such as material flows of heat, clean air, fresh water, fertile soil, electricity, fossilized energy, pollution, genetic mutation, disease, and nutrition. Human populations are dependent on the powers of populations of domestic farm animals. The human will may only operate in alliance with these other human and nonhuman powers. It is doubtful whether this alliance between the will and the host of other powers can ever be reduced to representation and mastery. There is, however, a third domain of relative impotence of the will. The subject is afflicted from the inside by beliefs and desires. While the subject may flatter itself that it has selected its beliefs and desires through its own sovereign and rational choice, beliefs and desires exert their own specific power of attraction. Flowing through populations as cultures, political opinions, religions, fashions, ideals, goals, or anxieties, for example, these autonomous flows of beliefs and desires may speak through the political subject like a ventriloquist. Reason may insulate itself against some of these flows when it finds inconsistencies between the order that derives from them and the order of perception. It has little power against the rationalizations that emerge from beliefs and desires when they act as subjects themselves, ordering representation according to their aims. Then, as David Hume remarked, reason is only a slave of the passions.[11] It is necessary to explore this third, meta-human dimension of power, for authority and right belong within the realm of belief.

THE PHILOSOPHY OF REPRESENTATION

An awakening to the active forces of these three broad ranges of power exposes the limits of subjective sovereignty. The mastery achieved through representation is an illusory mastery, for the quality — selectivity — through which representation achieves its power is also the cause of its impotence. In the presentation of the world to the mind, the mind is subjected to each perception, impulse, and orientation. It is helpless before the arising of each image, reaction, and desire. Yet in the representation of the world to the mind, the mind associates ideas, whether in accordance with their intrinsic nature or in accordance with its own understanding. In representation, ideas are liberated from the conditions of their arising in the course of time. They may be reproduced in the mind at will. In the act of selection, they are freed from external powers and subjected to the power of the mind alone. The mind imposes order on the represented world. Passing through an order of reasons, an association of representations, the mind may determine its own will. Reproducing objects in its own imagination, the mind invests and fixes its own desire. In short, through representation the mind becomes a subject to itself. In imagination it constructs its own sovereignty in reason, will, and desire. This selectivity is at once the construction of a limited domain of sovereignty and a broader domain of ignorance and impotence. The failure to represent and respond to every force in the order of the mind leads to its impotence before that which exceeds representation. There is always a remainder, epitomized by the force of the course of time itself, for if representation is a reproduction of images in the mind, it cannot include the contemporary presentation of perceptions, impulses, and orientations. Modern reason is a hesitation, a membrane, an interruption; it reproduces the world in the theater of the imagination, where the order of the sovereign subject is maintained. Yet the sovereignty of reason exists in the imagination alone. There is one thing that must be excluded a priori from the representation of the sovereign subject: its impotence. This is not to say that one cannot represent oneself as impotent, but this very representation of oneself as impotent is generated from within the mind. It is in practice an expression of the mind's power.

A belief in the sovereignty of the subject through its rational ordering of representation does not emerge without some external support or confirmation. Several social roles may serve as a model for imagining the mastery of the sovereign subject: the patriarchal father, the absolute despot, the chief executive officer, the owner of property, the artist, the animal trainer, the craftsperson, or the wealthy consumer, for example. Each may form the basis for imagining an unfettered liberty and power over a specific domain. On closer inspection, however, each of these social roles exists in a complex web of mutual influence and interaction with its correlative field. To attain true mastery in each case, it is necessary to hold the capacity to break off the relation with the mastered object. Thus, the owner of property is absolved from the corresponding obligations for care and maintenance of property by disposing of it, selling it in exchange, or allowing it to decay. Ownership is the right to dispose of property. The consumer exercises sovereignty in the selection of products by refusing to purchase others on offer. Choice is rejection. The craftsperson rejects recalcitrant materials. The despot exercises sovereignty through power over life and death. Sovereignty is destruction. Sovereignty is a relation that exists only in its suspension. It is exercised primarily as a threat, but the execution of the threat consists in dissolving the relation. Such power may be exercised through violence, through severance, or through flight. Yet as the image of negation, sovereign power exists only in the imagination. In practice, the mind may be subjected to both physical force and the force of authority.

POWER BEYOND REPRESENTATION

As a result, a political theory that takes sovereign self-determination as the primary expression of power suffers from a bad conscience. If power is to be demonstrated beyond the confines of imagination, it must be demonstrated in practice. Acts of violence, severance, suspension, negation, or flight must continually be repeated to demonstrate the reality of power. If the sovereignty of reason exists in the imagination alone, it must be supplemented by an exercise of will. The will demonstrates sovereignty when it converts representation into reality. It is a question of moving from the theater of imagination to the theater of life. Yet the body through which the will is exercised is less supple than the mind and is determined by physical forces and other subjects. The sovereign will can only act on the narrow stage where it concurs with or overpowers other wills. The sovereign subject pays little heed to the vast sphere of its impotence or to the construction of the stage where its action is possible. The causality of the will is only possible on the basis of cooperation or even a consensus between other wills and forces. Selection and consensuality form the basis for the illusion of sovereignty. There is a physical, social, and ecological coordination that enables all acts of will. It appeals, beyond sovereign representation, to physical, human, and meta-human configurations of power.

This mediation calls into question established notions of subjectivity, causality, and power. The essence of the political is at stake here. If there is active mediation in all human relations, involving the activity of a multiplicity of nonhuman powers, of human reactions and reciprocities, and of currents of belief and desire, then mastery provides a very poor model, ideal, or goal for power. The relation between subject and object is mediated by a host of powers, both past and present; its underlying orientation may be determined by belief and desire.

In addition, the essence of reason is at stake here, because mediation brings into question the dichotomy between the discovery and representation of order, on the one hand, and the imposition of order, on the other. If action is mediated by a host of additional active forces, then there is a sense in which order is both disclosed and emergent. Reason, far from trying to represent or master reality, would then be an attempt to cooperate with, nourish, and reorient reality. Far from being invested in the abstract and universal, reason would be invested in the concrete and local.

Finally, at stake here is the essence of theology, for absolute sovereign power is a theological notion.[12] Where even the tyrant depends on the credulity of his subjects, only the divine is supposed to possess absolute self-sufficiency. Short of true social models, the notion of unrestrained power is encountered, to varying degrees, in forms of monotheistic belief. The divine is the model for the essence of power and the essence of reason. Only the power of the creator can be unmediated. The sovereign subject of modern political thought—the basis for freedom and democracy—is not free from the constraints of belief and desire. Instead, it contains its own theological presuppositions deriving from the history of its emergence. Whether the subject is separated from divine power, as for the somewhat Arminian John Locke, or identified with divine power, as for the somewhat Calvinist Benedict de Spinoza, a theological model of power is the implicit heart of sovereignty and reason. The modern notion of the political remains contaminated by a theological problematic inherent in its very notion of power. Power rests on meta-human flows of beliefs and desires.

This notion of power as mastery should therefore be subjected to onto-logical, political, and theological critique. In essence, one may ask whether such a notion of power is true, powerful, or divine. This is not a simple inquiry, for at stake is also the practice of critique. What ideal or criterion can be used to assess this notion of power? What principle can take prece-dence? And what is the nature of the precedence of such a principle if it is not to be conceived in terms of a theology of sovereignty (understood as originality, independence, or mastery)? Any attempt to retreat to first prin-ciples leads to a vicious circle of self-presupposition. The meaning of being, of power, and of divinity is presupposed in modern models of rational, critical inquiry. Indeed, a theology of sovereignty, expressed in the exalta-tion of originality, independence, and mastery, is implicit within the entire tradition of thought deriving from Greek reason, whether this thought is classical philosophy, medieval theology, or modern critical reason.

There is, however, an alternative direction of thought. It is possible to enter the mediation of the concrete. The move from representation to reality requires the mediation of the theater of life. One may escape the the-ology of sovereignty by engaging with immanent problems.[13] The selection and coordination of active processes of nonhuman powers, of human inter-actions, and of orientations of belief and desire occurs in reality as well as in the mind. There is a social body that corresponds directly to the power of the imagination in representation. It proceeds similarly through selection and mediation and is a catalyst enabling physical, human, and meta-human configurations of power to interact. We are concerned here with a different kind of causality, a power external to both physical process and human will. It is here that a truly incarnate political theology is to be sought.

A specifically social form of power is necessary to support the public representations on which the will acts. Such a political body could be the marked and appropriated body of property, or the body of the sovereign, or money itself.[14] It is a material instance invested with ontological, eco-nomic, and theological presuppositions. It forms a stage for the collective exercise of will in the public theater of representation. It mediates causality. It is the body of power. Without this political body, little public exercise of power is possible. One may try to dispose violently of as much property as one wishes, but if one has no title to such property, one risks meeting resistance from counter-violence. One may issue as many decrees as one chooses, yet if one has no authority, this exercise of will comes to nothing.

One may make as many demands as one pleases, but if one has no money, then one will be unable to purchase. Political power is thus unthinkable without a body that supports it, whether such a body is a weapon of violence, a sovereign authority, or money itself. As Edward Leigh remarked in 1715, "Money, or that which supplies it, is the Sinews of Government both in War and Peace: where that is wanting, nothing can move regularly, the want of Money being the Root of all Political Evil."[15]

The conversion of thought toward concrete reason, by means of a consideration of these political bodies, has a dual effect: it changes the content of reason, turning away from laws and first principles toward concrete problems and mediations, and it changes the nature of reason, since reason no longer stands over and above the concrete but must itself pass through concrete mediation. Reason must go further than representation. The immediate relation of representation to consciousness is a product of the fantasy of omnipotence of an isolated subject, but power is always mediated by selection and by a body. Each political body may operate its own particular kind of causality. Then it is not only the case that a political body is invested with ontological, political, and theological presuppositions. Being itself, power itself, and the divine itself are not immediate representations. One cannot simply claim that being is, that power is powerful, or that God is divine. One cannot discover what such concepts might mean without the mediation of a concrete, political body. Ontological, political, and theological inquiries cannot proceed directly to impose their order, will, and desire on representation without being caught up in a narcissistic fantasy. Indeed, there is no reality or verification, no power or representation, no divinity or credibility without mediation. All ontological, political, and theological inquiries—concerning truth, power, and divinity—need to pass through the mediation of some kind of body that gives substance to their claims. As Jacques Lacan once said, "Man thinks with his object."[16] Contemporary philosophy, political theory, and theology can make no further progress without a consideration of money.

MONEY AS A POLITICAL BODY

In modernity, money mediates property and sovereignty: one comes into sovereign possession through exchange. Money is itself property belonging to an individual account. Money is also dispersed sovereignty: the capacity of the sovereign to repay debts through future taxation underwrites the value of money. The sovereign body itself, now in the form of the symbols of sovereign power, has become multiplied and dispersed among individuals. Each time money is spent, whether inside or beyond the limits of the particular nation-state, it expresses the sovereign power of the nation whose symbols it bears. Property, sovereignty, and credit become united in the body of money. Money participates in and brings together the realms of the nonhuman, the human, and belief and desire. In modernity, money is the political body par excellence.

Money acts as the living symbol of the sovereign individual. It expresses individual power as nothing else can. If the right to dispose of property is exercised to the full, and property is exchanged, then the value of that property is expressed in terms of money as its price. Money substitutes for property after severance of the bonds of ownership. Similarly, the liberty of the sovereign individual to enter into any obligation or contract at will is expressed in terms of money. It is only money that may trade for all other things. Money, in Fyodor Dostoyevsky's phrase, is "coined liberty."[17] Furthermore, money is effective demand, or, in James Buchan's phrase, "frozen desire."[18] It commands order. Without money, there would be no production in a society based on the division of labor. Money gives the motive for production. Money effectively symbolizes the value of property, the sovereignty of freedom, and the power of desire. It is the political body that stands before and represents the individual. Money is the tool through which democracy is realized. Money is the supreme instrument of political expression.

According to the old saying by George Savile, "They who are of the opinion that Money will do every thing, may very well be suspected to do everything for Money."[19] One must consider not only whether money effectively symbolizes the sovereign individual, but also whether the sovereign individual may not be the imaginary reflection of money. One must consider whether power in modernity operates primarily through the sovereignty of the will, or whether power in modernity operates primarily through the active force of money. One must consider whether the beliefs and desires that flow through individuals are not made possible by social institutions such as the market and the nation-state in which the individual's sovereign will can be exercised. One must consider whether the market itself is not founded on money as the basis for exchange and whether the state itself is not founded on money as the basis for taxation.

The turn of thought to the mediation of the concrete, therefore, has very little to do with the scientific study of empirical reality, which selects and analyzes reality on the basis of principles, concepts, and formulas embedded in the imagination. Life itself is deprived of its own embodiment, mediation, and fecundity. The consideration of money as a political body is a matter of theology rather than of economic science. This can be explained by means of a concrete example. In his introduction to *Grundrisse*, Karl Marx famously argued that "civil society," the society of free individuals detached from natural bonds in free competition, is itself a historical product. The producing individual, using tools and language, is a product of the family and communal society. Only in the eighteenth century did social relations confront the individual as a mere means toward private purposes.[20] For Marx, if everything—including social forms such as individuals and money—is produced historically, then the social structure is entirely determined by the structure of production.[21] The individual is itself a representation, a product. Marx attributed primacy to production because everything is produced historically. This seems to be the primacy of temporal order: process comes before product just as subject comes before object. Where the other classical economists took the individual as a presupposition, Marx argued that the individual possessed of property and liberty is itself a historical product—a product of collective labor.

It is not clear that "social production" or "historical production" are any less derivative than the individual will. Social production, of course, is dependent on tradition, command, or money.[22] We need to consider whether historical production is dependent on some mediating term that gives it orientation and direction. A few pages later, Marx answered the question differently:

Nothing seems more natural than to begin with ground rent, with landed property, since this is bound up with the earth, the source of all production and all being, and with the first form of production of all more or less settled societies—agriculture. But nothing would be more erroneous. In all forms of society there is one specific kind of production which predominates over the rest, whose relations thus assign rank and influence to the others. . . . In bourgeois society . . . agriculture more and more becomes merely a branch of industry, and is entirely dominated by capital. Ground rent likewise. In all forms where landed property rules, the natural relation [is] still predominant. In those where capital rules, the social, historically created element [is]. Ground rent cannot be understood without capital. But capital can certainly be understood without ground rent.[23]

The primacy of a natural or temporal order, implicit in the notion of "historical production," is undermined.[24] Three principles are enunciated here against what one might consider a "naturalistic fallacy." First, capital *predominates*—it exercises a sovereign power. Second, it does so as the historically created element, since social production now organizes natural production. This is only because of the first principle: that capital rules. Third, capital can be understood without ground rent; it is thus based on independent principles of the understanding. Capital is supposed to be independent of agriculture. It is capable of ruling, therefore, because of its independence. Sovereignty derives from a severance of relation.

What is at stake here is the specific power of capital, its mode of ruling. This power has something to do with independence, although it is in reality inconceivable that there could be capital without agriculture, just as it is inconceivable that there could be city-states without agriculture. The power would therefore seem to be independence in an order of principles or reasons. Yet this power also has something to do with offering itself as a representative body, "a general illumination which bathes all the other colours . . . a particular ether which determines the specific gravity of every being."[25] Indeed, the activity of historical production as well as the exercise of sovereign power may be impossible without such a representative body that mediates all causation. Marx himself broke with historical determinism: "It would therefore be unfeasible and wrong to let the economic categories follow one another in the same sequence as that in which they were historically decisive. Their sequence is determined, rather, by their relation to one another in modern bourgeois society, which is precisely the opposite of that which seems to be their natural order or which corresponds to historical development."[26] In bourgeois society, private property as a social reality is a product of money, since landed property is enclosed for the purpose of obtaining money through trade rather than simply obtaining grain through agriculture. Property is only private property when it is capable of being exchanged. Similarly, the liberty of the individual is a product of money, since an individual may be freed from the demands of community, tradition, and authority only by finding other sources to provide for needs, through trading for money. Furthermore, the individual becomes a subject of desire, capable of ordering production through demands, only when such demands are made effective through money. The abstract social relations of property, liberty, and desire, removed from their formation in a physical and social context, gain social consistency through money.

CONCLUSION

One can no longer consider the vital political problem to be that of political subjectivity. It is no longer a question of conscious self-determination, whether as an individual or as a collective. The sovereignty required for such a subject is itself an illusion. Instead, the concrete manifestation of physical and meta-human powers at the end of modernity requires elucidation. Once the context for contemporary intervention is clarified, two subsequent problems become urgent. The first concerns the way in which capital or money predominates, or the mode of exercise of a power that does not appear to be constrained by competing powers. It concerns the essence and exercise of power itself. The second concerns the possibility of bodies of representation. What political bodies can still be created that will attribute a different hue or gravity to all particular things represented under their light? What further concretions can be enabled? How may the value of such values be assessed?

Two

THE END OF MODERNITY

MODERNITY HAS ALWAYS been a utopian myth. The unique reordering of the surface of the planet over the past two hundred years, and especially over the past sixty years, has not occurred through acts of human will and knowledge alone. The contributions of physical processes and other life forms, of instinctive human care and provision, of captivating ideas, and even of money have been immense. One may even wonder whether the human will is a product of such a broader range of processes. Discussion of this point is somewhat academic, however. The end of modernity or the disclosure of modernity as an illusion, whichever is the case, does not arrive as a change in intellectual fashion. It is a brutal, physical, overwhelming reality. It is the breakdown of stable alliances between environmental, human, and meta-human processes. For those afflicted as a result of modernity—by war, contagious disease, loss of land and access to fresh water, loss of networks of social provision, and loss of employment and means of subsistence—modernity has always meant instability and impotence. Modernity has fed off and propagated geographical inequality.[1] And, as will be demonstrated in the chapters that follow, wealth is built on poverty, and knowledge is built on ignorance.

The impotence of the modern, rational subject is exposed by instabilities in both physical and meta-human powers. Modernity comes to a final end in the collision between economy and ecology. At the time of first writing (in November 2005), the vast majority of informed opinion has little sense of the inevitability or impact of such a collision. By the time this book reaches many readers, the end of modernity may be so evident that it is pointless to attempt to predict or explain it. For example, the end of modernity engulfed New Orleans in early September 2005 in the wake of Hurricane Katrina. The environment ceased to behave in a stable way necessary for prediction and control; damage was inflicted on the primary source of power for modernity, oil production and refining; the human bonds of modern society evaporated with the flooding of the energy and transportation infrastructure; and, most significant, a climate of fear invaded the otherwise undamaged public institutions responding to the crisis — the media, military, and emergency-management authorities — leaving many of them paralyzed and useless, at best, or positively harmful, at worst, for several days. Such is the end of modernity: a generalized state of emergency in which the stability of normal, modern life proves to be the exception rather than the rule. Indeed, the stability of modernity has always been exceptional. The emergency and chaos that are its inevitable by-product are the norm.

PHYSICAL INSTABILITY

Human agency can achieve mastery only if the physical world behaves predictably. Assumptions of continuity and gradual change have been axiomatic in the development of science from Newton up through the twentieth century, whether in physics, biology, or geology. At the limits, however, discontinuities arise. What is difficult to predict in a complex world, as opposed to an isolated laboratory, is where the thresholds of stable behavior might lie.

Dominant narratives of climate change designed to inform policy have until recently focused on the detection of trends rather than the prediction of possibilities. The narrative of abrupt climate change, by contrast, implies that surprises are inevitable.[2] The past ten thousand years (in geologic terms, the Holocene era) have shown a remarkable level of global climatic stability, but even during this period abrupt regional climate changes have been sufficient to wipe out civilizations.[3] Prior to the Holocene era, global average temperatures oscillated much more sharply, according to evidence from the Greenland ice core and from ocean sediments. Abrupt oscillations between colder and milder conditions lasting ten or twenty years were common; vast changes of temperature took place within five years.[4] The last warm age, the Eemian period of 135,000–110,000 years ago, had sudden plunges toward ice-age temperatures; only its last two thousand years were stable.[5] In comparison, the past eight thousand years have been strangely stable. Human agricultural and industrial activities have not yet faced the large and rapid climate oscillations typical for most of the last 110,000 years.

Projections of temperature rises over the coming century depend on the rate of anthropogenic forcing through the emission of greenhouse gases. The mechanisms that trigger abrupt change or establish global stability are as yet poorly understood and can easily escape detection. An abrupt climate change occurs when a threshold is crossed, triggering a transition to a new state at a rate determined by the climate system rather than by the initial cause. For example, the last ice age was followed by another cold spell that lasted for about thirteen centuries. The Younger Dryas period, as that cold spell is known, may have been caused by the melting of a glacier and the resultant change in the drainage pattern of a large freshwater lake in Canada from the Mississippi River basin to the St. Lawrence estuary. This change in route, in turn, redistributed salinity in the North Atlantic and disrupted the prevailing pattern of thermohaline circulation, changing the global climate. Such is the delicacy of the overall climate system. Anthropogenic triggers are potentially more significant. There are many potential candidates for positive feedback processes that trigger abrupt climate change. Greater evaporation from rising sea temperatures near the equator may disrupt the thermohaline circulation of ocean currents through increased precipitation and runoff, causing lower salinity in the Arctic. These changes have been postulated as a potential cause of past dramatic oscillations in the Earth's climate. The melting of the Greenland and Arctic ice sheets may have a similar effect. Rising sea temperatures in the Arctic may reduce the coverage of the Arctic with ice and, consequently, reduce the albedo effect by which solar radiation is reflected, leading to a self-perpetuating process. Methane gas, released from soils and bogs in the Northern Hemisphere as the permafrost melts, would intensify the greenhouse effect. The drying out of rainforests such as the Amazon as the temperature rises may lead to increased forest fires and the release of carbon dioxide. It has been estimated that small temperature increases would turn forests, oceans, and soils into net sources rather than sinks of greenhouse gases.[6] Increasing differences in temperature between ocean beds and surfaces could lead to greater stratification of temperature layers, reducing the flow to the surface of nutrients that feed the phytoplankton on which all sea life depends and that act as a major sink of carbon dioxide. News reports in 2005 and 2006 stated that most of these processes are already under way: Downward currents in the Arctic to drive the Gulf Stream have significantly decreased; levels of ice cover in the Arctic after the summer melt are significantly reduced; the defrosting of the western Siberian peat bog, the size of France and Germany combined, is releasing bubbles of methane; numerous forest fires have broken out; and the Amazon is suffering droughts.[7] In short, if the global climate is normally unstable, and anthropogenically induced climate change triggers a much larger release of carbon, methane, and nitrous oxides—whether from fossil fuels, industrial agriculture, forests, or degradation of the soil—then dramatic changes in temperature are inevitable. Less predictable are the extremes of regional temperature changes that will occur over a period of instability and whether a new stability will be achieved at a much hotter temperature or, as a result of processes yet unknown, a much colder one than the present. Climate models have not yet succeeded in simulating the abrupt climate changes of the past, and the summaries of scientific papers speak only in terms of uncertainties. The results of anthropogenically induced climate change may well include droughts, famines, floods, hurricanes, and forest fires. They may well include the permanent flooding of low-lying countries and coastal cities, which contain a significant proportion of the global population, as well as frequent flooding of a third of agricultural lands. They may result in dramatic and rapid oscillations in temperature or even another ice age. Prediction of the most basic conditions for continued human existence becomes impossible.[8]

At the end of modernity, a second, perhaps more imminent, catastrophe is also waiting to happen. The finitude of environmental resources such as fossil fuels, fresh water, fertile soil, forests, biodiversity, and pollution sinks threatens to destabilize the global economy. It is already possible to gain a sense of the scale of this collision course, if not its ultimate consequences. A paper presented in 2002 to the U.S. National Academy of Sciences, "Tracking the Ecological Overshoot of the Human Economy," aggregated the area needed for cropland, grazing, forestry, fishing, and human habitation, as well as for the absorption of carbon dioxide, and concluded that the human economy has exceeded the carrying capacity of the planet since 1980. In 2002, some 1.2 Planet Earths were needed to sustain levels of consumption. Moreover, if 12 percent of the planet were set aside for the preservation of biodiversity, which contributes to a wide variety of essential environmental services, then the figure would be closer to 1.4 Earths.[9]

We are consuming our own collective body. Because wealth is inevitably perceived in terms of physical consumption by embodied human beings, economic growth necessitates an increase in consumption. A global growth in wealth and consumption of 2.8 percent per annum (the average in 2000–2004) would be sufficient to double this load within twenty-five years. For low-income countries, with a total population of 2.3 billion and a growth rate in the gross domestic product (GDP) of 5.1 percent over this period, consumption would double in merely fourteen years.[10] Clearly, vital instabilities will arise at a global level within twenty-five years. Most of the effects of overshoot will be regional, since fertile soil, fresh water, forests, and even natural gas have limited transportability. The effects have comparatively little impact on the lives of the wealthy. The global crisis emerging from the collision between economic growth and ecological finitude must therefore arise from a deficiency of oil supplies. While an intelligent layman could have predicted this some years ago (it was in early 2001 that this reasoning led me to check the data on the remaining years of oil reserves at the current rates of production) there is now a burgeoning literature on the fossil-fuel crisis as the end of modernity.[11]

The carbon burned in fossil fuels amounts to the consumption of four centuries' worth of total primary plant growth each year. Oil deposits derive from a few epochs of extreme global warming when the atmosphere was filled with carbon dioxide, which fostered prolific algal growth that effectively poisoned the seas and lakes. Deposits of algae were later converted into oil. The geology of oil is well understood, and there are few deposits left to find; extrapolation from the rate of past finds suggests that 90 percent of recoverable reserves have already been discovered. Indeed, more oil has been produced than discovered for each of the past thirty years. With the peak of discovery in the early 1960s, and cumulative production lagging discovery by thirty-eight years, the final peak of oil production is approaching very shortly. For example, rates of oil and natural-gas production in the United States and United Kingdom are set to fall sharply over the next ten years. While some estimates of the date of oil's peak place it as far away as 2037, these are largely speculative.[12] Credible estimates place it in the current decade. Whatever the precise date, the peak of fossil-fuel production signals the end of modernity. During the twentieth century, the global population expanded sixfold, exactly in parallel with oil production.[13] Fossil fuels are an essential part of most aspects of food production, including transport, the construction and operation of farm machinery, the production and use of fertilizer and pesticides, the generation of electricity for refrigeration and storage, and cooking. Given the ease of storing and transporting fossil fuels, and the small amount of energy required to extract them from the ground, there are no effective alternatives for use on a similar scale.[14] At the same time, the world's level of energy consumption will double in a mere twenty-eight years, driven by population growth, industrial development, and increasing per capita energy use. The collision between supply and demand will take place within a decade.[15] (Indeed, I now regard the credit crisis of 2008 as the first phase of the collision: the rise in oil prices and consequent inflation led to the rise of interest rates, triggering the failure of subprime loans.) Given the extent of the degradation of the soil by industrial agriculture over the past century, the global population looks set to plummet toward preindustrial levels over the next thirty years.[16] The consequences will be worst in countries with poor soils and dense populations, as well as in countries heavily affected by climate change.

The end of modernity will be met by climatic instability, fuel poverty, food shortages, disease, social unrest, conflict, and war. In a time of shrinking rather than growing resources, few of the economic and political values of modernity can be preserved. A social order propagated through mass communications rather than personal relations will demonstrate very little resilience. Catastrophes and abominations of hitherto unimagined proportions are almost inevitable.

The aim of this summary is not to persuade people of the coming catastrophe of the end of modernity, as events themselves will do this more rapidly and effectively. The argument is, rather, that the modern age has been built on the power of fossil fuels rather than the human will alone. It is difficult to summon up political will when one is afflicted by physical instabilities, whether in the environment, in access to essential resources, or in health. Any account of the political that begins with the will alone must be deficient. Any account of the economy that begins with human labor, as opposed to the labor of the soil, of domestic animals, and of fossil fuels, is deficient. Moreover, once the self-referential circle of the human will is breached, the way is opened for other interventions and forces.

CONCEPTUAL INSTABILITY

In modern thought, concepts are formed by a process of abstraction and representation. Humanity can only achieve mastery if concepts retain their identities through this process. Should concepts dissimulate and nature prove to be unnatural, power prove to be subservience, wealth prove to be poverty, democracy prove to be tyranny, or freedom prove to be constraint, then concepts will be insufficiently stable to inform the will.

The normal procedure is to attempt to stabilize concepts through the sovereign decree of definition. Definition may establish a network of conceptual relations, but it does little to guarantee the authenticity of representation, as the existence of relatively more and less useful definitions shows. Instead, it is essential that the process of abstraction and representation preserve the nature of the abstraction designated by the concept. Abstraction cannot be allowed to compromise fidelity. Herein lies a peculiar difficulty: abstraction is a selective procedure. In the representations of the sovereign subject, the selection cannot be performed by the nature that is to be selected; it must therefore be performed in representation itself, with the abstraction as its own criterion. Abstract concepts precede the sovereignty of the thinking subject as the conditions and criteria for representation. They are at once what is represented and what enables representation. They are like the courtiers who flatter their sovereign as to the wisdom and originality of his decisions while at the same time they serve as his sole sources of information, manipulating an inevitable outcome. They are like the bureaucrats who govern elected politicians without those politicians' knowledge. This self-referentiality has the effect of self-confirmation, excluding all that is different from consideration. There is no longer a test of fidelity to the matter at hand.

The manipulation of concepts to appeal to immediate interests and passions is a perennial and widely acknowledged tool of propaganda. It is rarely acknowledged that reason will inevitably be supplanted in such a process. For if consciousness is informed by a process of representation, then one will only select for representation that which contributes to a judgment that will continue such representation. Imagination has its own process of natural selection, its own economy of survival. The vividness of concepts depends more on their conceptual coherence and self-referentiality in specific circumstances than it does on the nature of those circumstances. These paradoxes are well illustrated by the concept of democracy. Democracy consists in the identity of the governed and the governing. It is a reactive conceptual formulation, taking its notion of "governing" from the sovereign institutions, such as absolute monarchy, that it historically opposes. Carl Schmitt noted the paradox here: in a democracy, the sovereign, whether an assembly composed of or representing all citizens, can change laws and constitutions at will, without the limitations imposed on monarchy or aristocracy.[17] Indeed, in a democracy, where each consents to be governed by the collective will, there is a capacity for unrestricted domination. As Schmitt points out, it matters little whether the collective will is determined by the majority or whether it is determined only by a minority, perhaps even the executive, as in the case of war. The collective will must be obeyed without appeal. For Schmitt, the "people" — referring to those who govern and are governed — is a public category. Note the self-referentiality here. How can one have a public without a people or a people without a public? For Schmitt, then, ballots and opinion polls are insufficient to form the will of the people. The "unanimous opinion of one hundred million private persons is neither the will of the people nor public opinion."[18] The key issue is neither the will of the people nor the will of the executive but the process by which the public will is formed, both as a general will through a constitutional process and as public opinion through information and discussion. Democracy is fated to destroy itself in the formation of the will.[19] In the last instance, it is neither the people nor the executive that govern but the processes of formation of a public will. The public will is compatible with dictatorship or almost any other kind of government. Every significant political power can hope to form the people's will and so identify with the will of the people.[20]

Joseph Schumpeter has similarly pointed out that the will of the people requires a conception of a common good around which the will of the people can be unified.[21] For the collective will to be public, it must be represented, and in that respect it requires a determinate object. The problem for democracy here is that such a conception of the common good appears to be lacking. The mechanisms of liberal democracy, including freedom of speech, freedom of press, freedom of assembly, and freedom of discussion, produce an unrestrained clash of opinions. The role of mediation comes to the fore once more. It is one thing to have an abstract freedom of speech and another to be effectively heard. In the clash of opinion, opinions are not heard more vividly if they speak the truth, for the truth can be verified only by the confirmation of further vivid opinions. Instead, opinions must flatter the audience they attempt to attract; they must appeal to passions and immediate interests. The resolution of this competition—where liberal-democratic mechanisms give weight to the majority—must be a utilitarian conception of the common good, the greatest happiness of the greatest number. This is not the triumph of liberal ideology but the effect of mechanisms of conflict and competition. Moreover, this utilitarian conception can be little other than a materialistic conception of the common good as the creation of wealth, for no other conception can survive the test of liberal discussion. The creation of wealth alone has universal appeal to immediate interests.

The stability of liberal democracy depends on the stability of its concept of wealth. In a liberal democracy, the consumer appears to be sovereign. The people, governed by the vision of the common good of consumption, are fated to serve the creation of wealth. This vision might not, without considerable advertising propaganda and institutional conditioning, correspond to the private will. Yet no other outcome is possible. Capitalism is a process of continual restructuring for the sake of maximizing consumption. Consumption, of course, rests on production, and production rests on machines, resources, people, and organizations. The sovereignty of consumption results in the subservience of production; for each act of consumption there is an extended network of producers engaged in production, often beyond the confines of the democratic state. The inevitable outcome of a liberal democracy, lacking a collective determination of higher goods, is subjection to consumer desire. Production no longer has a universal representation like consumption; it cannot form the basis for agreement

on the common good. Wealth is necessarily dualistic and unequal. It involves domination and poverty. The stability of democracy depends on
keeping this poverty beyond the confines of expression in a political will.
As Schmitt noted, if democracy requires the equality of the homogeneous
on the basis of, for example, membership in a nation, it also necessarily
requires the elimination of the heterogeneous from political representation.[22] The foreign and unequal, but also the animal and nonhuman, as
well as higher values or spectral forces, are excluded from political representation. Democracy constructs the homogeneity of the collective will to
which it appeals. In sum, the concept of democracy dissimulates. Beneath
the ideals that it conjures up, it facilitates the domination of the people by
consumer desire and money.

Democracy is merely a polemical principle, an organizational form
without political content.[23] Historically, it has often been supplemented
by liberal norms of discussion and openness: persuading an opponent or
allowing oneself to be persuaded of the truth or justice of something. The
assumption is that truth or justice will predominate in free and open discussion. The problem of representation recurs here once again. Representation necessarily isolates an individual from its context. It separates the
object from its environment. It imposes a hierarchical dualism between object and environment. The environment is treated as background, excluded
from the value of the object, defined and explained in terms of the object,
stereotyped, and homogenized.[24] All representation is partial, obscuring
truth and propagating injustice. All representation is misrepresentation;
all representation imposes its own values in advance. Representation has
little facility for propagating truth and justice, because truth and justice are
independent of opinion and representation. The paradox of representation
is that, although matters that are true and right may be represented, the
truth or justice of such matters cannot be represented in their independence from representation. Truth and justice exceed all representation. If
one attempts to represent them, then they are produced by thought and
are no longer independent of representation. If one merely appeals to their
independence, then they are not represented at all. In short, democratic
discussion is doomed to fail—not because people are insufficiently ascetic
to pursue truth at the expense of their own interests, but because the interests of reason already exist that determine the conditions of representation.
All of the common complaints about democracy in practice emerge from

this structural problem: the degeneration of democracy into a struggle of party interests, the banality of debate, the politics of personalities, the irrationality of human behavior, the manipulation of opinion by propaganda, the secrecy of real decision making outside public debate, and the determination of politics by economic realities. None of these failings are new. Democracy is corrupted at the origin because it subscribes to an impossible ideal.

Similarly, the political ideal of freedom echoes modern humanism. It is freedom from public representations of divine command or the sacred common good; it is freedom to determine one's will by entering into contracts in the marketplace; and it is freedom to master a portion of nature or dispose of one's property as one pleases. Lacking public representations or manifestations of a common good, free and open debate must necessarily settle on such individual freedom as its lowest common denominator. Once guarding against threats to the individual or property becomes the essence of the common good, then manipulation of fear becomes the pre-eminent tool of governance, and absolute rule by the state may be sanctioned to defend against an emergency. Yet this very perception of the primacy of threat and consequent absolutism derives not from taking freedom and property as ontological points of departure. Instead, the positing of freedom and property as a basis derives from the mechanisms of representation and discussion themselves. For freedom and property alone have universal appeal to immediate interests.

Just as the collective will of democracy requires the creation of wealth as the object that makes it possible, it also requires an assumption of the free individual as subject of this will. Failing the public representation of truth and justice, however, there is no other form of persuasion than the manipulation of opinion. Just as in the sphere of economics, where freedom to consume is dependent on the constraint on others to produce, so also in politics, freedom of expression is dependent on the constraint on others to be persuaded. Universal freedom is only possible in an ideal world without context. The modern quest for wealth—the increasing domination of the natural world—and freedom—the separation from natural constraint and social obligation—are illusions, impossible ideals born of representation and abstraction, projections of an idealized condition in which humanity cannot survive or flourish.

In the last instance, representation rests on a utopian faith. Modern values are supported not by nature or reason but by nothing less than a secular theology. Theological questions may be reintroduced as soon as one places representation—that which abstracts from time—back within time. Saving time forms the essence of the modern project of emancipation. Only when one is liberated from the constraints of natural necessity that may foreshorten our life spans, and one is liberated from the constraints of social obligation that occupy our time, does one have the freedom to become what one wishes to be. The aspiration is for a condition of atheism where one is finally unconditioned by God or nature. Economic rationality depends on a symbolization of time so that a calculation can be performed that minimizes relative expenditure while maximizing control over nature through technology and maximizing control over social obligation through money. The certainty that attaches to economic rationality derives from its proofs in practice: technological invention and acquisition of wealth. Yet the knowledge, power, and wealth acquired are always local and partial. Projecting a future when liberation will be complete, economic rationality is faith seeking understanding. In this total future, abstract symbols of time will effectively represent time as open, empty, and undetermined in a glorious, heavenly future where the passage of time is no longer constrained by natural necessity or social obligation. Trust in the transcendent will vanish only when one finally attains the complete repeatability and universality required for scientific certainty, and when all knowledge is grounded on evidence. Only as such will the secular sphere be constituted, the sphere of the present age untrammeled by obligation to repeat the past or anxious expectation of the judgments of the future, where all causes are mediated to their consequences by knowledge.

To attain such a condition, however, it is necessary to short-circuit expectations and treat the secular age as though it were present, here and now. One projects hypotheses about the natural world before one can test and correct them. Similarly, in the sphere of value, one estimates the price of a commodity in relation to other commodities, needs, and interests. This very anticipation, this very faith, introduces a distortion into emancipatory practice, producing ignorance and slavery. For one has to project the secular utopia as already attained in order to construct the world of nature or the sphere of value. The result is a totalization that attempts to effect both a formal and a real subsumption of reality. Concepts of nature, value, society, necessity, power, wealth, freedom, and even money are abstractions that depend on a prior totalization, as though the system of exchange and relation that constitutes the world were universal. In each case, a representation of material life, which functions as a medium of social interaction, assumes an autonomy from social interaction as soon as it is posited as existing in itself. It maintains such an autonomy only by attempting to realize itself, by effecting first a formal and then a real subsumption of material life under its organizing categories. In short, the material, secular, natural, and social worlds have no ontological purchase. They are representations that exist only insofar as they attempt to realize themselves. They possess an abstract unity that can never be realized in practice.

The mechanism for the constitution of the secular order of nature, or the "*novo ordo seclorum*" celebrated on the dollar bill, is explained by money. We return to the problem of the specific power of money to venture a preliminary exposition. This mechanism, the dominant political "energy" of modernity, can be summarized briefly here. It will be elaborated subsequently. Failing the arrival of the universal, secular utopia, one substitutes a particular for the universal in anticipation of the universal. In *Grundrisse*, Marx noticed the "contradiction" that occurs between money as the universal unit of account and money as a particular commodity that can be exchanged: "Money—the common form into which all commodities as exchange values are transformed, i.e. the universal commodity—must itself exist as a particular commodity alongside the others, since what is required is not only that they can be measured against it in the head, but that they can be changed and exchanged for it in the actual exchange process. The contradiction which thereby enters, to be developed elsewhere."[25] The consequence of such a contradiction is that there is no longer such a thing as nature, society, or even history. No such universal terms are ever achieved or explained. One always substitutes a particular for the universal: a natural process for nature as a whole; a social institution for society; a historical event for history. Lacking access to knowledge of the full order of nature, one projects partial and particular images to substitute for the universal. Yet what are rendered invisible in a commodified, naturalistic, secular ontology based on evidence and information are not merely social forces, but temporal forces. In the very act of saving time, one loses time altogether. In the construction of secular knowledge, a knowledge of the "present age," one excludes the past and the future in favor of an imagined eschaton of perfect knowledge. This attempt to save time by attaining a partial vision of perfect knowledge in advance of the eschaton is the very move that at once eliminates all possibility of true knowledge of time and allows the entry of diabolical forces into human thought.

The consequences of the substitution of the particular for a projected universal have a significance that amounts to both the origin and the end of modernity. First, since there is no necessity that governs which particular should be substituted for the universal, this structure of thinking can capture all desires. All points of view can be represented here, for the substitution of the particular for the universal is a purely formal structure. It does not initially seem to matter which content will come to fill it. Progress toward the universal offers the promise of limitless possibility. In the secular eschaton, once progress has been achieved, people will have the freedom to do as they please with their time and money, since they will no longer be subjected to natural necessity or social obligation. As a commodity, then, money stands in for any specific will or desire; it is the material representation of a universal form. Second, however, those particulars that are best suited to occupying the place of the universal are those that are capable of universalizing themselves. A conception of the people as supreme power, for example, or a conception of human identity as self-consciousness, or a conception of truth as founded on empirical evidence, or a conception of money as supreme value — it is astonishing to consider the extent to which human activity has been regulated by such autopoietic ideas. The relevant characteristics of such ideas include both an openness to relation, so that the rest of the world is judged from their perspective, and a closed interior generated by self-reference, so that they become the sole measures of themselves. In the case of money, since it is both means of payment and unit of account, the best way to acquire what one wishes is to make money first. Thus, money posits itself as the universal, supreme value and the means of access to all other values. At the same time, money becomes a kind of encompassing membrane that determines what will count as valuable, just as empirical truth determines what counts as real, or self-consciousness determines what counts as experience, or the will of the people determines what happens in the course of history. Third, once significance has been delegated to the universalized particular, it then becomes the source of all

benefits, wealth, and significance. By saving time and borrowing a particular postulate from a future secular utopia, one owes a debt of gratitude.
One is under an obligation to demonstrate that one's idol will indeed appear in the secular utopia. In this respect, the extreme vulnerability of the
monetary system constitutes the very source of its power. Not only are
economic agents committed to making future profits to pay off current
debts, but governments are committed to preserving and restoring a fragile
monetary system as the very condition of all social activity. The devastating
effects of financial crises demonstrate how dependent the "real economy"
is on monetary systems.[26] Moreover, such devastating effects tend to impoverish and disempower ordinary people, while international bodies ensure that reconstruction gives prime importance to the re-stabilization of
the monetary system in the interests of international capital as the precondition for any political action.[27] Volatility and instability, the result of the
"internal contradictions" of capital, only strengthen the system as a whole.
The analogies hold with other universalized particulars. The absence of
clarity concerning the will of the people makes the determination of public
opinion all the more necessary. Failures of human self-consciousness make
self-knowledge all the more important. Errors and prejudices make empirical verification of the truth more urgent. The freedom of modernity entails
an unlimited debt to the future that it has created. Within the illusion of
modernity, life is determined by eschatology.

ECONOMIC INSTABILITIES

The end of modernity is a crisis of representation. Once nature is no longer
stable, it cannot be effectively represented and mastered; once concepts are
no longer stable, political decisions can no longer be taken according to
principles or pragmatic considerations. The humanistic representation of
two kinds of power — of the body and of the will — proves to be an illusion.
Humanity has always been at the mercy of other principles and powers.

The problem of the relation between the economic and the political
should be considered in relation to the crisis of representation. Where political power relies on a qualitative representation of nature and society,
economic power relies on a quantitative representation of exchange value.
This difference in representation is decisive. Debates about whether eco-

nomic globalization leads to the "end of politics" or the subjection of the nation-state to the power of finance capital may be resolved at an ontological level. If the principal power of the nation-state is sovereign legislation, or a restriction of liberty, then its power is limited. One may restrict the movement of bodies through force and shape the determination of the will through threats, but one can no longer legislate for rates of exchange value. Although the state may attempt to act in the economic field by controlling interest rates, the money supply, rates of taxation, borrowing, and spending, it remains one economic agent alongside others. The state merely has a power of economic intervention. Of course, the economy cannot operate very effectively without a set of market regulations enforced by the state and a currency supported by the state. Yet the state cannot operate very effectively without the economy as its source of wealth and power. There is a mutual dependence between economic and political power. This dependence is asymmetrical in one vital respect: where state power is localized in a people and territory, economic power is localized in money. One is static, the other is mobile. States may be heterogeneous, but capital is relatively homogeneous. Where capital can choose which states it does business with, a state cannot easily choose which capital will benefit its polity (leaving aside, for now, considerations of a hegemony of currencies). A state may regulate the movement of capital, in theory and in the past, subordinating economic power to political ends. Once the movement of capital is deregulated, however, it is like gas that has been let out of a bottle.[28] Capital cannot be restored without some stronger force of attraction drawing back inward investment. Once capital has been liberated, it will be reluctant to commit itself permanently to the economic fate of a particular nation and currency; exchange in search of better prices and profits is the essential power of money. In this respect, economic globalization is irreversible short of a breakdown in transport, communications, banking, or energy infrastructures. States that have released the movement of capital have little choice but to subordinate all other political aims to the attraction of investment or risk losing the source of their power. Money is the supreme political authority in modernity. It constitutes and expresses the will of the people. It forms the illusory autonomy of the political subject at the same time that such autonomy is undermined.

Money, in its essence, responds to the crisis of representation. For where representation within a polity corresponds to perceptions of truth or right, to observation or to habits, customs, and laws, money provides a medium for the representation of exchange value. The value that money represents, then, is merely the value that could be exchanged for it—in other words, a value that is represented by others. This, in turn, represents the value of other exchanges and other representations. There is no grounding of exchange value outside the specular realm of representation, in which representations can only represent other representations. Whereas political representation is constructed internally in relation to a culture where everything has a determinate place and value, economic representation reflects the activity of a set of exterior evaluations. Exchange value is never the value of an object in itself or the use value of an object to a particular person or culture. It is the value that may be substituted for the object in exchange. It is the value that remains when the internal relations of a polity or culture are broken by the alienation of property.

If politics concerns the construction of a public space of representation, economics concerns the construction of a different kind of public space: the market. In the market, goods can be found that have traveled some considerable distance from their sites of production. Such markets operate inefficiently by means of barter exchange; they operate far more effectively with the use of money. In Aristotle's account of the invention of money, metal was adopted because of its mobility and ease of transportation, and was stamped with a sign to save the trouble of weighing, for the purpose of long-distance trade.[29] In such trade, value is carried beyond the polis and its representation of values. In spite of the sovereign's stamp on the coinage, the value of money is determined by possibilities of exchange in other markets, not simply those within the polis itself. Even when used within a political space, money represents value that belongs outside. It is a representation of value that continues to function when all internal representations break down. Indifferent to the particular goods and values with which it may be exchanged, money represents the abstract quantity of an exchange value. Money is apparently neutral in exchange, indifferent to buying or selling, production or consumption. It merely facilitates exchange by measuring and storing value, having no intrinsic interest on its own account. Money has political and ethical neutrality. It produces and destroys nothing; it is indifferent to any exploitation, violence, appropriation, or exclusion carried out in order to obtain its services. Money continues to bear value through political crises and through nihilism.

Aristotle was prescient here. The use of money to make money, money that bears interest, and the quest for profits for their own sake have no determinate value and so no place within the polis. The condemnation of usury derives from this principle. For money that makes money leads to the acquisition of a power that has no political essence or limits. The power of accumulated money threatens chaos and nihilism by overpowering all existing values. It threatens to dismantle the social order piece by piece through appropriation, substitution, and exchange. Economic globalization is the completion of this anti-political process throughout the world through millions of minor acts of alienation between people and people, people and land, and land and its products or resources. It fragments the world of public representation through substitution and exchange.

Nevertheless, exchange value does not dissolve prior social relations without reconstituting its own public space of representation. As Adam Smith explained at the opening of *The Wealth of Nations*, trade is the condition of possibility of the division of labor and of economic interdependence.[30] Money facilitates the growth of a new social network of public representation. The market is the social form that replaces public representation. Values become local, variable, and purely quantitative in an extended system of markets.

Money mediates between representation and reality. While exchange value is represented in terms of a quantity of money, a quantity of money also represents demand. The degree of one's desire for any good or service is represented publicly in terms of the sum of money one is willing to pay for it. Of course, one's desire may exceed the money one has available for payment, but such desire is not publicly represented. In a market society, political values are irrelevant. If public representation occurs only in the form of abstract quantities, then evaluation can be represented only in the quantitative form of a degree of desire. There is no effective public representation apart from as a degree of desire. In the market, then, all evaluations must be invested with a degree of desire to become public; they must further be backed by a sum of money. Money, which renders demands effective, is a reality principle that realizes desire. It makes exchange possible. It does so, however, by being desirable itself. Money is acceptable in exchange because it is the means of exchange itself. Since it may be exchanged for anything, money mediates between and coordinates desires. As the means of access to the realization of desire, money is supremely to be desired; as that which is supremely desired, money is acceptable in exchange and so becomes the means of access to the realization of desire. It is this vicious circle that underlies the trust in money. Money has a dual role in representation. On the one hand, it represents the objective social value that could be obtained in exchange for it; on the other hand, it represents a degree of subjective desire for that value. It joins desire to satisfaction in representation itself. As such, it constitutes the very texture of market society. Market society is constituted not simply by exchange, therefore, but by the representation of exchange as a satisfaction of desire.

Representation takes on a different form in the market from that found in politics. In politics, representation reproduces a form or concept. In economics, representation reproduces a value or quantity. Nevertheless, there is a sense in which representation in money is already fractured and not itself. For money is at once, according to the economists, a means of payment, a measure of value, and a store of value.[31] Exchange value is at once acquired through money, represented by money, and preserved in money. While other commodities may be taken as representing their exchange value, money remains distinct from other commodities in a number of respects. It has a socially validated monopoly of equivalence, expressed both in its status as legal tender and in its being uniquely required for the payment of wages, taxes, interest, and dividends, and for the repayment of loans. Moreover, where other commodities have to be sold to realize their exchange value, money represents its exchange value without needing to be exchanged. As such, money is the object of an unlimited desire for accumulation. Furthermore, money is the measure of profits, yet it can yield a profit only through investment, flowing out and back through exchange.

To represent exchange value as a price in terms of money, therefore, is to synthesize three different considerations into a single quantity. In the first place, a price represents a sum of money, which represents the value of all sorts of other goods that may be acquired through money. Value is formed through an imagination of exchange, generated by all kinds of desire. In the second place, a price represents a sum of money, which represents a specific degree of the demand for money. In the third place, a price represents a sum of money, which represents a certain degree of power for making profits through investment. All three of these desires find public expression in a price: a desire for goods, a desire for money, and a desire for profits. Money is a source of perpetual dissimulation and equivocation. At one and the same time, money is that which makes desires effective through exchange, that which makes desires achievable through accumulation, and that which makes desires more effective through profits. As a means of payment, money participates in the sphere of objective reality through circulation; as a measure of value, it participates in the sphere of subjective reality as a degree of desire; as a store of value, it participates in an impersonal sphere of credit or the possibility of expressing desire and realizing value. As the universal mediator, money substitutes its own desire as the secret essence of every heart's desire.

Money therefore reconstitutes the social order as an order of interdependence, of desire, and of credit. As the means of realization of the social order, facilitating interdependence, desire, and credit, it is that which is the supreme principle of reality. In a market society, there is no higher aim than making money, for money is the reality principle. Within a market society, there is an unlimited demand for profits. This power of realization and this demand are purely social forces, subsisting outside the human will in society itself. It is an impersonal and abstract force, beyond the pleasure principle. Indeed, as the means of access to pleasure, the means of making desire effective, money must be acquired through profits or hoarding. One passes through that which has no intrinsic desirability — the acquisition of money — to gain access to pleasure. This is the profound link between capitalism and the structure of the Oedipus complex. More than this, it calls on desire as the only mode of evaluation capable of structuring market society. It constructs an abstract and impersonal politics in the interstices, faults, and ruins of existing political orders: a politics of desire. Economic flows destabilize politics by fracturing existing relationships by means of appropriation, substitution, and exchange. Modernity is always already anachronistic, constructing its ineffectual representations on a base that is economically destabilized. Economic flows, then, re-stabilize a market society, using representations that may be ineffective from a political point of view within an economy of desire.

It is vital to differentiate, therefore, between the self-representation of modern political society as deliberately ordered according to the rationality of the collective will and a market society shaped by irrational flows of desire and money. Of course, the two forms only exist together and in mutual presupposition. Yet modern political society is purely formal; economic society is real. If there are cases of successful subsuming of actual societies beneath rational political projects, they are exceptions rather than the rule. They are islands of stability in an ocean of instability. The extraordinary consequence is that political judgments—whether of the state, of the citizen, or of a revolutionary minority—remain largely impotent. An entire model of political thought and action remains anachronistic. In the face of money, even sovereignty lacks power. Modernity is at an end.

MARKET INSTABILITIES

Economic society does, of course, also have its own intrinsic instabilities. In a purely market society, a degree of wealth can be measured by one's accumulated assets. Assets gain their value from exchange. When a market society is inhabited by a capitalist society, by contrast, assets may be regarded as capital stock and therefore as factors for the production of value. The value of an asset is no longer given by exchange alone. Rather, it is given by speculation on a rate of profit. Value no longer measures an accumulated stock in relation to desire. It measures a differential rate of profit. Fixed quantities are destabilized by underlying rates of return; asset values fluctuate wildly and become subject to speculation; speculation inflates values in a self-perpetuating cycle, guaranteeing the short-term success of speculation as a further form of destabilization and re-stabilization. On the one hand, money is a determinate quantity, entered on bank statements and balance sheets, circulating in finite units; on the other hand, capital is a rate of profit or credit, a differential rate, value in motion, independent of the material form that it assumes. Capital destabilizes the representation of value in terms of money from within. Under normal conditions of capitalist representation, all knowledge is quantifiable information. Science and management become purely matters of bookkeeping, as though the world were under the sovereign control of the rational subject. Yet all movement, creation, and selection happen elsewhere. Every step in the construction of knowledge may be rational, but the whole enterprise is entirely delirious, shaped by interdependence and flows of desire, belief, speculation, and credit. In spite of popular assumptions, however, speculation effects a limited degree of destabilization because it tends to enclose unstable positive feedbacks within stabilizing negative feedbacks. If prices rise too high, it is time to sell; if prices fall too low, it is time to buy. The principal forms of economic instability lie elsewhere.

In the first place, there is the relative strength or weakness of currencies insofar as this exceeds political control. Instability may be expressed in comparisons with other currencies in the form of devaluation or in comparison with the same currency across time in the form of inflation or deflation. Such effects are central to economic analyses of the politics of money. Such crises are geographically determined; they may be the principal form of expression through which the absolute limits of capitalism are actualized. They may also be the principal forms through which contemporary warfare is threatened or enacted. The dangers of the use of force may be avoided by achieving economic domination of another nation-state. Even the U.S. military remains helpless before the buyers and sellers of U.S. Treasury bonds: devaluation of a currency is at once devaluation of that nation's purchasing power and a partial enhancement of its productive power. It is also a devaluation of the entire nation's assets, leading to an initial flight of foreign capital investment, followed by the purchase of a nation's assets at bargain prices, eventually resulting in a continual economic drain in the repatriation of profits. Currency crises are good for speculative investors who may reap the benefits several times over.

More significant for our purposes, however, are the absolute economic crises. In the second place, there is the unlimited quest for profits characteristic of capitalist society, with its consequent requirement of increased consumption. As previously mentioned, the mechanism for the creation of wealth depends on a quest for monetary value driven by the threat of exclusion or poverty, by the self-positing of money as the supreme bearer of power, by the enhanced power of those institutions that habitually acquire money, and by the exploitation of those who are compelled to labor for subsistence. This process of continual growth or economic colonization drives the increase in both production and consumption. It produces instability when consumption uses up resources and reaches its physical limits. As previously discussed, economic crisis results from physical instability.

The physical limits to the growth in capital as the means of production are absolute, although capitalism itself may survive and prosper even within a context of rapidly shrinking GDP. Here, again, speculators may profit from the rise in commodity prices as well as from shorting the stock markets.

In the third place, money is gradually replaced by credit, or credit comes to take the form of money itself, for it is necessary to produce both goods and money. An unlimited quest for profits is made possible both by the production of value through industry and enterprise and by the production of money for circulation and reserves. For every quantity of exchange value produced, it is necessary that sufficient money be available that can be exchanged for it. In large part, this problem is solved by recirculation, since what is produced is later consumed, whereas money can continue to circulate. Economic growth, however, does result in an increased demand for money, since the timing of the production and distribution of goods and services may not match entirely with the timing of their consumption. In practice, such accumulated stocks may be immense but such inefficiencies are mitigated by all the varieties of financial intermediation. Financial intermediation places a value in purely nominal assets in order to facilitate the temporal process of market exchange. Credit here functions effectively as money, as a store of value that has perfect liquidity and can be exchanged at will. Growth in production is therefore matched or even exceeded by a growth in credit. A capitalist economy is supplemented by a credit economy. Money itself is largely displaced by credit; indeed, as a mere token of exchange value, money itself is revealed in its essence to derive from credit rather than from a hypothetical and unlimited process of exchange.[32] As Geoffrey Ingham concludes, "Capitalist credit-money is nothing more than a network of claims backed by banks' and states' promises to pay that are fabricated into a hierarchy of credibility by foreign exchange markets and global credit-rating agencies."[33]

The creation of credit has a curious effect on production, for it marks the emergence of a further layer of spectral financial power. Money as credit, whether in the form of paper money or an electronic record in a bank account, is created as a simultaneous asset and liability. Money is created in the form of loans as a claim against property. Such loans have limited inflationary effects that apply to speculative assets such as property; they are guaranteed by an undertaking to make sufficient money to pay back the loan. The money added to the economy must be withdrawn; economic agents who have taken out loans must act as economic deflators, seeking to withdraw money from the economy, for loans are repaid in the currency of their issues, not in terms of pure exchange value. If they are repaid at interest, then more money eventually must be withdrawn from the economy than was originally added. Since the money was newly created, then it must be replaced by the creation of further money elsewhere in the form of a loan. The entire economic system functions as a spiral of increasing debt, with individuals, businesses, and governments committed to ever increasing levels of overall debt in the system as a whole. Such has been the case throughout the history of modernity, even if concentrations of debts have always been localized. The result is that the quest for profits is less an aspiration than an obligation. The global economy, within capitalism, has always already been destabilized by a credit economy that functions as its internal milieu and condition of possibility. The spiral of debt can increase indefinitely, progressively enslaving democratic citizens to contracted debts until the physical limits to economic growth are reached. Debt will then need to be redeemed by massive levels of inflation, devaluation, and impoverishment. The illusion of accumulated wealth is displaced by the reality of accumulated debt. Economic collapse, often regional in its most intense effects, is the outcome of the end of modernity.

In the fourth place, there is also a more subtle form in which the economy is undermined from within. While a market society gives birth to capitalism, and this in turn is driven by a credit society, the credit society opens the possibility of a further economic form. This may be considered under the unprepossessing rubric of financial disintermediation: the separation of forms of credit and speculative value from their productive roles within capitalism and intermediary roles within a market. While the trade in derivatives may facilitate market activity by providing a means to hedge against risk, it may also become a means of profit seeking in its own right. While buying shares may contribute to investment, betting on the movement of share prices has a limited effect on production. Speculation on derivatives and currencies, despite the vast profits and sums involved, may be considered a specialist activity, the prerogative of expert investment funds. The common wisdom is that it is nearly impossible for amateur traders to beat the general rate of return in the market. About 90 percent of amateur traders fail to make profits. As such, derivatives trading has little impact on wider society, however lucrative it may be for the successful few. The advent of Internet communications and of speculative tools such as contracts for difference, options, and covered warrants, however, allow the opportunities provided by disintermediation to become available to the ordinary investor who is willing to take large risks. By means of charting, or the technical analysis of price movements; short-term trading; high rates of gearing; and compound interest, extraordinary rates of speculative profit may soon be available to the privileged common person. Even if considerable expertise is required to trade successfully, such expertise is already for sale at affordable prices. This process is significant for a number of reasons. By means of selling short—that is, agreeing to sell an asset one does not possess at the current price so that one can later buy it at a lower price before delivery—one can make large profits when the markets are falling. Profit-making becomes detached from the productive economy. Once this means of making a living becomes available to a large class of people apart from the productive economy, it signifies the emergence of a new economic class beyond capitalist relations of production—a class of unlimited power that can thrive when all other classes do not. Capitalism therefore undermines itself from the inside with the growth of derivatives trading. Rates of profit from rapid price fluctuations, amplified by gearing and compound interest, far exceed the rates of profit achieved by production and investment. The productive, capitalist economy is becoming subservient to the speculative economy of casino capitalism. Capitalism is evolving once more. It is becoming a society of speculation and credit operating in the service of a parasitic class who control access to profits. The full implications of such an evolution are not yet clear. Such a class requires only a conventional economy of sufficient size to fulfill its demand for consumption and to provide a spectacle of predictable price movements from which it can reap a profit. Its continued existence is otherwise autonomous.[34]

CONCLUSION

Modernity has never achieved human mastery of nature or the liberation of the human will. Striving for wealth and freedom has had the effect of subordinating humanity to the impersonal and abstract force of money. Once money becomes the condition of possibility of society as such, whether in the form of market exchange, capital accumulation, credit intermediation, or speculative disintermediation, then the value of money, however fragile, must be maintained at all costs. Indeed, the very fragility of the financial system, its vulnerability to frequent regional crises, is the very source of its power. Traditional political means have no force against its spectral power. No institution, whether in the form of a state, a revolutionary vanguard, or a people, is able to control it. The power of money cannot be seized by physical force, even if a finite quantity of valuable assets can. The power of money cannot be restrained by legislation or an act of will, for the locus of its value is always reflected elsewhere in future exchange. Attempting to control money is like attempting to seize hold of an image in a mirror or a ghost. The spectral power of money, for all its ephemerality, is no less real. It is even invulnerable to enlightened critique, for there is no mode of social representation that escapes its power. The specter of money hangs over democracy as its inner principle or truth. Only money gives effective public representation to the expression of desire.

Money is not the sole principle of social reality. In contemporary society, however, it does have a peculiar dominance, a spectral power. It mediates between representation and reality. Attempts to counterpoise a different social order to the present are therefore caught in a dilemma. It is one thing to represent a different social order; it is another to make that order effective and real. It is one thing to will that an alternative be realized; it is another for that will to be effective. Politics cannot circumnavigate the problem of money without acquiring its own political "energy," without acquiring the authority to make a political will effective. In the economic world of natural selection, capitalism expands because of its own internal dynamism, its own spectral power. Any challengers would have to demonstrate a greater capacity for survival, colonization, and appropriation than that present within capitalism. The unique advantage of a society mediated by money is that it represents value in an external milieu, in a form that may be reflected and appropriated by all others, independently of their own political preferences. Money succeeds in shaping society because it is the element of the exterior, beyond political representation. No genuine political alternatives are possible without a new mode of representation, a new political body—one capable of redemption from debt at the same time as that it constitutes the texture of an entirely different social order. Progress cannot be achieved by turning back to older, pre-market society models for these will remain forever vulnerable to the market's corrosive power. Political progress can come only from passing through the internal logic of the political body of money, appropriating its soul and distinctive power while subordinating it to newly created ends. Such a political problem requires a careful analysis of the theology of money.

A first radical conclusion is ontological. It is no longer sufficient to oppose will and matter, representation and production, being and becoming, the one and the many, transcendence and immanence, for the relations between these dualisms are always mediated by a spectral power that authorizes their realization. It is a question of belief and desire. Belief and desire are everywhere. Even if no one really wants money—it is always a means, never an end—everyone believes in money, everyone desires money, or, rather, money is the reality, the interiority of belief and desire in which we dwell. It is not we who desire money; it is money that desires in us. For where thought as representation is an abstraction from time, an attempt to master a given space, money as credit is an abstraction from space, an appropriation of time. Credit offers value in advance; in doing so, it functions as the condition of the creation of that future value. Credit posits itself as a spectral, temporal force. In addition to the determination of bodies in space through physical power and the representation by means of concepts in imagination through the power of the will, there is also the power to determine time. It is the power to determine attention. Money produces nothing—not even desire. It gives credit. It appeals to the future. To put it another way, it prays. Ontology is determined by eschatology. Life is determined by a possible future that attempts to actualize itself in us, even if the outcome of this actualization bears little resemblance to the future as conceived.

A second radical conclusion is political. It is no longer sufficient to oppose political forces of the state in the name of autonomy or self-determination. At present, the powers of inhuman ecological forces and meta-human forces of demand and debt are rapidly growing, leaving little scope for self-determination through political activity. The sphere of human freedom has narrowed. Even at this level, possibilities of resistance to a dominant credit capitalism are confronted by more formidable powers than ever before in the alliance between the military, industry, finance capital, corporate media, informationalized knowledge, and consumerized subjectivity. Any successful resistance to the dominant power structure would have to face destabilization by external forces, economic sanctions, direct military opposition, or simple exclusion from the means of production. The global history of modernity, and especially the history of the twentieth century, has repeated the same drama throughout the world with almost a single outcome. When dealing with ecological and spectral powers, it is useless to aim at seizing or abolishing the power of the state. Powers have to be engaged at their own level: ecological adaptation to new environmental circumstances, for example, or the creation of new structures and practices of belief and desire.

A third radical conclusion is that the "energy" of the political is inhuman. It is a spectral power that may insert itself into human life through belief and desire. Such may be the political significance of the world religions; such may be the political significance of money. The question is no longer one of a transcendent power of divinity intervening in nature; nor is it of immanent powers that are produced entirely within nature. For "nature" itself is indeterminate and incomplete, opening itself out onto temporal and spectral forces wherever the complexity of life opens itself onto multiple possible connections and determinations. Such virtual potencies, while absolutely prohibited in modern thought, may form the substance of a politics of the future. Such a politics must begin with an ontological, political, and theological inquiry into money.

A TREATISE ON MONEY

A PARABLE

The nature of money is not generally understood; it is accessible only to the exceptionally wealthy. We are convinced that economic governance is scrupulously determined in accordance with the nature of money; nevertheless, it is an extremely painful thing to build our cities upon a substance whose nature we do not understand. I am not thinking of the disadvantages involved when only a few and not the whole people understand the nature of money, and the opportunities this affords for deception. Such disadvantages are perhaps of no great importance. For the wealthy have obviously no cause to be influenced by personal interests inimical to us into deceiving us about money, for the nature of money was made to their advantage from the beginning, and they themselves stand above the need for money since they can rely on mutual credit. This seems to be why the understanding of the nature of money is entrusted exclusively into their hands. Of course, there is prudence in that, but also hardship for us. Such hardship is probably unavoidable.

The very existence of economic laws deriving from the nature of money, however, is at most a matter of presumption. Some of us have attentively scrutinized the behaviour of the wealthy, and claim to recognize among the countless number of transactions certain main tendencies which permit of formulation in terms of principles. Yet when in accordance with these scrupulously tested and logically ordered conclusions we seek to adjust ourselves somewhat for the present or the future, everything becomes uncertain, and our work seems only an intellectual game, for perhaps these laws that we are trying to unravel do not exist at all. There are actually some who are of the opinion that if there is any economic law, it is simply this: the laws of economics are what the wealthy do. The overwhelming majority of the people, however, account for discrepancies and failed forecasts by the fact that the science of economics is far from complete, and that the material available, prodigious as it looks, is still too meager. This view, so comfortless as far as the present is concerned, is lightened only by the belief that the time will eventually come when the science of economics is complete, and the nature of money is fully understood. Then wealth will belong to the people as a whole. It is not that the wealthy are despised; on the contrary, we are more inclined to despise ourselves for our failure to understand and acquire money. And this is the real reason why those who doubt the existence of economic laws remain so few — even though their doctrine is so attractive — since it unequivocally recognizes the right of the wealthy to do as they please.

The problem can be expressed in a sort of paradox: any party that would repudiate all belief not only in the laws of economics, but also in the necessity for money as such, would have the whole people behind it. Yet no such party can come into existence, for nobody would dare to repudiate money. The sole indubitable law that is imposed on us is the need for money, and must we deprive ourselves of that one law?

Adapted from FRANZ KAFKA, "The Problem of Our Laws," in *The Collected Short Stories of Franz Kafka*, 437–38.

Three

ECOLOGY OF MONEY

CAPITAL

3.1.1 CAPITAL IS THE MEANS of production that has itself been produced. Since everything has been produced, all means of production are capital.

Production is inherent in the natural order. Stars, planets, elements, compounds, cells, genetic codes and living bodies, for example, form the means of production for more complex forms. Natural capital is produced independently of human activity. Human activity modifies existing processes of production by selection and extraction, by juxtaposition and assembly, and by fueling and catalysis. All economic production involves the cooperation of natural and human-produced capital.

The production of capital involves accumulation, invention, and assembly. It is one thing to produce and accumulate; it is another to produce a means of production. An accumulated stock of product does not become a means of production until a productive machine is invented into which it may be assembled as a part. Stock is only potentially capital in reference to a determinate machine or productive process. Potential capital only becomes capital when it is actually assembled into a productive machine.

Nevertheless, it is insufficient to simply accumulate stock, to invent form, and to assemble parts. The machine, to become productive, has to be switched on. It has to be powered, whether by electricity, combustion, human skill, animal strength, or solar power. Production consumes a flow of energy. If a common modern metaphysics represents the world in terms of matter, information, space–time, and energy, then these dimensions are represented in the production of capital as the accumulation of stock, the invention of form, the assembly of parts, and the supply of energy.

Money is a form of capital. An ecology of money explains the role of money as a means of production in terms of the relations it forms with other modes of capital. Yet a difficulty arises when one tries to represent money in relation to capital. Money is an accumulated stock. It is not, however, assembled as a material part of a productive machine. Instead, it is exchanged for an accumulated stock, for an invented form, for the labor involved in assembly, or for a supply of energy. Money is also an invented form. It does not, however, govern the arrangement of parts. Instead, it is a form that measures the value of the stock, form, labor, and energy used in production. Money also plays a decisive role in assembly. The availability of money determines whether investment in capital can take place. Money does not, of course, stand alongside the workers to assemble the parts. Instead, it promises value and so enables itself to be exchanged for stock, for plans, for labor, or for energy. Moreover, money is invested for the sake of a profit. The value promised by money may take the form of products that fulfill needs and desires or the form of profits in money.

Money may therefore be differentiated from other forms of capital as a stock that is not assembled or consumed, as a form that does not order or arrange, and as an act that accomplishes nothing other than promising. As an object of pure exchange, it is not an object of use. As a pure quantity, it imposes no conditions on form. As a passive instrument, it takes no active role in directing assembly. Money is a condition of production that is not itself productive. It defies the metaphysical categories of representation by means of its anomalous participation in each category. The question of whether money participates in the category of energy is more perplexing. Money is inert; it contains no physical or potential energy. The role of money in capital production remains a philosophical conundrum.

The common solution is to regard money as a symbol of human evaluation and desire.[1] Money is treated as an ambassador for the private human will in the public and material world. Money expresses the effective demands of the sovereign, rational subject. If money leads to accumulation, invention and assembly, this is because it expresses the agency of the human subject. Money is the instrument of desire; desire is required, alongside energy, to realize capital production.

Such a solution leaves open the question of how human capital, itself a product of processes of reproduction, nutrition, and evolution, can become a human subject. Moreover, these subjects are inaccessible apart from their material and symbolic expressions and their representations in consciousness. There is a weight of philosophical argumentation that questions the existence and autonomy of such a subject.[2] Although one might observe agreement between private consciousness and material and symbolic expression, one cannot observe a strict order of causality between these in either direction. One cannot therefore be confident whether money expresses desire or desire expresses money. The common assumption that money expresses desire arises from the observation that one can desire without money, and money itself evidently lacks energy, qualitative form, or active will. The human subject is invoked to explain how money can accumulate value, measure value, and promise value. Money is treated as a substance, a standard, and an instrument. The problem that remains to be explained, however, is that of the objective nature of the value that the subject is supposed to act on through the symbol of money.[3]

Nevertheless, we need to decide in advance whether such value is the precondition or the product of money. This problem can be easily resolved by a consideration of the difference between representation and production.[4] A productive machine can be represented in imagination in terms of its accumulated stock, invented form, and assembled parts. It may even, by extension, be represented in some malleable material or symbolic medium. A represented machine, however, will never function to produce because its new medium lacks its own source of energy. Indeed, media of representation are chosen precisely for their malleability, which involves inertness and a lack of energetic process. An imagined machine is reproduced under the force of the imagination alone: instead of bearing its own energy, it bears the energy lent to it by the vividness of the imagination; instead of bearing its own force of attraction and selection, it is subject to the force of attraction and selection by which the contents of the imagination are composed; instead of bearing its own power of evolution and invention, invention is regarded after the fact as a product of a fertile mind. Thus, when the world is reproduced in imagination, it is no longer reproduced as productive capital but as passive and inert. Such is the source of the theology of the human subject as creator. Since the world is only known as represented, it must be supplemented by the transcendent decrees of a human subject.

There is no reason to extend the power that a mind exercises over the imagination, or that a hand exercises over malleable materials and symbols, to the relation that humanity has with the world as a whole. The notion that the production of capital occurs outside the sphere of human activity is sufficient to dispel this modern myth. Energy, force, attraction, selection, and invention are not the sole preserve of human culture. Representation itself must be explained. Representation is a process of abstraction that reproduces forms without their material substance. It separates forms from the context in which they dwell and function; it separates forms from the passage of time and from their own productive processes; it separates forms from the forces that impinge on them to give them orientation and direction.

When money is represented apart from its context, then the accumulation of relations that give it meaning is neglected in favor of its residue of a material or symbolic substance. When money is represented apart from time, then its role as an agent of investment is neglected in favor of its role as a store of value. When money is represented apart from credit, then its role as producer of value is neglected in favor of its role as a standard measure of value. In short, the entire nature of money as productive capital is occluded by representation. Since the mystery of capital production remains unexplained, the human imagination merely extends its own power, a free power of imagination, so that it appears as though the human subject exercises its power through the malleable instrument of money. Such a power is extended in imagination only. The one who believes that he can do anything through money ends up doing anything for money.

It is not necessary to assume the imposition of value as a transcendent form on nature. Value is an abstraction that derives from representing nature in terms of money — or at least, in terms of a form that is assumed to be composed of discreet, inert units, independent of the temporal work of thinking or representation and entirely passive, subject to the sovereign decisions of the will. Value is represented in a form that is taken to be independent of evaluation. If it emerges that such a form has an active role in evaluation, as is the case with money, then even the highest values are devalued.

An alternative is to represent nature in terms of productive capital. This does not eliminate the dangers of illusion. It does, however, liberate thought

from subservience to the form of representation by enabling the direction
of attention to relational context, to temporal process, and to orientation to
the future. For, as we shall see, money contributes its own specific determination as a promise of value. The power of such a promise exists in addition
to energy and desire. Consideration of money as productive capital enables
the elaboration of an ontology, a politics, and a theology of money.

3.1.2 Capital is the source of all wealth. Wealth derives from accumulation,
invention and assembly. It also requires a supply of energy, instigation by
desire, and facilitation by the promise of money. Wealth is poorly understood when it is considered in terms of products alone. An accumulation of
stock or assets provides a very limited conception of wealth. Accumulated
stock is subject to consumption and depletion. The process is entropic: it
begins in wealth and ends in poverty. If, by contrast, accumulated stock is
assembled into a productive machine, then the output may be consumed
without harming the integrity of the machine. Machines may continue to
produce so long as they draw their inputs from the outputs of other machines. While the entire system may be entropic, drawing energy from the
sun, machines may continue to produce in a sustainable process for as long
as the required inputs can be produced by other machines, and all products can be inputs for further machines. Sustainable economic production
concentrates on the production of capital rather than the consumption of
accumulated stock. Capital itself is negentropic: it is the production rather
than the depletion of wealth.

Accumulated stock, therefore, cannot be considered capital until it has
the potential to be incorporated into a productive machine. Nothing in
itself may be considered a means of production; it becomes a means of
production only in relation to the machine that may incorporate it. Capital
is therefore a relative notion. The value of capital appreciates to the extent
that capital becomes capable of entering into viable processes of production. The invention of new processes of production and the assembly of
productive machines make vital contributions to the creation of wealth. An
increase in wealth occurs through accumulation, invention, and assembly.
Capital also involves energy, desire, and promise. It is a process of intermediation. Capital is the site and occasion where parts of a machine can
interact productively. It cannot be reduced to a set of material parts, an

ideal form, or spatial contiguity. Capital has the mysterious power to convert assembled parts into an active process.

The creation of wealth, therefore, is poorly understood in terms of an accumulation of value. The creation of wealth is more properly considered the creation of capital. While the creation of wealth expends energy, it may be understood in terms of the accumulation of resources, the invention of forms, the assembly of machines, the intensification of desire, and the increase in the credit of promise.

3.1.3 Capital can be exchanged for money, just as money can be exchanged for capital. This process of exchange facilitates the assembly of capital and so contributes to the process of production. Exchangeability itself is part of the means of production, even though the process of circulation involves products that are not in themselves part of a productive process while in circulation. Money may therefore be regarded as capital insofar as it stimulates production through facilitating exchange.

The exchange of capital for money has another effect: capital may be represented as having a determinate value in terms of the quantity of money that is exchanged for it. Moreover, to be exchanged, capital, like anything else, must be represented in this way as having a determinate price. A price, like a hoard of money, produces nothing. Yet the act of pricing, through considerations of exchange, facilitates exchange and therefore production. Then as a represented quantity, money has no productive role. Yet as a quantitative representation, money facilitates production. In precisely the same role, money is both unproductive and productive. Money becomes active and productive through making itself into a passive body for representation.

This paradoxical nature of money is the source of some significant illusions. On the one hand, the representation of capital in terms of money as an exchange value obscures its specific nature as capital. When capital is represented in terms of money as an exchange value, it is represented as already sold. In other words, it has been disappropriated or alienated. It is no longer part of a productive machine. It is reduced to an accumulated stock. Capital is represented, then, in terms of the product of a process of production rather than in terms of the productive process itself. It is represented without energy, desire, or belief. The distinctive element that makes it capital has been removed; even the product or accumulated stock has been removed. All that remains in representation is a sum of money. To measure capital in terms of an accumulation of exchange value is to miss the decisive ingredient of capital as capital.

On the other hand, the representation of capital in terms of money facilitates its nature as capital. For the purchaser of capital, such a representation holds out the promise that capital may be acquired and assembled and so become productive. The representation of capital in terms of money increases its promise, its capacity to be incorporated into new assemblages. Money promises production. It delivers this promise through the illusory representation of exchange value. Money effectively functions by concealing its nature as capital. It is therefore hardly surprising that it is normally treated as an accumulated stock.

3.1.4 It is not essential to identify capital with money. Money may indicate the presence and operation of capital in terms of its effects. A rate of production indicates the activity of capital. A rate of profit, or the difference between the exchange value of outputs and the exchange value of inputs, measures the effects of capital. Instead of valuing capital assets according to their past accumulation of value, therefore, it may be preferable to value capital assets according to their rates of profit. Assets may be valued according to the time taken to earn their purchase price. If capital is regarded as a value that increases, or as money that makes money, then the value of capital may be regarded as a rate of profit.

Such a move is not altogether sufficient to escape from illusion. Inputs and outputs are only priced according to their exchange values. Their value in the process of production is irrelevant except insofar as it contributes to the market price as a whole. What is measured by a rate of profit is not the value produced by capital production but the outcome of a particular trading strategy of buying one set of goods and selling another. Capital is valued, by this means, in terms of external measures of exchange rather than in terms of intrinsic productive power and significance. When rates of profit are taken as indicators of the operation of productive capacity, there is a danger of a fundamental dissimulation: *income may derive from the consumption of capital as well as from new production.* An enterprise may destroy the conditions that make it possible in the very process of production. For capital itself includes all the means of production, including the prevailing conditions that make production possible. If these conditions are provided by nature and society, then they may not need to be regularly purchased. If they are not represented as internal costs of production, capital may be consumed and depleted. Without an independent measure of capital, it is impossible to tell from the rate of profit whether wealth is being generated or depleted by any particular process. Indeed, all processes generate some forms of wealth while destroying others. When reduced to a single rate of profit, this ambivalence is no longer represented. All economic activity is accounted as positive if it yields a profit. An increase in stock of exchange value replaces all measures of the increase of capital.[5]

This dissimulation is the crucial error of modern economic activity. Modern economic activity only measures rates of profit. Since it is more profitable, in the short term, to consume the means of production than to preserve them, then economic activities that do so will outstrip economic activities that aim for sustainability. Since they are more profitable, they will survive, grow, and prosper in the short term, forcing their sustainable competitors to adapt or be forced out of business. In such an environment, sustainable practices in ecological terms are not sustainable in economic terms; similarly, sustainable practices in economic terms are not sustainable in ecological terms. An economic system that is constructed around the maximization of short-term profits will necessarily consume its capital. For in such a system, consumption of inherited and accumulated assets is measured only as an increase in wealth. Such a system will necessarily destroy its long-term conditions for survival. It is inevitably bound for crisis.

All social systems involve the production of means of production. *Capitalism may be regarded as the social system in which capital is measured as an accumulated quantity in terms of exchange value.* It matters little whether the means of production are privately owned, or owned by the state, or owned by workers' or buyers' cooperatives. Each is a form of capitalism. Each measures the means of production in terms of its exchange value. Each will necessarily deplete its capital insofar as it seeks to maximize profits. In capitalism, investment itself, guided by the maximization of profits, is directed toward the maximization of rates of depletion. Such is the inevitable contradiction of capitalism: it is necessarily self-destructive.

3.1.5 The production of natural capital depends on the finite rate of flow of nuclear energy from solar radiation. This energy may be stored in highly fissible or fusible chemical elements; it may also be stored in fossil fuels. Such stores are finite. Once depleted, the overall rate of energy for production is that which can be captured from renewable sources. Natural capital imposes limits of past accumulation and present rate of flow on the energy use of any economy.

Natural capital uses this energy for the circular flow of matter. The hydrological cycle, carbon cycle, and nitrogen cycle are the most basic and significant circular flows. The waste products of one part of each cycle are the nutrients of another. Similarly, metabolic oxidation in living creatures is balanced by photosynthesis. The rates of recirculation within such cycles also place limits on the rate at which any organic or economic system can function. If such cycles are not maintained, the result is the depletion of natural capital. Within such bounds, however, organic systems have evolved an unlimited proliferation of forms adapted to specific environmental niches. The limits on flows of energy and matter do not impose limits on the creation of forms. Such is the accumulation of natural capital.

Capitalist economic systems, by contrast, aim at a single primary product: exchange value. Exchange value, once reinvested, aims at the production of an unlimited quantity of exchange value. The motive power of capitalist reproduction is compound interest. A national economy that grows at a rate of 4 percent per annum over three centuries would increase in size more than one hundred thousand times. A capital sum invested at a 6 percent rate of interest per annum would increase in size nearly four million times. A successful day trader who earns an average daily profit of .6 percent from small variations in asset prices would, if starting with a sum of $1,000, be capable of buying the entirety of global assets within twenty years. Material production cannot keep up with such rates of growth.

Economy and ecology are mathematically incompatible.[6] Economic growth is incompatible with ecological finitude. It must necessarily reach its limits and collapse before rising again to a lesser extent in an oscillating pattern of decay. Capitalism is unsustainable. Global capitalist development is impossible. Such a logical fact strikes at the heart of faith in capitalism.

3.1.6 The incompatibility of economy and ecology meets with much resistance. One strategy of denial is to attempt to mitigate the depletion of energy and resources by means of efficiency gains through technological improvements. Yet since large and unnecessary inefficiencies may be removed first, levels of efficiency gain tend to decrease with each successive stage. Compound interest, by contrast, increases exponentially. The collision cannot be postponed for long. Moreover, efficiency gains reduce overall costs and improve profits. The additional income will be used for consumption and investment. Both consumption and investment stimulate production, resulting in an overall utilization of energy and resources at a similar rate to the previous one. Efficiency gains, in themselves, contribute nothing toward ecological sustainability.[7]

In practice, efficiency gains have to be enforced by a rise in prices of the relevant energy and resources. The suppliers of energy and resources, especially the oil, gas, and mining sectors, gain a greater share of the relevant wealth. This wealth, again, will be used either for investment or for consumption. The same is true for government taxation, which supplies an additional source of revenue to increase government spending, leading to a multiplier effect throughout the economy.[8] In short, neither efficiency, prices, nor taxes can significantly reduce energy use. Energy consumption can only be reduced in the system as a whole by "demand destruction" through economic recession.

A second strategy of denial is to attempt to separate non-material from material production. There is no absolute limit to the production of ideal forms. Economic growth can continue through the production of ideas, knowledge, and virtual or silicon-based entities, as well as through growth in the nominal value of speculative assets. Economic growth can and does continue on a shrinking ecological base. Nominal economic growth can and does continue on a shrinking base of material production and consumption. Non-material economic entities can continue to thrive under conditions of material scarcity. Nevertheless, this strategy does not reckon with the material reality of consumption: consumption remains an essential part of economic growth. A human consumer, possessing money, will possess a free choice as to what he or she consumes. Being material beings, people will wish to consume material goods, should they be at all available. Price signals derived from depletion rates may do something to restrict material consumption. Yet prices reflect costs of production, as well as overall demand. They do not directly signal absolute rates of depletion. Moreover, if compound rates of economic growth continue, they will be matched by compound rates of consumer-spending power. To reduce consumption, prices of material goods would have to rise sufficiently to destroy demand. In practice, this would mean that those with little spending power would be unable to afford the necessities of life, while those with plenty of spending power would be able to continue to consume at a similar rate. Demand destruction is also tantamount to reducing production and thus reducing economic growth as a whole. It means economic collapse. While some non-material sectors of the economy may in theory continue to thrive, they will in practice be inhibited by a lack of wealth in the rest of the economy. In short, there are two fundamental restrictions on the dematerialization of the economy. Embodied human consumers will find that material consumption takes priority over other forms of consumption, leaving it as the last form to suffer from demand destruction. In addition, there are very few real forms of non-material production. Even the computing, entertainment, research, and education sectors require an ever increasing throughput of material resources to sustain their non-material production. Any continuation of nominal economic growth on a shrinking material base can only be accompanied by the material impoverishment of the majority.

A third strategy of denial is to argue that the market will take account of ecological limits through price signals. Yet prices respond to the scarcity of supply, not to absolute rates of depletion. Prices do not distinguish whether supply derives from sustainable production or a depletion of finite reserves. For example, natural gas remains cheap while it is forced out of the ground under pressure; when the pressure drops through depletion, the fall in production rates is rapid and terminal. Price signals only come into force at crisis levels of depletion, when demand exceeds supply. It is too late by then to conserve natural gas. Indeed, when production levels fall and prices rise due to continued demand, it becomes much more profitable to engage in further and more rapid depletion of the remaining stocks. The ultimate result is demand destruction, with a consequent shrinkage in the economy.

A market economy necessarily leads to a deficit in capital growth. In a market economy, capital is measured by prices and therefore in relation to effective demand expressed in money. The only demands measured are from those who have money. Those who control the most money are those who invest money for the sake of a profit. Capital is therefore priced in relation to its profitability. It is priced in relation to a set of competing investments in terms of the single quantity of a rate of return, measured against risk. Measurements of capital, then, do not take into account the distinctive varieties of capital and their need for maintenance. For example, the renewal of depleted resources and the recycling of waste may be restricted in important respects by physical limits. Without infinitely powerful technology, price signals will be insufficient to achieve substitution and recirculation.

Moreover, positive feedback effects arising from the destabilization of capital may outpace the growth in the relevant forms of economic activity that respond to such change. Only in limited circumstances does supply rise to meet demand. For example, the high demand for good governance and social stability does not express itself, at times of extreme instability, in terms of available money for investment in governance.

Furthermore, markets are unable to deal with the free-rider problem.[9] Waste is discharged; its toxic effects are not restricted to the economic entities that generate it. While the removal, recycling, and disinfecting of waste is a public good, the costs of waste are widely distributed across the public. For any economic entity that generates waste, then, the costs of toxicity may be relatively minor compared with the potential benefits of the toxic process of production. A cost–benefit analysis at a microeconomic level is incapable of accounting for the external costs of toxicity.[10]

Finally, price signals only give value to activities of detoxification to the extent that toxicity reduces profits. The total amount available to be spent on detoxification, whether by the private sector or by governments, is limited to a perceived potential reduction in profits should toxicity be allowed to continue. It bears no relation to the costs of the actual work of detoxification needed to maintain capital. Indeed, as long as similar profits may be acquired through substituting new areas of capital for depletion, leaving behind exhausted capital and polluted ecosystems, a market economy will necessarily prefer such substitution over efforts toward detoxification. Exhaustion and substitution is more profitable than maintenance. In short, a market economy will necessarily produce successive and increasing toxic effects.

The problem of the clash between economic growth and ecological finitude derives from a capitalist system that is based on perpetual growth.

All growth is represented positively as a profit. Little account can be taken of the need for conservation and recycling material. A market economy is a monoculture aimed at the growth of profits alone; it does not facilitate the development of reciprocal and complementary systems that recycle its products. A market economy is necessarily toxic. It matters little which political system is imposed to support such a market economy or the extent of its redistribution of wealth. Once capitalism reaches its limits, it will necessarily shrink as a sphere of circulation, leaving those who are now outside its parameters bereft of essential resources.

The error derives from a simple illusion: if capital is measured in terms of exchange value as an object of accumulation, then no account is taken of capital as a differentiated and interdependent means of production. An alternative economy will be required by those who live outside the margins of a rapidly shrinking capitalist mode of production.

3.1.7 Means of production can be divided into four approximate categories: those that contribute primarily to the accumulation of stock, or physical capital; those that contribute primarily to the invention of processes, or creative capital; those that contribute primarily to the assembly of processes, or constructive capital; and those that contribute primarily to the execution of processes, or dynamic capital. Physical capacities for production include natural resources, such as fresh water, sunlight, air, fertile soil, fossil fuels, minerals, seeds, and livestock, and artificial resources, such as roads, buildings, and machines. Creative capacities for production include human capital, which is itself dependent on health, knowledge, skills, adaptability, and motivation. Constructive capacities for production include human labor, institutions that facilitate cooperation, shared cultural practices, mutual obligations and interdependence. Dynamic capital includes physical energy, desire, and credit. In a complex, interdependent world, accumulation, invention, assembly, and execution are all necessary for economic production. Physical, creative, constructive, and dynamic capital must be combined.

Capital necessarily exceeds capitalist representation. Representation is the product of a process combining physical capital as the medium of representation, creative capital as the invention of forms of representation, constructive capital as the practice of representation, and dynamic capital as the power of representation. Representation is itself a form of produced wealth. It is not its own capital production. Representation is a simple product of a complex process of synthesis. It does not disclose its own substance, form, construction, or energy since it directs attention to the substance, form, construction, and energy of that which it represents. Moreover, even when the power of the object of representation is represented, the power of the representation is not identical to the represented power. As an active force of mediation, capital is inherently unrepresentable. Hence, the true nature of money exceeds all possible representation. It is a dynamic power, not an object of knowledge.

Capital necessarily exceeds measurement. It is less significant that capital should be measured than that it should be sustained, enhanced, and developed. If wealth consists primarily in capital, in capacities for accumulation, invention, and assembly, then it does not consist in the speculative value of assets, in prices determined by demand, or in rates of income or profit. The speculative value of assets reflects the behavior of traders in the market more than it reflects the accumulation of capital. Prices reflect demands for consumption more than they reflect possibilities of invention. Rates of profit and income reflect the consumption of capital more than they reflect its construction. Money that is represented is not money in itself. In short, wealth cannot be properly assessed by an experience of available pleasures or by an evaluation of assets, income, or prices. Capital generates prices and pleasures. It cannot be assessed by them.

A price is formed within a market by comparison with the prices of other commodities or assets that could be substituted for the one in question. Such representation depends on a dissimulation: it assumes that all capital can be appropriated, exchanged, and substituted. It assumes that the complex relations between physical capital, human capital, constructive capital, and dynamic capital can be reproduced by the logic of market relations. It assumes that there is always an alternative or a substitute. It assumes that value only appears insofar as it is replaceable. It assumes an infinitely disposable world. It assumes that everything that contributes to wealth can be given a price — that is, that it can be appropriated, exchanged, and substituted.

Nevertheless, appropriation, exchange, and substitution involve the removal of the thing from its networks of physical, personal, and social relations. They involve the disassembly of capital. Adaptation for the market by rendering all things in the form of exchangeable property is essentially antithetical to the production of capital. Market relations may be the condition for new forms of assembly and invention; they always come at the cost of existing relations of production.

The generation of wealth cannot, therefore, be reduced to the generation of quantities and prices, for wealth is generated by the set of natural, personal, and social processes that compose the entirety of human experience.

EXCHANGE

3.2.1 In economic representation, money is considered in terms of value. The subjective process of evaluation is accorded priority; money merely represents the values given by subjective choices. According to Georg Simmel, the subjective estimate of value becomes representable through exchange: "The value of an object acquires such visibility and tangibility as it possesses through the fact that one object is offered for another. This reciprocal balancing, through which each economic object expresses its value in another object, removes both objects from the sphere of merely subjective significance. The relativity of valuation signifies its objectification."[11] Money expresses this value of exchangeability: "If the economic value of objects is constituted by their mutual relationship of exchangeability, then money is the autonomous expression of this relationship. Money is the representative of abstract value."[12] One may observe that money represents such value in a triple sense. It represents or symbolizes actual value when it functions as a means of exchange; it represents or measures ideal value when it functions as a standard unit of account; and it represents or promises potential value when it functions as a store of value.

No market, or institution of exchange, can function without subjective choices being represented in some kind of object or symbolic medium. One cannot presuppose, however, that such subjective choices are independent of the operations of the market. Even if desires pre-exist their expression in a price or an exchange, it is doubtful whether subjective evaluations pre-exist their expression in a price.[13] For values cannot enter consciousness without some symbolic medium of representation through which desires may be expressed. Such a scale of comparison is provided by money. The market effects its own disciplining and ordering of desire, just as language effects a disciplining and ordering of thought, providing the condition for what is thinkable. There are desires that are not represented in the market because the bearer has insufficient money to make demands effective. If the realization of desires is entirely unrealistic, then little attention will be paid to them, and they may hardly figure in consciousness at all. Someone who participates in a lottery can imagine how he or she would spend the winnings and so nourishes his or her desire for the benefits of wealth. Since the market offers the possibility of the realization of some desires, it has an effect on desire and subjective choices and so on represented value. The value represented by money is not independent of money itself. Money makes certain evaluations effective. This effective power of money demands a reconsideration of the role of money in representation. It will be necessary to critically examine the standard functions of money in exchange discussed in the textbooks of economics.

3.2.2 As a means of payment or medium of exchange, money is believed to facilitate a process of exchange that already exists in the form of barter.[14] Money is able to mediate between differing demands that exist in different places. Money makes transactions between two parties possible that would not be otherwise because money is able to represent an unspecified demand. Money is acceptable because it can later be turned into a particular demand: it represents all available objects of desire. It may be exchanged for all things. There are, however, significant differences between purchase with money and barter exchange.[15] A barter exchange takes place between two parties. Barter is comparable to a reciprocal gift, where the obligation to return a gift is effected immediately. Each gift is of a dual nature: a present is given at the same time as an honor and an obligation. Giving has both a physical and a social significance. Depending on relative status, such an honor may be regarded as tribute, patronage, or a bond initiating an obligation to give back. Indeed, if the relative status is uncertain or flexible, the choice of returning a gift, including its nature and timing, may be elements of political strategy.[16] The exchange of gifts is inseparable from a relation of power.

Here lies the significant difference between the social form of value and the social form of honor. Values are estimates constructed by autonomous subjects. Even if a subject accepts or imitates received values, the work of evaluation is still an expression of the subject's power. Honors and obligations, by contrast, must be given or acknowledged where they are due.[17] They express the incorporation of the subject into an existing social form of representation. They express a mode of piety. Power lies outside the subject in social customs, and although these may admit some flexibility, any transgression risks punitive measures, exclusion, or the wrath of the gods.

In barter exchange, by contrast with gift, the obligation to return is effected immediately. Barter exchange may presuppose a relation of relative equality; alternatively, barter exchange may be conducted to construct relations of relative equality, averting potential hostilities. Yet if each gift is regarded as the equivalent of the other, such equivalence may not signal an absence of social difference so much as the limit of a process of negotiation through which differences of potential are enacted. The actual exchange may be the outcome of differences in relative power and status. Only after the event may the gifts be regarded as equivalent in value because they were indeed exchanged for each other. Prior to the agreement of exchange, however, the resolution of a bargain may be the expression of differing levels of power. Barter exchange is not neutral in relation to other systems of social power; it may be an expression of it when such power is enacted to the full in exchange. Although both parties may gain what they wish in barter exchange, the relative quantities of what they gain may be augmented or diminished by the exercise of social power.

The social elements of power and status call on factors external to the simple relation between two parties. In the same way, monetary purchase is not simply a physical exchange of goods. It also has a social dimension that is compressed into the actual values agreed while obscured by the notion of value itself. For exchange never takes place between two parties alone. Barter exchange may only be possible in the rare coincidence of complementary demands. Monetary exchange changes this significantly. By vastly augmenting the occurrence of possible exchanges, it also enables each transaction to be compared with a set of alternative transactions that could be substituted for it. In addition to the two parties, there is a range of possible exchange relations with third parties that each of the two parties has preferred not to pursue. These have an impact on the actual exchange insofar as they determine the agreed price. The logic of exchange is not complete as a two-way transaction; it also includes comparison and substitution. In every monetary exchange there remains a third, inactive party whose presence determines the outcome. In this respect, monetary exchange remains a social relation. The possibility of transferring one's business to a third party tends to neutralize effects of social power. Social power is not entirely removed, however, for it is now assumed by those who have the highest mobility or the option of transferring their business. Those who have access to the most markets, whose assets are most liquid or in demand, have the opportunity for a greater degree of comparison and substitution. They have the most social power.

The possibility of a transfer of business enables those who buy to choose a partner who has the weakest level of social power and will therefore be willing to offer the most advantageous terms of trade. As a result, all trading partners will be reduced in power to the weakest available on the market. Exchange effects a stripping away of invested social powers, dissolving prior inequalities. It leaves one principal inequality between those who have the power to transfer business and those who have the most urgent demands for the trade to take place. Power lies with money, in the hands of the buyer. Money dissolves other social powers, therefore, but it retains its own social power. The power to transfer business — whether this reflects the social properties of the commodity for sale or pertains to the reputation, mobility, or knowledge of the market actor — trumps all other social relations in exchange. It is the power of disassembly or flight, abandoning one set of mutual dependencies for the sake of establishing an equivalent elsewhere.

The overall effect of exchange, then, is not merely to dissolve all previous social powers, leaving equality in exchange. It is to remove the reciprocal balances on social power so that one party who profits most from transactions because of his or her superior mobility can act with progressively less restraint. Market exchange creates the illusion of social equality at the same time that it brings about the reality of social inequality. Yet social power circulates through exchange. The seller acquires both the exchange value of money and its social value of liquidity. Patterns of circulation and recirculation, then, will be more significant in determining the overall balance of power expressed in money than will the accumulation of money at any one time.

Money does, however, have a considerable effect on the nature of exchanges. What might be considered a delicate social negotiation within barter takes on the appearance of a simple exchange within the market. Yet money does not simply facilitate exchange. It also dissolves a prior social order, with its obligations, reciprocities, and interdependencies, and replaces it with the social order of the market. Money generates markets at the same time that it facilitates exchange. The function of money is not, therefore, reducible to a medium of exchange. Money is an active principle of social change. It has effects that are not reducible to its designed function. Money cannot be represented fully by the function of a medium of exchange or means of payment. It does more than merely symbolize value. It imposes its own scale of evaluation through which profitable activity, as the source of social power and means toward all other ends, is valued more highly than other activities.

3.2.3 Money may also be represented in terms of its function as a unit of account. Money facilitates the representation of exchange value. In relation to this function, money also acts as both condition of the market and product of the market.

Markets are not given in advance. Like all forms of constructive capital, they have to be invented, assembled, and accumulated. Markets may be accumulated when a particular location acquires a reputation for the buying and selling of certain assets, goods or resources. Such a market is open to those who have access to that location, as well as to the assets, goods, or resources that may be traded there. There is therefore no such thing as a single, global market. Markets are differentiated by location, reputation, and what is bought and sold.

Markets are also facilitated by the acceptability of a single commodity or asset in exchange for all other items traded there. Money enables goods within a market to be compared directly with each other in terms of a price. In addition, money mediates between markets, joining them together, crossing boundaries of location and types of items traded. Money facilitates exchange between markets that are differentiated in respect to distance, time, reputation, and category. As the single principle that enables markets to interact, money enables values within markets to be measured in relation to values in other markets. By enabling trade and comparison between markets, money effectively functions as the medium for the invention of markets.

Markets may be facilitated further when a dealer undertakes to buy and sell a particular asset or commodity to anyone who wishes to sell or buy it. While all traders may buy and sell money, some traders take it upon themselves to buy and sell another asset or commodity. Such dealers aim to balance quantities bought and sold by controlling the price. These dealers are market makers. To facilitate throughput in the market, and thus to increase the profits achieved through a small spread between bid and offer price, such dealers need to hold a certain reserve of the asset in question. The dealer makes the market by controlling a reserve, a spread, and a price.

In practice, therefore, markets are not simply composed of a large number of two-way barter transactions. One cannot fully represent the form of the market by the exchanges that take place within it. Markets are made possible by their own distinctive infrastructure. Such an infrastructure is not itself an object of demand within the market. The location and reputation of the market differ from what is traded there; the money used within the market is acquired not for its own intrinsic use, but simply for the purpose of further exchanges; and the dealer's reserve must be maintained overall, not accumulated or depleted. Reputation, money, and reserve are the factors that facilitate markets.

Money, in its role of generating exchange between markets, acts as a vital component of constructive capital. Since money, unlike other products, is not consumed, it provides a sustainable vehicle of circulation. In this way it differs from reputation, which is not alienable but accumulates, and from reserves, which do not circulate as reserves. Exchange values are represented in terms of money rather than in terms of reputation or reserves of stock, since money may actually be exchanged for them. In this way, money becomes a unit of account.

Money does not merely circulate, however. While reputation and reserves are not money, money contains within itself the functions of reputation and reserves. It is portable reputation and portable reserves. Indeed, it has to retain these properties to function as a unit of account. Values have to be measured in terms of some reputable standard of measure. Values also have to be measured in relation to a value that is stored or reserved. Neither a two-way exchange nor circulation alone therefore explains the true nature of money.

Debates over the true nature of money derive from emphasizing only one of its characteristics.[18] If the value of money is taken as deriving from its intrinsic content, as in metalist theories of money, then its function as a reserve of value is exaggerated at the expense of other functions. If the value of money is taken as deriving from its reputation as a means of circulation, as for those who derive money from banking and credit, then its reputation is exaggerated at the expense of other functions. Yet money cannot be acceptable in exchange, possessing a real value, unless it is capable of reserving value. Money cannot reserve real value without being acceptable in exchange. Reputation and reserve are mutually dependent; neither explains how money acquires value and becomes capable of generating a market.

There are two main approaches to explaining the value of money: money is regarded either as a commodity or as a unit of account. Commodity theories of money derive money as an emergent product of barter. In barter exchange, one seeks to acquire goods not only for immediate use but also for their liquidity or exchangeability. The commodity that is most widely accepted in exchange plays the role of money. Faith in its acceptability enables it to become an effective store of value. There is a logical circularity here: money is a means of payment because it is a store of value, yet money is a store of value because it is a means of payment.[19] The most exchanged commodity may still have multiple exchange ratios in different circumstances. It does not become a standard unit of account.

Unit of account theories of money explain money in terms of its extrinsic imposition on the market by a political agency such as a state. According to state theories of money, money is issued by the state in the form of payments and demanded by the state in the form of taxes.[20] The endless, circular flow of the market is replaced by a model of efflux and reflux.[21] Money maintains its reputation in line with the power, prestige, and prudence of the issuing state. It is acceptable in exchange as legal tender, supported by authority. The difficulty here lies in explaining how money tends to circulate freely beyond the territorial boundaries of the state. Beyond political boundaries, money embodies the economic prestige of the respective state. It has a market value only where it becomes a means of payment because its reputation stores value, and its reputation stores value because it is a means of payment.

The commodity and unit of account theories of money are not mutually incompatible. Indeed, they are complementary, each supplying the deficits in the other.[22] Money does not belong solely to the market or to the state, because each institution is incomplete without the other. The question is: to what extent do the two together explain the function of money as a unit of account? A third factor, in addition to market and state, will also need to be invoked.

As a medium of exchange, the value of money is thought to derive from the quantity in circulation relative to size and speed of the market as a whole.[23] Yet since it possesses a reputation, money also accumulates or depreciates in value apart from changes in circulation. Indeed, the "market as a whole" is an abstract ideal. There is no possible way in practice for prices to be assessed in relation to the market as a whole.[24] The value of money does not depend on the quantity in circulation alone. It is not an absolute standard of measure or even a measure internal to a closed system. The value of money also derives from beyond its territory in associated markets. Moreover, money is a reserve of value that promises the delivery of a certain quantity of value at a future date. The value of money, as a reserve, depends on future expectations. It embodies a degree of credit. The nature and value of money therefore do not derive solely from factors within a market or from factors provided by a state. The value of money as a unit of account depends on its acceptability in external markets and in future markets. The use of money as a unit of account is not simply a means of valuing commodities against other commodities within the market as a universal equivalent. There is no universal market. The pure market is itself a utopian abstraction. Such a process of comparison is never completed; commodities are not compared in value directly with each other through the medium of money. Instead, commodities are valued in terms of money — that is, in relation to expectations of evaluations in external and future markets. Money is not simply a unit of account because it also embodies reputation and credit. The nature of money is not properly explained as a unit of account within a closed market. While money may function as a unit of account, it also opens evaluation up to exterior and future factors.

3.2.4 Money also represents value through its function as a store of value. Money is regarded as storing or reserving the exchange value of goods, assets, and services. As a reserve of value, money is a passive object of human control. Money is comprehended under the form of property. For the one who possesses money, money is a passive instrument of desire. Yet for one who seeks to acquire money, money has an active power of command. The value of money as a reserve of value lies in its capacity to express an active power. Once again, this active power is not comprehended when money is treated as a passive object of exchange. Money proves to be more than a machine designed for the preservation of value.

In reality, value is not reducible to the situation of exchange alone. In exchange, value circulates. In reality, the value of goods, assets, and services may undergo significant transformations outside exchange. It is important to distinguish between goods and services acquired for the sake of consumption and assets appropriated to be held. Reserved assets may be property or stock and therefore subject to subsequent exchanges; they may be capital that produces additional value; or they may be speculative assets whose value is expected to rise as demand outstrips supply. Whereas consumption cancels out the value of production, appropriation preserves or even increases value. Whereas in exchange, value is preserved by definition, since the market value is determined by the price paid for it, such exchanges take place for the sake of consumption, production, or speculation. Market value is subordinate to other processes that affect value. The value arrived at in exchange will depend on intentions and expectations regarding the future progress of value. Money enters into relation with the value of the goods, assets, or services for which it is exchanged. Money also enters into relation with activities of consumption, production, and speculation that it makes possible. In relation to exchange, money is a passive store of value. In relation to consumption, production, and speculation, money is constructive capital.

The true nature of money, as constructive capital, has to be uncovered from beneath the illusion that money functions purely for the preservation of value. Money as an active force exceeds its apparent functions. It makes a difference whether money is used to purchase goods and services or for production or investment. If money is used for purchase, it is simply a means of payment; if money is used to pay for production, whether in the form of rent for physical capital, wages for labor, or interest on financing, then it actively stimulates production. There is a significant difference between production and distribution: production adds an absolute value,

a stock of product, whereas distribution adds a relative value, expressed as
an increase in price. When all values are expressed as exchange values, this
distinction is concealed. Moreover, distribution is itself part of the activity
of constructive capital, since it facilitates the assembly of the means of
production. Nevertheless, absolute values are heterogeneous, expressed in
terms of various stocks of product, while relative values are homogeneous,
expressed in terms of prices. When money is exchanged for existing goods
and services, then it merely functions as a means of distribution. When
money, by contrast, is used for rent, wages, or interest, then it stimulates
the creation of value. Such value would not be created if money were not
paid for it. Money, therefore, has an active role in the process of production. It is a mode of dynamic capital.

It has been assumed that it is demand, rather than money, that stimulates production. The productive power of money would then be merely an
instrument in the transmission of demand. One can distinguish between
demand itself, which originates with people, and money, which is the signal of such demand. Nevertheless, however strong people's demands may
be, they remain ineffective until they are supported by money. Demands
are only effective to the extent that they are expressed in money. Money
has the distinctive power of making demand effective. The active power of
money is a power of purchasing, of making demands effective. This active
power has a different nature when it constitutes physical capital as capital
by means of the payment of rent; when it commands human capital as
labor in the form of wages; and when it enriches constructive capital in
the form of interest. The metaphor of exchange for these forms of payment conceals the active power of money in making demands effective
and stimulating production. For money facilitates the release of potential.
There is always an excess of productive capacity that could be released if
money became available. Rather than an exchange, the relation is more
like a contract or mutual obligation. Rent is paid if capital is constituted
for production. There is always an excess of potential demand over effective demand. Labor is contracted rather than purchased. Wages are paid if
labor gives itself to be commanded. Similarly, money capital is borrowed
rather than purchased. It is given to be invested and spent in return for an
agreed payment of interest. Indeed, in this process capital does not strictly
leave the original owner, even if money does, for capital is converted from

money into an asset such as a share, bond, or loan. Such assets are often highly liquid and can be exchanged as easily as money. Investment therefore should be regarded not in terms of an exchange but in terms of the contracting of assets and liabilities.

An essential difference remains between exchange and contract. Exchange is an instantaneous swap of private property; contract is the agreement of mutual obligations that endure for a period of time. Property itself rests on permanent implicit or explicit contracts. A village market where products are exchanged as property provides a poor paradigm for the comprehension of economic behavior.[25] Most economic behavior endures over time rather than consisting of a series of instantaneous transactions. Most economic behavior involves the agreement of contracts. Where exchange retains the physical dimension of gift giving, contract belongs to the sphere of social power and obligations. Where exchange is subjected to the sovereign choice of the owner of property or the consumer, contract imposes obligations. Money, as dynamic capital, has to be understood in terms of the social sphere of contractual obligations rather than in terms of a village market where products are exchanged.

3.2.5 In a productive economy, capital is heterogeneous yet interdependent. Land, labor, and finance are not constituted as capital until they are assembled for production by the intermediation of money for the payment of rent, wages, and interest. Capital is composed of absolute and heterogeneous values, yet it is paid in terms of a homogeneous value. There is no way to determine a just division of payments between rent, wages, and interest, since the contributions of land, labor, and capital are absolute rather than relative. Production would not take place without each of them. Instead, rates and proportions may be determined in practice through the market, in terms of exchange and substitution, according to supply and demand. In practice, then, the price paid for capital has little relation to its intrinsic capacity or productivity. It is determined in relation to exchange, in which the original capital is no longer constituted as capital, since an alternative is substituted for it. Capital as capital disappears from the measure of prices to the extent that it is treated as an object of comparison and substitution. Relative values take priority over absolute values. Relative values are formed by substituting anticipated profits from future constitutions of capital for those modes of capital that are already actually constituted in a determinate location. Relative values are anticipated; they do not assess values that exist in reality except in relation to anticipation.

The power of money is effectively neutralized when money is regarded as a passive instrument of exchange. When an asset is exchanged for a quantity of money, the exchange values of the asset and the quantity of money are equated. An asset is worth a certain price because it may be exchanged for that particular quantity of money; the money is also worth that price because it may be exchanged for the same quantity of money. As pure liquidity, $1,000 is tautologously worth $1,000. The illusion here is to treat the unit of account as a commodity. As a commodity or object of exchange, money has no distinctive power in exchange. It appears to be neutral. Yet as a unit of account, money has an active power of pricing. Money is not neutral in exchange because it has an active power of intermediation. It makes exchanges possible.

The effect of reducing exchange value to prices is to reduce exchange to an equation between the value of a quantity of one commodity and the value of the quantity of another. The perspective that predominates here is that of the seller who judges all things in relation to the quantity of money desired. In selling, capital is liquidated as capital, even if it may be reconstituted as capital by the buyer. The seller's perspective excludes the perspectives of other parties in an exchange. The buyer must compare the proposed purchase to a set of alternative purchases, weighing these against each other in an attempt to find an optimum rather than an equivalent. In addition, any exchange always involves a number of other participants, even if their positions remain unchanged by the exchange. Such participants may include alternative sellers, whose products are refused; alternative buyers, who offer too little or arrive too late; conveyancers, who may facilitate the transmission of property from one owner to another; and market makers, who make exchange possible. Even if intermediaries may not be required, money itself or banks facilitate and intermediate exchange. By facilitating exchange, intermediation makes exchange possible. It therefore has an impact on prices.

In the formation of exchange values, then, this complex social situation is eclipsed by the imposition of the hegemonic perspective of the seller. While the power of liquidity may remain in the hands of the buyer, having a significant impact on prices, the dominant perspective in pricing belongs to the eyes of the seller. Exchange value is formed from imagining a condition in which capital is disassembled and sold. It is constituted entirely by anxiety or anticipation. Exchange value, rather than reflecting past accumulation or present productivity, embodies a future orientation. If prices are represented in terms of money, then money itself represents anticipations of the future. Money therefore stands in the place of and represents credit. As the advance that is offered on the basis of credit, money, as the measure of prices, is essentially credit.

MONEY

3.3.1 The nature of money explains exchange; the nature of exchange does not explain money. How, then, are we to understand the function of money? Adam Smith famously described money as the "great wheel of circulation": "The great wheel of circulation is altogether different from the goods which are circulated by means of it. The revenue of society consists altogether in those goods and not in the wheel which circulates them."[26] As a mere vehicle or means of exchange, money contributes nothing to the overall output of a society. Money carries value, but the value that it carries is that of the goods, not its intrinsic value as money. The revolutionary insight here derives from Copernicus: money has become a mere token of value.[27] The use of money, as a sign of value, carries more ontological and economic significance than its substance. Smith can therefore make a sharp distinction between money itself and the value of money. If money is merely a vehicle, then Smith could argue that the substitution of paper for gold and silver replaces a very expensive instrument with one that is much less costly. The value of money is its value as an instrument or vehicle. It is not the value of the substance of which it is composed but the value of the goods that can be had in exchange.

Smith's image of a wheel of circulation presupposes a closed economy. Money can recirculate only if it remains in the economy without being spent elsewhere. The distinction between goods and vehicle of circulation holds only to the extent that there is a circulation. In practice, however, goods do not circulate but are produced and consumed. Similarly, money does not continually recirculate if it is also produced and consumed. Yet to the extent that money recirculates, it can be replaced by abstract value. Assuming that money is functioning effectively as a wheel of circulation, it can be displaced by a consideration of abstract value until the wheel breaks down. Money needs to be considered by economics only when it fails to function as an effective vehicle for circulation. There would appear to be an optimum quantity of money for an efficient wheel. If too little is present, exchange will not take place, because there is nothing with which to pay for it; if too much is present, prices will rise until the excess is absorbed. If there is too little or too much, exchange is restricted either through lack of means or through loss of confidence in the vehicle of circulation due to inflation. Monetary economics may concern itself with the optimum quantity of money. It does not concern itself with the accumulation of money as such. The object of economic activity, then, would be not to acquire money but to accumulate exchange value.

The "great wheel of circulation" does, however, provide a poor image of economic activity. As has often been noted, Smith's understanding of money as a wheel of circulation does not explain the quotidian facts of economic life: the striving after money, the desire to accumulate money.[28] Exchange value is accumulated, but for this to occur, exchange value must be converted back into money. Money is required for the payment of rent, wages, interest, and taxes. Capital investment takes place in the form of money, and profits are realized in the form of money. There is a cycle of production, then, but it begins in money and ends in money. While the cycle of exchange may begin with goods and end with goods, the cycle of production begins with money and ends with money. Each cycle operates in and through the other. Each operates according to independent principles. The demand for goods, expressed through exchange, drives production; the demand for profits, expressed through production, drives exchange. Each liberates the other to achieve a greater potential. Investment in production leads to the discovery and satisfaction of more wants; increases in consumption lead to greater profits. Economic activity originates in complementary drives: a pleasure principle and a will to power. There are different circuits of money and goods, even if they operate only through each other. Since prices are arbitrary, the circuits of goods and money merely provide the occasion and means for the flow of the other. They do not determine the rate of flow.

Smith's image of a circulating vehicle in a closed economy depends on the presumption of a finite amount of gold and silver in circulation — an amount that adjusts in relation to the size of the economy. Nevertheless, as soon as variability of the total quantity of money in circulation is admitted, such variation may be influenced by factors extrinsic to the endogenous requirements of exchange. In particular, if money is issued as paper or in the form of electronic bank records, then it can be created to stimulate production. Money, created in the form of loans, passes through its own life cycle before being canceled when the loans are repaid. Money here is an active stimulant of production. It is therefore insufficient to regard money as merely a technical instrument of exchange whose quantity can be adjusted to maximize the facilitation of exchange. It is insufficient to regard the economy as the sphere of circulation of exchange values, whether these are borne by goods or by money. Instead, the common-sense perspective holds more weight. On the one hand, goods are produced, distributed, and consumed, flowing in one direction; on the other, money is created, circulated, and canceled, flowing in the reverse direction. An economy requires a production of money commensurate with its productive output, even if money endures and recirculates for longer than do the goods for which it is exchanged. Both directions of circulation need to be considered. One concerns the circulation of goods; the other concerns the circulation of social power.

A more subtle cycle, however, must be considered. As a means of payment, a sum of money has a particular purchasing power expressed in terms of the value of goods that may be obtained for it. Yet goods themselves are heterogeneous. Their relative values can be established only by comparing them with a sum of money that could be exchanged for them. The price of goods is expressed in terms of money, while the value of money is expressed in terms not of the goods themselves, but of their prices. There is a vicious circle of reciprocal presupposition here. Just as money physically circulates as a means of payment in acts of buying and selling, it also mentally circulates as a measure of value in terms of possible acts of exchange.

The effect of this vicious circle is that prices are real and determinate yet arbitrary. Lacking any independent or absolute standard of value that would establish economics as a science, such as the one sought by David Ricardo, prices are open to arbitrary fluctuations. Then the purchasing power of money, the quantity of goods that may be exchanged for it, is entirely relative. Just as one may distinguish between money and the value of money, one may also distinguish between an absolute power to purchase, the power inherent in money itself, and a relative value that is purchased—the exchange value of money. Money possesses both an absolute and a relative purchasing power. Relative purchasing power is a passive object of exchange. Moreover, whatever price is agreed in exchange, relative purchasing power remains unchanged in the act of exchange, since the value of the goods and that of the money exchanged are defined as equivalent to each other. Exchange value, whether expressed in goods or in money, remains constant by definition in exchange. Exchange value does nothing to measure increases or decreases in value that always occur outside the sphere of exchange, whether in the accumulation of goods or in the appreciation in prices. There is no need to consider money separately, according to such a perspective.

Money does have an absolute purchasing power, and it is this power that circulates in the reverse direction to goods. It is a question not of how much value is purchased—or relative purchasing power—but of the power to purchase that much value. It is the power, the potential to acquire value, that makes demands effective. Whereas relative purchasing power requires that one view the exchange with hindsight as though it had already taken place, establishing equivalence between a sum of money and a quantity of goods, absolute purchasing power requires viewing the exchange with foresight, as a power to acquire value. Whereas exchange value or relative purchasing power is instantaneous, absolute purchasing power endures until the exchange. Money, as constructive capital or an absolute power of purchasing, is essentially a promise of value. It is a power to enter into exchanges or contractual arrangements. It is an embodied social power.

The power of a promise is not represented in account books. It escapes accounting and the empirical investigation of economic science. As a promise, the power of money is subject to uncertainty, confidence, and even strategy. It may perhaps best be understood through theology rather than economics, for the absolute purchasing power of money consists in the power of a promise. It consists in credit. A promise involves the suspension, yet determination, of a value in time. It is therefore necessary to differentiate between what is promised, or the relative value of money, and the promise itself, or money's absolute purchasing power.

3.3.2 Money promises value. It does not specify the form that such value will take. Used for consumption, money promises pleasure. Used for exchange, money promises property. Used for investment, money promises more money. The value of money, or the value that is promised, has no exact or fixed measure. It is an indefinite potential.

The promise provided by money, then, is more than simply the value of the goods and services that it can buy. Money promises access to other markets. Money promises future profits. Money extends purchasing power to distant places and future times. It is pure, unqualified potential. It has the capacity to generate markets. Money has the power to acquire pleasure, to appropriate property, to constitute capital, to command labor, and to repay interest and loans.

The selling of goods and services is driven by the desirability of this purchasing power. Money gives the freedom to select and refuse within the marketplace. Money gives the freedom to disassemble current relations of mutual dependence to replace them with future, more desirable relations of mutual dependence. Money, as the promise of freedom, generates the demand for money. Freedom is a kind of social entropy. Once possessed of money and freedom, and thus financial independence, few would be willing to enter into onerous obligations, except to acquire more money. Money is therefore the great liberator. The promise of freedom and independence empowers money. It makes money acceptable in exchange. It gives money a relative purchasing power, since it is acceptable in exchange. Yet the absolute purchasing power of money that is embodied in its promise exceeds its relative purchasing power, which is expressed in terms of a determinate set of goods. Money opens value out onto an unlimited future. It is irreducible to finite spheres of exchange.

This is not to say that money is primarily an object of hoarding. It is not essential to possess money; it is merely essential to have access to money. This is consistent with money's nature as promised. Exchange value can be hoarded in the form of profitable assets that are highly marketable. With a high degree of liquidity, profitable assets are one step removed from money. They bear the promise of money and so represent the promise that is available in money. Since exchange value is normally hoarded in the form of profitable assets, the will to power expressed in the desire for profits may be concealed beneath an apparent demand for the pleasure provided by assets and goods. Money itself is left out of account. Such an illusion can be left to economists. In practice, it is all too obvious that assets are valued by the amount of money that they promise, by the amount of money that may be offered in exchange for them. For the consumer, driven by the pleasure principle, money is the promise of goods. For the speculator, driven by a will to power, assets are the promise of money.

3.3.3 Distinct drives open up distinct perspectives of evaluation. In economic life, all things hold their value through something else. All things have value only insofar as they are capital, capable of being incorporated into some productive activity, even if it is only the production of pleasure. For example, living beings function effectively only in an environment that meets their needs; they have no value in isolation, for they cannot survive in isolation. Similarly, property, goods, and services hold value only as objects of desire and use. There is no value without the invention of form. Even in representation, use values are imagined in relation to some desired process. An imagined world of use values is substituted for prior values within an ecological context: use is value in relation to a human agent. Moreover, such an invention and imagination of form is the precondition of productive economic activity. Desire appears to constitute the very texture of society.

A different perspective is expressed in exchange. Considered in relation to exchange, a thing holds value only in relation to possible substitutions. The intrinsic properties of the thing, whether in relation to its ecological context or in relation to its human use, are put aside. One replaces a field of forms and uses with one of exchanges and prices. This is essentially a change in perspective: use and exchange are differing perspectives through which the world may be seen. They are not neutral but have determinate optical effects. If one examines the world from the perspective of use, then the entire world is colored and distorted by one's own demands, needs, and desires. If one examines the world from the perspective of exchange, then instead of seeing things themselves, one sees that which can be exchanged for things. Moreover, these things in turn are not seen, but other exchanges are substituted for them. It is as if one looks only at the shadows. Only intensities of shade are expressed in terms of exchange value. Money, as the unit of account, is the screen on which all shadows are formed. All of one's demands, needs, and desires that find confirmation in things are temporarily suspended; no satisfaction is immediately visible. The world, as seen from the perspective of exchange, offers itself to a single desire: the desire for an increase in profit. No other desire or thought is represented in exchange value.

The use of money as a screen against which the world is projected has a peculiar optical effect: all demands, needs, and desires are kept in suspense. They remain private and do not impinge directly on social relations. Social relations become constituted by a sole public demand: the demand for money. It is only by fulfilling the demand for money that other demands can come to fulfillment. The texture of society appears to be constituted by the promise of value expressed in money. Hence, money functions as more than just a screen or support for the projection of exchange value. The demand for money maintains the perspective through which exchange value may be seen. In a relative sense, the exchange value of commodities is measured in terms of money; in an absolute sense, exchange value is constituted by the perspective through which it is seen, the demand for money as such. The demand for money, in turn, is constituted by the promise that is offered by money. In exchange, the texture of society is constituted by credit.

Such perspectives of use or exchange are only maintained if they answer to particular needs, desires, and demands. To answer here means to offer a promise. A perspective must produce images through which the demand finds satisfaction — imaginary satisfaction or satisfaction through images. The power of money, then, does not ultimately lie in its capacity to deliver promised value. Money gives trust that the image can be achieved. The power of money is its capacity to hold and maintain a perspective in the mind. As a promise, it focuses attention on the power it promises. As a screen, it veils and withdraws attention from all other modes of social interaction. None of the competing perspectives promise the liquidity, flexibility, and freedom available to the one who has money. The power of money is a power to control attention, to absorb mental energy, to shape the spending of time. The power of money as a promise consists in its ability to capture attention and desire. Money promises freedom and power. As a screen and a perspective, it does not draw attention to itself so much as to the freedom and power acquired by its means. Withdrawing itself from attention, its hold over attention is all the more secure. As the principle that makes demands effective, the supreme means of freedom and power, money is a reality principle: it promises the power to realize all other desires and values. It offers itself as the universal social means. As the supreme means of access to value, money is that which is of most social value. It is the precondition for the realization of all other ends. All other ends must be suspended until sufficient money is obtained for their realization. Money thus posits itself as the supreme being, the focus of attention and desire, the principle for the realization of capital projects. Money posits itself as God, the principle of all creation. Its hold over attention is the worship it demands. As long as the world is regarded from the perspective of exchange, the power of money is absolute.

3.3.4 It is an apparent paradox that money, a mere sign or token, can become the supreme principle of power. It does so through the theological power of a promise. The power of money is expressed through exchange. In a market society, money makes markets possible. Money is the condition of possibility of society as such, of the division of labor and mutual interdependence, insofar as society is constituted by exchange. Moreover, since exchange involves the dissolution of prior social forms of power through disassembly and the constitution of new forms through reassembly, it replaces other social forms with exchange. Since exchange values are measured in relation to external or future values, they cannot be constrained by existing orders of power. Money possesses the power of flight. Any attempts to contain it will drive it out of the territory.

Exchange values are derived from comparison. A price indicates the lack of availability of cheaper substitutes or alternatives. A price also indicates the lack of stronger effective demands. Under such conditions of comparison, then, one is always threatened by one's competitors. For every exchange facilitated by money, there are a host of possible exchanges that do not occur. Competition requires winners and losers. There will always be some who cannot pay more or sell for less. While such competition has the relative effect of equilibrating prices, it also has the absolute effect of threatening lack.

Money, as an absolute sign of wealth, combines the promise of wealth with the threat of poverty, for the wealth promised by money is only temporary. Only capital promises enduring wealth. For one who holds money and buys, the freedom to satisfy demands is a promise of wealth; once the purchase has taken place, however, the condition is replaced by one of the absence of money. The threat of poverty follows the promise of wealth. For one who sells to acquire money, money holds out the promise of freedom to satisfy demands. Yet failure to sell holds out the threat of poverty. The threat of poverty precedes the promise of wealth.

In a market society, therefore, relations of interdependence are opaque and unstable, threatened with termination at any moment. One can have security in such a society only if one has a dependable source of income. One can participate in such a society only to the extent that one has access to money or credit. While money promises the freedom of the market, it also threatens the constraint of exclusion. The power of money is not embodied in its promise alone; it is also embodied in the threats present within a market society. It would seem that no one could be more free than an economic agent in a marketplace with unlimited opportunities to exchange, make profits, and satisfy demands. In reality, such economic agents suffer from an immense discipline. For the freedom to exchange is a freedom to command labor; such freedom can be realized only if labor is available to be commanded. The freedom of the wealthy can be acquired only at the expense of the servitude of those who work. Market society, while appearing to promise liberty, imposes itself as a rigorous system of discipline. One is always under an obligation to acquire money. Such an obligation is independent of any drive for pleasure or will to power. One may be under an obligation to produce for sale to acquire money; one may be under an obligation to repay debts to remain creditworthy; one may be under an obligation to invest so that one generates an income. While appearing to offer the promise of the security of wealth earned through the division of labor, market society imposes a condition of general insecurity, facing each of its members with the threat of exclusion from relations of interdependence.

Just as the fear of market failure as a whole generates a demand for money as liquidity at the onset of market panic, so the fear of failure within the market also generates a demand for money. Money, as the source of market society, announces a promise but delivers a threat. This threat, in turn, reinforces the demand for money. The more extensively society is constituted as a market, the stronger the demand for money and the further the constitution of society as a market. Few political forces can resist such power; few political forces can mobilize the productive power of capital in the way that money can.

The value of money derives from the demand for money. Money holds value because it is acceptable in exchange. According to the simple image of society as a closed market, abstract exchange value derives from substitution and comparison in terms of a universal equivalent. Society is constituted as the limit of a process of comparison of possible values. Things hold exchange value, and thus social significance, to the extent that they are compared with all other values. In practice, of course, such a process of universal comparison can never complete its large number of permutations. Relative prices are estimated in relation to their nearest alternatives. Such prices are also estimated. Instead of tending toward equilibrium under ideal market conditions, therefore, prices can only be compared to other estimates, leading to an unending process of fluctuation and oscillation, since each correction of an estimate leads to a correction of other relative prices. There is no absolute standard against which prices may be measured, and there is no universal market in which prices can be determined. The value of money can never be fixed in relation to the overall level of prices, therefore, because prices never achieve an overall level. The value of money is determined from without. It is, in part, an expression of the demand for money. The demand for money derives from its promises and threats. Money is acceptable in exchange because it is an object of demand; it is an object of demand because it is acceptable in exchange. Money gains value from the trust in money; it holds its value through imitation—that is, it is widely accepted in exchange.[29] Yet although such imitation can spread by contagion, it also needs explaining by means of an initial impetus. The initial impetus giving value to money is nothing less than its promise and threat. If, prior to the marketization of society, the promise carries more weight than the threat, then subsequent to the marketization of society both promise and threat are intensified: more relations can be reconstituted than ever before through the market; fewer relations can be reconstituted at all outside the market. Through the agency of money, the market effects a progressive colonization of society. Through the colonization of society, the market intensifies the demand for money.

The social reality of money as constructive capital is that of a self-fulfilling promise. Money has a relative purchasing power expressed in terms of the value of goods that could be exchanged for it. Money has an absolute purchasing power, which is the power of a promise. In addition, money has an absolute power to impose itself on society expressed in terms of its power to fulfill itself as a promise. Money gains power because it has power. It is a dynamic force, a pure promise, a spectral reality emergent from nothing, yet ordering everything. It offers no surface to resistance; it accepts no limits on exchange. It exceeds all other social forces. Such is the engine of modernity.[30]

DEBT

3.4.1 Economic production is driven by energy, desire, and belief. The distinctive feature of the modern era is the liberation of copious quantities of energy, desire, and belief from natural, social, and religious sedimentation for the direct purpose of production. Only at the end of modernity are the limits to the accessibility of energy for economic production being explored. Given the possibilities for unlimited accumulation, invention, and assembly, the immediate limits to production are largely given by a shortage of available money for investment. Since in a market society materials, expertise, and constructive labor may be acquired through money, the primary shortage is always of money. The possibility always exists of an increase in the productive power of capital if there were more money.

At the same time, each economy has unlimited potential demand. While demand for some particular goods may reach its limits, as in the theory of marginal utility, there are other demands that in principle are unlimited. While there may be limits to quantities of consumption and appropriation, there are no limits to improvements in the quality of goods and services that may be desired. Alternatively, if no other use for money is more urgent, it may be invested speculatively for further profits. There is always an unlimited demand for money. Therefore, there can be no general problem of over-accumulation.[31] If available money exceeds immediate opportunities for productive investment, that money can be spent on higher-quality goods and services, driving up prices, or on speculative assets, also driving up prices and thus leading to speculative profits. There are merely dangers of over-production in specific sectors or dangers of lack of confidence in specific speculative markets. Practical limits to demand are set, once more, by the shortage of the availability of money.

Every economy, then, has unlimited capacity for production and unlimited capacity for demand. Even the clash between economic growth and ecological finitude leads to opportunities to profit from the extraction of scarce resources (especially in the mining, oil, and gas sectors) and from adaptive technologies. Even devaluation of a currency leads to opportunities to profit from reliable stores of value such as gold; even a fall in the stock market leads to opportunities to profit from selling short. Limits to economic growth are always experienced as limits to the availability of money. There is an unlimited quantity of socially useful work that could be done; there is usually a number of unemployed laborers who would be willing to do it. There is always a lack of money. Money is dynamic capital. Without it, productive possibilities are left unrealized. If there are limits to the capacity of the state to organize labor to meet demand, these limits are ones of credibility. Money offers in credibility what the state lacks. It offers the power of freedom; it offers itself for possession. In return for its commands, it gives its power of command. Nothing promised by the state can match that which is promised by money.

An increase in the supply of money can increase both production and demand. Moreover, the presence of additional money stimulates the economy by the multiplier effect. When an individual spends money, the money is lost unless it is traded or invested for a profit. In an economy as a whole, however, the same money can be spent again and again. If investment is balanced against consumption, then a supply of additional money can unlock a supply of potential production, as well as a supply of potential demand. For an economy to grow effectively, then, it requires the production of goods and services, as well as the creation of money, to express demand. In a closed market society, an increase in the supply of money merely increases inactive reserves. The excess money may fail to recirculate and be hoarded; it may be spent abroad and not return; or it may lead to a general increase in prices. In a capitalist society, by contrast, an increase in the supply of money can lead to investment in production and an increase in consumption. Money may stimulate economic growth. The investment of money in capital for the sake of profit is the essential strategy of capitalist society. It demands the accumulation and creation of money for investment via purchase, rent, wages, and interest; it produces the accumulation of money in the form of profit. There is no question of an optimum quantity of money; there is merely the question of an optimum use of money. Money used for investment may subsequently be used for consumption, leading to a rise in prices if production does not increase as quickly. If too much money is directed to consumption, then there is the danger of inflation; if too much money is directed to production, then there is the danger of over-supply. Irrespective of this balance, money remains a productive force.

3.4.2 The demand for money is unlimited. One can never have enough profit, enough economic security, enough investment, or enough consumption. In spite of the general scarcity of money, the supply of money is also unlimited. In response to such demand, money is created by banks in the form of loans to businesses, government, and individuals. While the demand for loans may be unlimited, there are always limits to the effective demand for loans, for loans—both the principal and the interest—have to be repaid in money. Loans are effective, then, only if there is some guarantee that they can be repaid, either through the sale of assets, future earnings, or investment. The offer of a loan is quite simple: one can have the freedom of money in one's pocket now if one shows the capacity and undertakes the obligation to engage in activity that will yield a profit. A loan is a contract, not an exchange. Where the money that is spent, and the power and freedom it embodies, passes on to others, the contractual obligation to repay the debt remains with the borrower. Where money seems to be a passive, neutral substance or sign in exchange, it is an obligation in contract. Money functions as a transferable debt, passing freely through any number of hands, yet the value that underwrites it is the contractual obligation to repay interest on the loan. It matters little whether such a debt is underwritten by governments, who guarantee the payment of interest by means of taxation; by businesses, who guarantee the payment of interest by means of profits; or by individuals, who guarantee the payment of interest by means of future income. In each case, money is created as a debt.

It may seem important to distinguish between pocket money, whose value is reserved in its substance; paper money, whose value is reserved at a central location such as a bank; and debt money, whose value is a reserve advanced from future taxation, profits, or income. Marx, for example drew a sharp distinction between money and credit, since in a financial crisis credit is devalued, and there is a rush to hoard money or even gold.[32] Nevertheless, gold holds value only as an object of belief. All money is credit. In a financial crisis, there is merely a shift in credit from a centralized reserve maintained through the banking system to a reserve that can be held individually. A financial crisis means the disassembly of credit as constructive capital. It is more important to distinguish between money as a transferable asset — an embodiment of exchange value that can be freely used for purchases and investment — and money as a contractual debt. While money as an asset is transferred, that asset remains guaranteed by a debt that remains largely tied to the one who undertakes it. Money has two sides: a sovereign head that gives power and freedom, and a reverse side that speaks of social obligations. Assets embody social claims; they are always accompanied by liabilities. Any analysis of the operation of money that treats it as an asset alone, therefore, will remain deficient. One who accumulates money as an asset, who possesses power and freedom, enters a market that is already filled with liabilities and demands for money. More significant, since money is created as a debt, the one who enters the market with accumulated money encounters not merely a collection of sellers, but a collection of sellers who are already indebted to a sum in excess of that accumulated by the purchaser. The sellers, then, will be under an obligation to sell to such purchasers, to treat them as a source of sovereign commands. The indebted seller may have some choice between such purchasers but is under an obligation to provide some service to some masters.

The effect of the creation of money is not neutral on the economy as a whole. Since loans are spent before they are repaid in the form of money, they tighten the demand for money as such. While a loan adds to the total value in circulation, it also tightens the demand for money within the system as a whole by the rate of interest. For those who do not have easy access to credit, the tightness of the demand for money means that there is always a shortage of money available. For those who do have easy access to credit, the need to repay more money than one has borrowed means that there is always a shortage of available money. The creation of money through loans is the reason for the perpetual shortage of money. The more money that is created, the less money will be available. The greater the shortage of money, the greater will be the obligation within the economic system as whole to prioritize activities geared primarily toward the making of money. The greater the degree of accumulated wealth, the greater will be the enslavement to debt.

There is no more significant social force within the contemporary global economy than debt. Economic behavior is driven in part by the fulfillment of wants, or desire. It is also driven in part by the struggle for survival. It is driven in part by the speculative demand for profits, or a will to power. It is driven furthermore by the social obligation of debt. Such drives are not in competition with each other but come to fulfillment through each other. It is therefore impossible to divide them up into respective degrees of force. It is not easy to compare their respective degrees of impact on the economy, since each magnifies the effects of the others. Survival is obtained by fulfilling wants. Wants are obtained through market exchange. A market filled with products is available because of activity resulting from the quest for profits. The investment of profits in rent, wages, and interest makes money available for use in consumption, augmenting effective demand. Debt drives the quest for profits. It would seem that such drives have a relative order of independence. The struggle for survival can continue without the fulfillment of desires; the fulfillment of desires can continue without a quest for profits; a quest for profits can continue without the existence of loans and debts. It therefore seems natural to attribute priority to that which is historically and logically prior: debt is a means to the end of profits; profits are a means to the fulfillment of desire; desire is a means in the struggle for survival. Nevertheless, to treat these as "means" is to treat them as instruments entirely subordinated to the prior drive. In practice, the market enables a complex mutual dependence. The struggle for survival causes some to work for wages, serving another's desire. The desire for pleasure causes some to buy, yielding profits for another. Profits are made for their own sake at the same time that a proportion is used to pay interest.

Debt is a means that becomes an end, for to repay interest on a loan, it is necessary to produce exchange value for sale in order to acquire money. It is not sufficient for an economic system to produce wealth in the form of goods and services for it to pay back its loans, for loans are repaid in the form of money, not of goods and services. To repay interest on a loan, someone else must have created the money elsewhere as debt, so that the original loan is repaid and the debt is canceled. The amount of debt money in the economy spirals ever higher. The force of debt grows ever stronger. Instead of spending money on desirable public services, it becomes ever more necessary to spend money to make profits in order to repay loans. The availability of money for worthwhile activities becomes ever tighter while the availability of money for making profits becomes ever larger. With financial disintermediation, the circuits of profitmaking can take place through speculation alone, repaying debts acquired through high levels of leverage. Money can be gradually withdrawn from productive circulation to service the higher levels of profit available to speculation. In a world of increasing wealth, restrictions on the availability of money grow ever tighter.

3.4.3 It is important to clarify the difference between two kinds of debt. Private debts may be contracted between consenting parties by means of the temporary loan of existing assets. Such debts do not add to the money in circulation; they merely facilitate the efficient investment of reserves. The banking system functions as a market maker for such debts, facilitating the transfer of sums between borrowers and lenders. The system of credit changes essentially, however, when banks retain their reserves. In fractional reserve banking, a bank does not lend the money deposited with it; it retains such money in its reserves. Instead, it may issue a loan in the form of a check or a bank account. When the lent money is spent and deposited at another bank, a transfer may take place between the two banks' reserves. Yet in a large economy with a few central banks, a large number of such transactions will take place each day. The vast majority of these will cancel out; if there are temporary inequalities, the reserves can be lent between banks at the inter-bank rate of interest for overnight loans. In short, each bank will need to retain only a small proportion of the loans it issues in the form of reserves. The majority of this money is newly created; it is temporary debt money that eventually will have to be repaid at interest and canceled out. Such credit facilitates productive activity that would not otherwise be possible. It also locks all new productive activity into a quest for profits.

Debt facilitates mutual dependence. Interdependence increases wealth at the same time that it increases vulnerability, for when the value reserved in money can be carried in one's pocket, it is safely dispersed throughout the economy. Yet when the value reserved in money is retained in a central bank, it is, as Adam Smith pointed out, vulnerable to hostilities: a key strategic objective in any invasion is the store of money and gold reserves.[33] When the value reserved in money is no longer reserved in a physical location but instead consists in the network of private credit between banks, it becomes as fragile as a reputation. Value is vulnerable to monetary crises. This very vulnerability of debt is the source of its power. For while debts may be reduced by devaluation and inflation, such a move undermines credit as constructive capital and reduces the production of wealth. In a complex economy, the stability of money, credit, and the banking system takes priority over all other concerns, for constructive capital is the source of cooperation and wealth. In a complex economy, interdependence replaces self-reliance. Any disruption of energy supply, transport, communications, or banking brings the entire system down. While less wealthy societies are more subject to currency crises, the wealthiest societies are those that are most vulnerable should such disruption occur. When the distribution of provision is mediated almost exclusively by markets, society lacks any other forms of constructive capital through which provision can take place if the market fails. It is this very vulnerability of the system of credit that gives financial interests the supreme political power. If credit fails, which it can so easily, then the entirety of society fails with it.

PROMISE

3.5.1 Money is a promise of value. The essential issue that needs to be determined is whether such a promise is dependent on value or whether such a value is dependent on a promise. The question to be determined is whether the value of such a promise is determined in exchange according to supply and demand or whether the value of such a promise is a transcendental category that is irreducible to exchange. The distinction between money and the value promised by money is well established; the relation between money and the value promised by money is not.

As has been discussed, the value promised by money is not independent of money. The value promised by money is embodied in the goods, assets, and services that can be bought with it; the value of such goods, assets, and services is measured by prices, embodied in the amount of money that is paid for them. Prices are determined by comparing goods, assets, and services with each other within a market. A market is made possible by the existence of its reputation, money, and a dealer or reserve. Two kinds of comparison are possible within a market: a comparison of qualities of the items for sale where items significantly differ, the outcome of which is expressed in terms of a difference in price, and a comparison of prices of items deemed to be substitutable for each other, where differences in prices are compared. Use or exchange may be compared. The expression of qualitative comparisons in terms of price differences is significant here: a difference in quality is established not in relation to an absolute standard but in relation to the promise contained within money, for a price difference signifies all of the other possibilities available for that sum of money, whether in different or future markets. Far from being a universal equivalent through which all commodities are compared with one another, money represents the promise of value that can be obtained from other markets.[34] There is no universal equivalent or universal market. There is no valid macroeconomic perspective on the market as a whole. There are only perspectives of agents within the market, whether they are householders, merchants, landowners, workers, capitalists, bankers, speculators, or the excluded. All markets and comparisons are local and finite. Price is measured in relation to promise and opportunity, not in relation to an absolute standard. Prices are not fixed in relation to the world of commodities in general, because such a world exists only as a promise. Value depends on promise, not vice versa.

Money is distinctive among commodities in that it is a promise. When the value of a commodity is compared with money, it is compared with a finite power to enter external markets. Decisions on pricing are always strategic, contrasting knowledge of and confidence in a local market relation with the uncertainty and opportunity of external markets. Since the work of comparison with all commodities in all external markets can never be completed, a particular price must be substituted in place of a universal price and in advance of a universal price—perhaps in the hope that, through fluctuations in supply and demand, a universal price resulting from such external comparisons may one day be achieved. Where supply and demand are relative to local and finite markets, money provides the means by which the limits of the local market may be transcended. Value, then, is an effect of comparison and exchange. It treats an exchange as if it has already taken place for a determinate sum of money. Prices may be variables that fluctuate in time, but they always appear with hindsight, after the event; they discount the temporal dimension of promise. During the process of evaluation in which prices are formed, prices hold all of the uncertainty of a comparison of competing promises. Value is not an object to be appropriated or possessed; value only becomes value in exchange. While objects can be possessed, their value cannot. Value always belongs elsewhere. It is offered or taken, not held. Value, then, is a relational and temporal entity. It cannot be comprehended on the basis of the quality of objects or an accumulation of units.

3.5.2 Money created as debt can be analyzed into the following separable components: an asset, a liability, and a reserve. These components are separable to the extent that they can circulate between differing parties. An asset is a promise of value; a liability is an obligation to offer value; and a reserve is a security that guarantees value. Reserves are also usually assets, whether they take the form of money, property, or capital. In practice, then, money emerges from a contract that allows for a threefold division. Money is the promise of value. Yet such promises are worth nothing to those who make them. At best, the return of an IOU note signals redemption from a liability. Money bears value as a promise, therefore, only if the promise is trusted by others and value is advanced on the basis of that promise. Money exists only in relation. It consists in a promise: a value that is promised, trust in the promise, and value advanced on the basis of trust. Furthermore, a promise by itself does not generate trust. Trust is not based on the promise itself but on the reserve as a guarantee of value. The asset, the liability, and the reserve each indicate value. The reserve is typically held by a bank; the liability is typically held by the person who takes out the loan; and the asset is typically held by the person who currently possesses the money. From another point of view, value is advanced in the form of goods by one who accepts money on the basis of trust; value is promised in the form of money to the person who accepts money in exchange; and value reserved, signifed by the form of money, is underwritten by both the existence of bank reserves and the specific security of the one who has undertaken the loan.[35]

It is important to understand that this complex of money is an impersonal social structure. The value of money does not inhere in the objective value promised by money; nor does the value of money inhere in the subjective trust inspired by the promise. While the value of money may derive from exchange value and trust and be expressed in exchange value and trust, the value of money depends on the social power of money itself. The question of the origins of the value and trust in money are of less significance than its ultimate orientation and destination. It matters little how money first acquired value. It matters only how money maintains and intensifies its value. Questions of origins, of the universal, and of the necessary are subordinate here to the transcendental power of a promise. The distinctive spiritual power of a promise is the object of a theology of money.

In practice, money gains its value not from the promise alone, or from the existence of trust in the promise, but from the fact that value is advanced on the basis of such a promise, whether it is in fact trusted or otherwise. One does not have to believe in the value of money in order to seek it out and spend it; one merely has to believe that money will be acceptable in exchange. There are several reasons for using money in exchange that constitute the source of its value. If money promises an ability to participate in market society, it also threatens exclusion from access to capital for those who are unable to participate through lack of money. Any decision taken regarding trust in money is not taken independently of the decisions of others. To decide for money is to decide for the market; it is also to accept the reality of the presence of the market and the dangers of trying to ignore the opportunities provided by the market should they be accepted by others. Once decisions are taken to extend markets to new regions and sectors of social life, few resources are left to reconstruct social life in those regions and sectors apart from the market. The advance of monetary mediation is an irreversible process proceeding by imitation and its threat of exclusion. The advance of money is an entropic process, dispensing with prior obligations. Since money disperses the freedom and power of effective demand, it cannot be renounced without such freedom and power proving to be illusory. It is one thing to decide in the abstract whether the market offers an effective institution for organizing social cooperation in any particular circumstance; it is another thing to accept money that is offered. Decisions are made in practice by the acceptance of money, whatever one thinks about market relations as a whole.

The existence of money as such therefore imposes a peculiar dynamic on market relations. Prices may rise and fall within local and finite markets in relation to supply and demand. Yet prices are also determined in relation to anticipation of future or external markets. This relation with the outside is comparable to a slope on which price fluctuations take place, always tending in a certain direction; it is comparable to the tendency for an increase in entropy. While the slope may reflect anticipation of future markets, its gradient is driven by the actual power of money. Money draws its value from the will to survive that is threatened by a lack of money; money draws its value from a desire for pleasure that is threatened by a lack of money; money draws its value from the promise of advances that can be made on the speculative anticipation of profits; money draws its value from its creation as debt and from the obligations it imposes to convert value into money to repay loans and interest. Money, as the principle of mediation that makes demands effective, demands that the creation, acquisition, maintenance, and investment of money take priority over all other demands. By all of these means, money becomes the supreme social force.

3.5.3 Money has the power to make demands effective. Demands, like all economic forces, have a dual nature. On the one hand, a demand is a demand for the realization of an objective, such as possession or consumption of some good or service. On the other hand, a demand is an expression of an evaluation. It is a demand for attention; a demand that the provision of a good or service is worth some socially validated time, labor, and resources. Just as demands remain private impulses within individuals until they can be made effective through money, evaluations remain private thoughts within individuals until they can come to expression or social recognition. Lacking money therefore is like lacking the opportunity to vote, to speak in public, or to publish. It is to lack an opportunity to offer one's evaluations for acceptance as socially validated evaluations.

The economic effect of money, that it prioritizes the making of profits over all other economic activities, has a similar political effect: it prioritizes the making of profits over all other political values. It may take a long time before other political values are conceded to the market. Once conceded by the deregulation of markets, however, the advance of the political power of money is almost irreversible.

Money makes a dual promise of freedom. Money promises the power to make one's demands effective, liberating one from the constraints of natural and social obligation. Money also gives freedom to express one's own evaluations, offering them for adoption as socially validated evaluations. In both cases, such freedoms are bought at a price: one is only freed from natural and social obligations if the obligations are fulfilled by others. One can have political influence on a society only if that influence is accepted by others. The more that society is mediated by the market, the more extensively are the evaluations made by those with wealth imposed on society as a whole, for the mediation of influence occurs through money. Moreover, since those who have wealth are often constrained to make profits and repay debts, the existence of debt imposes its own political requirements. The curious effect is that even the wealthy classes have little control over the value of values in a society based on the market, capitalism, and credit, for once freedom to act positively, expressing one's evaluations as social forces, becomes constrained to acts of buying and selling, then such freedom has limited effects. One may, through wealth, gain freedom over one's time. However, one has little command over social time as such, except insofar as society spends time providing one's goods and services. One's evaluations, expressed through purchases, remain simply one's own evaluations; there is no reason for them to be adopted by others. They may even hold little significance for the individual, since the value of values is not grounded or recognized beyond the individual. One's evaluations could easily be substituted for other choices, with little overall economic impact. Since the evaluations have so little weight, they are easily subjected to social manipulation through fashion and advertising. Frequent or large expenditures can be made for the lightest of reasons, not because these are "what the consumer wants," but merely because the consumer has no basis for giving value to value, apart from the value of money.

It is a paradox, then, that the utopia of freedom achieved in a wealthy capitalist society offers very little effective freedom. Everyone may wish to impose his or her evaluations on others, or prove how valuable his or her evaluations really are, but few can achieve this effect. Just as the one who is formally free but has no money has little effective power of action, the one who has money but no socially validated evaluations has little power of expression. Everyone may wish to be famous—to be an actor, a writer, an artist, or a musician—but few can find a sufficient audience. Even the audiences that can be found may simply seek distraction rather than an engagement with the value of values. If money facilitates a social order composed of sovereign individuals, then there are no subjects. There can be little agreement on the value of values beyond the creation of wealth. Economic freedom excludes the possibility of constructing a shared ground for shared evaluations. It excludes the possibility of genuine social activity. While such social activity can continue through public discourse and inquiry, it is limited in power if it is not supported by money. Indeed, if such public evaluations are limited in power, they will command less acceptance, since it makes little difference whether they are accepted or not.

Economic freedom is deeply constraining. What is lost is a certain depth of human communication, a collective inquiry into the value of evaluations as such. For value is not an object to be appropriated or possessed; an evaluation is not simply held like an opinion. Value only becomes valued in relation. A matter must matter to someone. Money promises value and freedom, yet it delivers an absence of value and an absence of freedom. The promise offered by money is fundamentally false and deceptive. Yet the structure of money reveals the social structure of promise as such. It reveals a structure for collective evaluation. It reveals an ecology of credit.

Four

POLITICS OF MONEY

CONTRACT

4.1.1 MONEY, AN INSTRUMENT of exchange, is inseparable from the institution of the market, for money holds value only in markets where it may be exchanged. Conversely, markets enabling free exchange are only possible where money is present. Where the behavior of participants in a market who seek to accumulate wealth can be assessed by economics in the quantitative terms of exchange value, the relations of power that occur in the market have to be assessed in qualitative terms by political economy. For, as Adam Smith noted, "Wealth, as Mr. Hobbes says, is power." Money gives "a certain command over all the labour, or over all the produce of labour, which is then in the market."[1] It is a question of determining the relations of power that are expressed through the institution of the market, and so through money.

A person who trades in a market may be characterized by three essential features: a person is an owner of goods that may be exchanged; a person is an owner of labor that may be contracted; and a person is a free agent capable of entering into voluntary exchanges and contracts. Since all have the same freedom of voluntary contracting, and the same obligations to honor contracts and to respect property, all people may be regarded as equal in the marketplace. This egalitarian distribution of a purely formal power corresponds to the formal distribution of political power in a democracy, even if it is in practice compatible with dictatorship. For if all participants have an equal power in respect of form, then any differences between them in regard to property, networks, or ability to make profits appear to be purely economic. Such an economic perspective on the market

excludes considerations of power in advance because they are not represented in the market.[2]

Nevertheless, the same person, before he or she arrives in the market
and after he or she leaves it, may be characterized by three contrasting
features: in contrast to nominal ownership of property, a person is dependent on relations with his or her material environment for location, shelter,
sustenance, and enjoyment; in contrast to ownership of labor, a person is
subject to birth, maturation, illness, and death, and so required to undergo
physical processes over which he or she has no control; and in contrast to
the freedom to enter into contracts, a person has a set of dependencies and
mutual obligations to others, especially parents, children, relatives, com-
panions, educators, and all others connected in a web of relations not mediated by exchange.

Yet it is not simply the case that the concept of the free agent in the market is an abstraction. Such freedom does indeed exist, at least temporarily
or insofar as the market is able to provide sustenance, health, and compan-
ionship via the mediation of exchange. The person who can achieve this
for a temporary period, who effectively dwells within the marketplace—
normally a wealthy adult male as the model for the person—is conceived
within the social institution as a bearer of rights. This concept of the person as a bearer of rights is an abstraction that coexists with such people
and takes their mode of existence as the norm, for it is by right that one
claims the benefits accrued through exchange. In an act of exchange, property is alienated from one party and appropriated by another. One party
renounces any ongoing rights of use over the property; the other makes a
claim to use and dispose of property at will. Founded on private property,
the market is an institution in which claims are made or transferred. The
physical movement of resources does not compose a market. Instead, the
market is purely ideal. It is an institution that records the claims that over-
lie the physical distribution of resources, including habitual practices of
labor, usage, and consumption, as well as physical relations of theft, giving,
violence, and exchange. The market is a social practice of representation.
It represents not all physical processes, however, but merely the legitimate
claims made by people who participate in the market that are expressed in
explicit or implicit contracts. Such claims and property rights come after
the fact. They do not determine the distribution of property but merely en-

sure that the prevailing distribution, which has been achieved by whatever physical means, is granted the force of law.

In the market, then, all people are equal before the law. Their legitimate claims to property are granted an equal right. Yet if the market is purely an institution of representation, nothing actually happens in the market. All significant events, including political relations of force, happen elsewhere. This is not to say that the market has no effect on what happens. On the contrary, the presence of the market is determining in the last instance. This is because the market appeals to the threat of sovereign power to enforce contracts and to safeguard property. Private property has a purely social or public significance. Claims to property are valid only to the extent that they are generally recognized by others. Property requires the institution of sovereignty to sanction the right of possession. There can be no right to property without public sovereignty.[3] Similarly, there can be no right to dispose of property without the public institution of the market through which it is exchanged and claimed. Thus, there is no right to dispose of property (as distinct from usage of property) without money or some substitute for money in the form of credit or contract.

Sovereign force safeguards claims to property. If the market is the institution in which claims to property are respected as rights, then markets are inseparable from the sovereign threat of the use of force. The difference between interactions outside the market and those within the market is that within the market the person asserts a claim to safeguard property by appealing to the sovereign power. In other words, rights are claimed within a market by the threat of violence. A market is a social institution that constitutes itself by means of the threat of violence. One enters into the market by internalizing this threat of violence, accepting that any improper claim for the property of others may be met by force.[4] Once within the market, the community of those who respect private property, one is in a peaceable community where relations of trust are possible. Such trust, expressed in credit and in willingness to enter into contracts, is founded on the threat of violence.

4.1.2 The market as an institution sustains a range of different relations with external and heterogeneous social formations. In the first place, people in the market—and thus markets as a whole—are sustained by material, personal, and social dependencies. Because they are relations rather than properties, and because the person has no freedom to transfer or dispose of them (as opposed to abandoning them), such dependencies cannot be represented as rights within the market. Such dependencies, since they cannot be enforced as rights, are not represented at all. The market only represents the sphere of human agency and control; people exist in the market only to the extent that they have some mastery over their relations. A market society is composed of a set of sovereign individuals who are owners of property. It simply disavows or fails to nourish other relations and dependencies.[5] Such relations and dependencies, then, can be maintained only by the effective demands of those who trade within the market, should they happen to be conscious of them.

In the second place, there are social institutions beyond the market that limit the freedom of people to dispose of their property as they please, that make demands on a person's time and labor, or that impose non-voluntary obligations and contracts. These may take forms as diverse as local indigenous communities, imperial formations, socialist dictatorships, or religious traditions. Historically, capitalist market society constructed itself in opposition to an increasingly powerful monarchy whose wealth rested on the capacity to restrict and charter trade.[6] As a consequence, any social claims that limit property rights are treated within the market as a tyrannical infringement on liberty. They directly conflict with the market and its conception of justice insofar as they challenge the absolute right of the individual (or corporation) as owner of property, labor, and freedom to make contracts. The market tends to be opposed to these in principle insofar as they restrict abstract freedom, and it consequently claims the right to call on its sovereign power to make war on such social institutions as enemies of freedom, democracy, right, peace, and justice, should it seem advantageous to do so.[7] By contrast, the market has no opposition to dictatorships that respects the rights of property and trade because it requires a strong state.

In the third place, the essence of market exchange involves the transfer of rights over property and labor. If each individual within the market is at once sovereign over his or her property and labor yet also capable of freely entering into contracts, then in contracting one transfers that sovereignty and right to another in a specified respect. Individual rights do not exist by themselves in isolation. They are only claimed insofar as they are capable of being transferred. The social institution of the market is inseparable from other social relations such as contract, employment, and debt in which freedom over property, products, and labor is suspended and sovereignty over the property, products, and labor of others is claimed. The social situation of free, sovereign individuals has to be supplemented in practice with social relations of command. Alongside the equality of the market there is necessarily the inequality of debt, contract, and employment. These may involve despotic relations of command that are indistinguishable from those regarded as the antithesis of freedom and democracy. The market does not make war on these commands because such rights are established through market exchange itself. The market is thus not opposed to despotism in principle and even depends on and sanctions despotism. Indeed, freedom does not exist without its suspension in the form of contract. All that is required is that rights should be publicly represented according to a due process.

In the fourth place, rights are claimed within the marketplace by acts of appropriation. One may attempt to appropriate the property of others by theft or fraud. In such cases, it is necessary for society to defend the prior right. Yet where no preceding claims exist—that is, where no preceding claims are lodged by recognized recording procedures within the market—then one may attempt to appropriate property by claiming a right through, for example, discovery, invention, or construction. If there are no prior claims or acknowledged rights, then there is no reason to reject claims to appropriate property. It is property rather than money that is created ex nihilo.[8] This has significant implications for relations with non-market societies. Since the social institution of the market recognizes only claims that are lodged within its procedures of recording, then it recognizes no right beyond its own. Moreover, any resistance to acknowledged rights has to be regarded as theft and opposed with violence. The social institution of the market, recognizing no rights but its own, is geared toward universal colonization in the name of property, freedom, and democracy.[9] By means of the appropriation of rights to the means of subsistence, those who are newly incorporated as people in the market have no choice but to reconstruct their lives around market exchange. To survive, they have to take the best opportunities available to them in the market. Such opportunities usually involve a transfer of rights to their property and labor to others.

Impelled by the need for survival, they are no longer able to negotiate terms and have to accept whatever is offered. The theft and exploitation of property and labor is rendered legitimate when it is voluntarily contracted. It is voluntarily contracted when accompanied by the threat of starvation.

The market appears to be a peaceable social institution founded on justice. It recognizes the right of all participants to freedom and property. It mediates potential conflicts between its members by law, contract, and exchange.[10] Yet people maintain their status as participants in the market only to the extent that they acknowledge the sovereignty of the market system. They become free in the market by renouncing the freedom to form any social institution that has a superior claim to that of the rights of property and submission to contracts. The market is a despotic social institution founded on violence. Since such violence is enacted in the name of peace and justice, its effects are unlimited, for the market recognizes no countervailing claims. The market proclaims a total and universal war.[11] Where other forms of conflict are often finite, acknowledging the right and power of the enemy, the market acknowledges no conflicting rights. The market can aim at total annihilation of conflicting social formations. The sovereign states that safeguard the market justify themselves in inflicting unlimited violence on their enemies in the name of the freedom, democracy, and progress that they may establish in place of existing social formations.

The absolute claims of rights in the market transform a system of balance, measure, and justice — when considered purely in terms of the market's internal relations — into its dialectical opposite: an absolute system of total war. Yet physical violence is not the sole strategy of negation pursued by the market. Disavowal of dependence, suspension of freedom when submitted to contract, and appropriation are the daily strategies of negation pursued in practice by the market system. The freedom of exchange and contracting forms a very limited segment of social life within the market system as a whole at the same time that it is the only segment that is represented positively. What is truly significant, however, is the extent to which the market monopolizes strategies of representation, for any representation of alternatives tends to be written to advise free, sovereign subjects on voluntary courses of action. The conception of the human person prevalent within the social institution of the market has already been conceded. Such a representation has to compete directly with the advantages promised to the individual by accumulation of wealth through the market.

It is easy to protest against the tyranny of the market, which at once safeguards the liberty of those with property while imposing extortion and violence on those without. For the market defends people insofar as they conform to the abstract conception of a person as an owner of goods, labor, and freedom while ignoring, destroying, or appropriating people insofar as they have physical and social dependencies. Protest alone, however, is insufficient, because insofar as the institution of the market exists, it holds out the promise of opportunities to acquire wealth. By means of exchange, it offers an unparalleled promise of freedom and prosperity to each individual. Money does not merely create markets. It calls individuals out of prior social institutions and dependencies by promising their hearts' own desire. The power of money is spiritual, not purely social. It calls individuals into the state of subjectivity of the one who participates in the market; it calls them out to be individuals, characterized by violent claims to property, the self-discipline of labor, and enjoyment of freedom and prosperity. It is not sufficient, therefore, to point out the destructive effects of market society and to advise people to return to local or traditional economic activities, for the blessings of enhanced productivity and prosperity available to individuals through the market can always be contraposed to the curses and limitations of traditional life. The morality of the market will always prove more attractive to those who stand to benefit from it than other bases for morality. The theology of money, with its promises, its narcissistic self-positing as the supreme standard and measure of value, its speculative detachment from current conditions, and its despotic power expressed in debt, can be transformed only by a stronger spiritual power.

The strategies of negation pursued by anti-market or anti-globalization politics rarely take this course. The strategy of disavowal or forgetting, which recommends that we leave the market behind, merely reproduces the strategy of alienation by which people are abstracted to become agents in the market. For such a strategy is recommended as a voluntary and collective choice, as if we did not already live in relations of material and social dependence on the market and as if that dependence could simply be disavowed. It depends on the market conception of sovereign freedom, even if rendered in a collective form, that supposes we are free to choose how to determine our lives.

By contrast, the strategy of direct, violent confrontation in the name of an alternative social institution and practice appeals to imperial conquest, a strategy that has been subsumed into the sovereignty of the market institution. Success in such imperial adventures depends on military power, and military power itself depends on wealth, obtained through appropriation, accumulation, and exchange. It is difficult to conceive of amassing a superior power for military confrontation with the forces underlying globalization, even if one could gather a superior power in terms of numbers.

The strategy of renewed legislation limiting the power of capital and ensuring human rights reproduces the claims to sovereignty made within market society. Such sovereign power gains its strength from the will of the people. Yet the question of how the will of the people is formed remains to be determined. It may not be sufficient to appeal to reason and call on truth and justice if other, more partial truths and other justices may easily be propagated and gain the upper hand. The option of sovereign legislation presupposes that sovereign action remains possible despite the threat of capital flight. It also assumes that the formation of public consciousness on the basis of truth and justice remains possible, given the capitalist domination of the media and educational institutions.

4.1.3 If the market is a recording of the social order, it is a recording that is rather partial. The social order appears as a collection of sovereign individuals, each with a determinate set of property claims. A snapshot can be taken of society as a whole, where each is possessed of a determinate degree of wealth. Society appears to be an atomized collection of sovereign individuals. After exchanges have taken place, there is a different distribution of property, yet society remains represented as a set of property claims.

The absoluteness of such a conception, including its claims to property, results from its atemporality. At the same time that it is a set of property rights, the market enables a complex division of labor and a ramified network of interdependencies. Beneath the atemporal and synchronic recording of private property, the productive activity of land, labor, capital, and contract takes place. Such diachronic activity, the source of all wealth, cannot be recorded directly in the atemporal form of property and prices. Its value can merely be estimated and discounted, not recorded. Social relations that are eliminated by the atemporal form of private property based on the threat of violence reemerge into experience as soon as production is considered.

The notion of a market or a market society is therefore an atemporal abstraction. It imagines society in abstraction from all social relations apart from respect for claims to property and threats to enforce such claims. In practice, economic society is never composed simply of a market. It cannot be reduced to exchange.[12] Alongside the exchange of property there is also the payment of rent for land, the payment of wages for labor, the payment of interest for money capital, and the payment of taxes. Such relations are not simple, instantaneous exchanges but contracts that have enduring force. Economic society is not simply a network of exchanges; it is not a market. Economic society is composed of a network of enduring contracts. The primary object of political economy, therefore, should not be the distribution of property and productive resources but the resolution of social forces in the form of contracts. Moreover, the temporal nature and function of money is obscured when it is analyzed in terms of exchange. The function of money as a medium of exchange derives from its function as a facilitator of contracts (a standard for deferred payments). Since the market is a form of recording, contract, not physical exchange, is the primary phenomenon.[13] The political economy of money must be deduced from its role in contracts rather than its role in exchange.

4.1.4 Property may be explained in terms of contract rather than contract in terms of property. Private property is an implicit contract for possession and exclusion agreed between consenting parties. Such contracts are highly selective in their form of representation. While they are usually agreed between two parties, the outcome of the contract may have significant implications for others, for the physical environment, and even for the social environment. Property is a contract for rights without obligations. The property is a passive, silent partner in the contract, unable to assert its rights, needs, or power. This is especially evident when the property in question is a slave, an animal, or the labor of a woman to be employed for domestic or sexual services or where the precise nature of the labor required is not fully specified by the contract. In practice, the contract is drawn up by consenting parties under the tacit agreement that force should be used to render the object of exchange passive. A contract is rarely simply between two parties. The remaining members of society remain silent witnesses to the contract, tacitly agreeing that the parties should be undisturbed in their right to dispose of their property.

Market transactions form a public record of such exchanges. The property is simply designated. Its wider significance, its conditions for production and subsistence, its power, and its will are not represented in the contract. In practice, should these conflict with the will of the owner, there is a tacit agreement that they may be suppressed by the owner or by society on behalf of the owner. Sovereignty over property amounts to this. Market transactions, far from determining a just distribution, are necessarily partial; they consider only the respective claims of the consenting parties. Moreover, society as a whole is complicit with such injustice. Dissenting voices are suppressed. Private property is a contract consisting of rights without obligations that is extorted by force or the threat of force. Similarly, exchanges of property are contractual agreements to deliver property at a specified time and place. All exchanges are forms of contract. Yet not all contracts are forms of reciprocal exchange. As the example of property makes clear, rights may exist without obligations. Numerous parties are affected by each exchange, yet not all of these parties are represented in the exchange.

4.1.5 Money, likewise, is an implicit contract rather than a commodity. Like a title to property, money is a mere token of value. The social contract of market society involves a willingness to accept money in payment based on the confidence that others will also accept it in payment. Money is a form of transferable and implicit contract whose value rests on a determinate set of other contracts. Contracts have an effect on the distribution of physical capital, the activity of labor, and the availability and use of constructive capital. Contracts underwrite social cooperation.

Money, like other financial assets, is a contract that can easily be appropriated and exchanged. It is a form of public contract that has become private property. As property, it appears to have no substance, no force, no life of its own. It appears to demand no conditions for its maintenance. It appears to impose no temporal force directly on its owner. This is so because the implicit contract involved in money is not subject to individual renegotiation, even if it is continually subject to collective renegotiation according to its relative market value and rates of inflation. Yet to treat money purely as property and to determine exchange values in terms of money as prices is to construct an atemporal representation of value. It matters little that such prices may fluctuate in time; it matters little that expected variations in value are discounted in the price. Exchange value represents social relations apart from temporal contracts in the form of private property. Exchange value is an abstraction that results from inverting the priority of contract and property, as though enduring contracts were an effect of atemporal property rather than the reverse.

The study of exchange values therefore gives a partial representation of economic society. Social bonds in the form of contracts and social powers exercised in the agreement of contracts are not directly represented. They must first be represented in an atemporal form by assessing their exchange value. Their effects may be inferred from movements of prices and modeled in the form of temporal functions. Time is first excluded from social representation before being added later on as a transcendent model in the form of an equation of motion. The political reality of economic relations is concealed and excluded, for social reality in practice is composed of a vast number of temporal contracts and habitual interdependencies that are qualitatively determined. They cannot be accurately compared on a single abstract scale of exchange value or on a single, abstract scale of uniform time.

While many claim the right to money as private property, such claims do not effectively reduce money to property in practice, for as a promise or debt, money remains a contract. The market no longer furnishes an adequate image of economic relations. Any economic theory constructed under the assumption that the economy behaves as a village market will be largely worthless.[14] If contracts are evaluated in terms of exchange value alone, then an attempt is made to evaluate them in terms of property. In other words, the contract is observed from the perspective of one who has rights without responsibilities—from the abstract perspective of the one who is capable of buying himself out of all preceding contracts or agreements. To interpret society in terms of exchange value alone is to assume that all dependencies may be substituted for by an alternative deal that will always be available on the market. It is to suppose that the market is capable, at will, of embracing and representing all dimensions of reality. Since physical capital, human capital, and social capital operate according to their own laws of dependence, rather than according to the freedom of the market, such a representation will be necessarily false. Instead, the temporal process of supply, labor, service, or contract is treated as if it were a commodity or a slave. For production, labor, contract, and money are never private property, even if they are treated as such.

Where the abstract market seems purely economic, concerned with exchange values alone, a contract society is inseparable from the political form of the state. Such a state has three essential functions. First, it must safeguard property, or, more precisely, it must ensure that existing contracts are respected. Second, it must legitimate rights and claims to appropriation, making legislative or executive decisions on the propriety of such claims. And third, it must maintain confidence in the value of contracts by ensuring the value of a dominant currency. While it may not be essential that a state issue its own currency, it is vital that the state contribute to the stability of currency by pursuing appropriate monetary and fiscal policy. The three functions of the state concern right, liberty, and credit (or piety). Charged with maintaining a state of general social belief, the state remains a religious institution within secular modernity.

DISTRIBUTION

4.2.1 In terms of exchange, all things bear an exchange value. In terms of contract, there is no equivalent between what is offered and what is received. What is offered is always time, whether time is spent in a certain manner or is taken to deliver a product. One enters into an obligation to spend time in a determinate way. What is received is always nutrition for some desire or process. Things bear relative value if they provide for the "necessities, conveniences, and amusements" of life. Instead of considering buyers and sellers in exchange, therefore, it is necessary to consider nutrition and time. This transforms the entire perspective on the economy. While in principle an unlimited amount of exchange value and an unlimited amount of money may be available, a finite amount of nutrition and a finite amount of time will always remain. Political economy should therefore be concerned primarily with the distribution of nutrition and time, not with the distribution of exchange value.

Nutritional value is itself derived from underlying physical processes such as photosynthesis. Nature is an efficient gardener: its unlimited proliferation of forms leads to the existence of species to occupy each environmental niche. There is little scope for improving on the primary production of nutritional value. Human labor does not create nutritional value; it merely redirects the production of nutritional value away from ecological circuits that do not include humans to circuits that do. On the whole, through deforestation, soil degradation, and desertification, human agricultural activity has a negative net effect on the primary production of nutritional value, even if it is capable of temporarily increasing the production of nutritional value for humans by the use of irrigation, farm machinery, and fertilizers and pesticides and by exhausting finite stocks of fresh water and fossil fuels.

A theory of nutritional value may be derived from the work of Adam Smith. The supply of the means of subsistence remains scarce. Contractual offers of nutritional value command labor because labor requires nutritional value to survive. Labor theories of value consider acquisition in terms of weighing the benefits of satisfying desires against the toil and trouble of labor. Smith therefore proposed that labor is the only universal and accurate measure of value, equal quantities of labor being at all times and places of equal value to the laborer.[15] That which is dear costs much labor to acquire; that which is cheap costs little. In practice, of course, value is measured directly not in terms of labor time but in terms of money. It is important to understand the kind of labor Smith is discussing. He is concerned primarily with agricultural labor, paid at a subsistence rate, for the profit of tenants and landholders. For such labor, the only benefit of labor is the wage.[16] The rest is all toil and trouble. Such labor theories of value can maintain the illusion that all productive value is generated by human labor at rates that vary depending on efficiency gains introduced by machines. This is no longer credible when most energy for work is provided by fossil and nuclear fuels rather than by human labor. Moreover, it was not the actual view of Adam Smith: "No equal capital puts into motion a greater quantity of productive labor than that of the farmer. Not only his laboring servants, but his laboring cattle, are productive laborers. In agriculture, too, nature labors along with man; and though her labor costs no expense, its produce has its value, as well as that of the most expensive workmen. The most important operations of agriculture seem intended not so much to increase . . . as to direct the fertility of nature toward the production of plants most profitable to man."[17] Nature here is the source of value, while labor is its measure. Labor becomes a universal standard only when wages are maintained at a subsistence level. The source of wealth, including labor, is food: "As men, like all other animals, naturally multiply in proportion to the means of their subsistence, food is always, more or less, in demand. It can always purchase or command a greater or smaller quantity of labour, and somebody can always be found who is willing to do something in order to obtain it."[18] While Smith notes that wages as well as levels of subsistence may vary in relation to the wealth of the country in question, he writes against a norm of high child mortality among the laboring classes, with the "scantiness of subsistence . . . destroying a great part of the children which their fruitful marriages produce."[19] The consistent unit of value, then, is the subsistence level of nutrition. Smith explained how corn rent could maintain its value much more successfully than rent paid in money, even though the price of corn might vary significantly with seasons and harvests.[20] If the rent of land attracts a monopoly price so that workers will necessarily be paid at a subsistence level, and if the quantity of workers maintained is in proportion to the production of food, Smith sketched the outlines of a nutritional theory of value that grounds the labor theory of value: "Every other commodity, however, will at any particular time purchase a greater or smaller quantity of labour in proportion to the quantity of subsistence which it can purchase at that time."[21]

In this formulation, a standard unit of value is formed by measuring the natural relationship between a consistent quantity of nutritional value and the life of a worker. Value emerges from a conjunction between nutrition and time, not from simple exchange. When the benefits of nutrition are weighed against the spending of time, a different formulation of value emerges, for although time is limited, it cannot be hoarded. Time must be spent, and different modes of spending time nourish differing desires and differing aspects of a human being. For a person with time, energy, and desire to spend, work need not be regarded as toil and trouble. Work itself may have numerous nutritional qualities for the human being, just as leisure may have numerous debilitating qualities. If the art of living well involves constructing a balanced and varied diet of forms of nutrition, including more urgent physical desires and more subtle social desires, then the cost of labor is both the sacrifice of opportunities for other forms of nutrition and the danger of an excessive input of certain kinds of nutrition.

An economy of nutritional value operates throughout nature, as well as throughout the human economy. In practice, the human economy of nutritional value operates mainly outside the formal sphere of contract in local and informal economies of provision and distribution. Provision, like all forms of economic behavior, has a dual nature: as food nourishes the body, care nourishes the soul. Yet where forms of physical nutrition are limited and exclusive, forms of social nutrition have no intrinsic limits. Caring for others nourishes the emotional health of all, building a culture of generosity, trust, and interdependence. There are no intrinsic limits on informal social capital; there are, however, limits to the extent to which such provision can be spread.

The formal economy may be understood more fully against the background of the informal economy in terms of nutrition and time, provision, and care.[22] Where bonds of trust and interdependence do not yet exist, the formal economy can extend the benefits of social capital to strangers, for money represents a right to claim nutritional value. Although the use of money may substitute for bonds of social care and provision, it does not exclude the creation of such bonds. There is no need for loyalty and amicability between those who trade with each other in the formal economy, yet the formation of contracts for exchange enables such a possibility. To exchange or labor for money is to acquire a reified and de-personalized bond of provision, even if money does not bring emotional relations of interdependence with it. Yet a society based on commerce may construct a general culture of good faith and openness to interaction, building a veritable degree of social capital as collective goodwill. Given the scarcity of time, it is impossible that all relations will be personal and intimate. Money adds to overall efficiency by enabling relations of provision where none were formerly available and by enriching personal interdependencies with impersonal interdependencies. Money extends the effects of social relations of provision and care beyond their normal boundaries.

4.2.2 Given the scarcity of nutritional value, ownership of the means of subsistence tends to attract monopoly rates of rent, rather than equilibrium rates of exchange. Appropriation of the means of subsistence leads to economic inequalities. As Locke has shown, where there are natural limits to individual usage, money enables the possibility of accumulation leading to inequalities.[23] The appropriation of more land than one can use oneself is ineffective unless there are those who lack the means of subsistence and will therefore agree to work the land. Once the informal economy of care and provision is insufficient to meet subsistence needs, then those who lack nutrition under conditions of scarcity may be exploited through monopoly rent. The effect of accumulation is dual. On the one hand, the means of subsistence are appropriated, excluding access by others to the means of subsistence; on the other hand, the means of subsistence are made available once more but as private property. The distribution of nutrition can no longer be determined by traditional social structures of provision. Property overrides informal and traditional modes of social capital to make available those of the formal economy. Participation in the formal economy is driven by both promise of accumulation and threat of exclusion. Thus, monopoly is the norm and equilibrium is the exception within a market society. As Adam Smith was well aware, "In every different branch, the oppression of the poor must establish the monopoly of the rich, who, by engrossing the whole trade to themselves, will be able to make very large profits."[24] The scarcity of nutritional value is expressed in the scarcity of land, leading to monopoly rates of rent for land: "Rent, considered as the price paid for the use of the land, is naturally the highest which the tenant can afford to pay in the actual circumstances of the land."[25]

Significant inequalities of wealth accumulate a surplus value in the form of monopoly rent. In the informal economy, wealth consists in social bonds of honor, trust, care, and mutual obligation. The accumulation of stock has little value in itself except as a means of provision, a reserve against misfortune, a means of patronage, or a means of building a network of obligations. Against this background, the extraction of surplus value substitutes the formal economy for the informal economy; it substitutes contractual relations of obligation for the reciprocal bonds of care or patronage. It substitutes impersonal for personal bonds. Where personal bonds involve a complex interweaving of care, obligation, and social power, impersonal bonds are secured by power alone. Contractual bonds are enforced by society as a whole, embodied in the form of the state; they replace on ongoing process of negotiation between differing powers with a fixed agreement enforced by a vastly superior power. The precise terms agreed in a contract will depend on the relative status of the contracting parties. Those who are confident of maintaining their means of provision, whether from property or from an existing network of mutual obligation or contracts and those who have access to alternative contracts on more favorable terms, will be in a position of relative strength in contrast to those who seek the means of subsistence. The term "usury" may be appropriate here. In the Middle Ages, "usury" was widely used for any economic relation that exploited another's misfortune.[26] It makes a wealth of difference, however, whether debts are contracted voluntarily in pursuit of personal gain or they are contracted as the only remaining alternative under conditions of misfortune. It is the latter condition that is truly usurious. A contract agreed on the basis of a monopoly over means of subsistence may agree terms that extract unlimited quantities of time, claiming ownership over another's life. This is the source of debt bondage that is effective slavery. Those who are evicted from their land and deprived of the means of subsistence are offered an ambivalent deal in a contract of employment: the opportunity to work for a living is charged at the monopoly rate of the market. Such "generous" terms signify the true meaning of usury: turning the necessity of another into one's own opportunity.

In the formal economy, property must be accumulated before it can be exchanged. Exchange value derives from desire expressed in demand and from the security that desire will continue to be available to find nutritional value in what is available to be exchanged. There is a certain security in nutritional value in that it is likely to continue to remain an object of desire. There is a certain security in contracts in that they can be enforced by society with the threat of violence and exclusion. The production and accumulation of value is secured, ultimately, on usury. It is guaranteed by the need of those without access to the means of provision to seek employment in labor.

This is the political perspective from which globalization and the liberalization of trade may be judged. The liberalization of trade is a liberalization of opportunities for contract. It liberates opportunities for those with power in the market to make the most of their potential. Free trade facilitates an increase in production through the division of labor, for labor may be differentiated qualitatively according to available resources, skills, customs, and education. Nevertheless, the very principle through which free trade generates wealth—maximizing efficiency through the division of labor—is also the principle that prevents free trade in labor. Labor can find an equilibrium price in the market only if it can achieve the same degree of mobility between markets and flexibility over production as money itself. Since labor is often tied to a locality or a set of skills, it cannot move freely within the market to meet demand. There will always be an imbalance in labor, with certain forms of skilled labor always in demand and carrying a higher price, and other forms of labor commanding a lower price or none at all. In practice, then, free trade profits from a reserve army of the unemployed who drive wages down to subsistence levels in certain employment markets. Such free trade facilitates economic growth not for all but for the few based on growing inequality. It amounts to a liberalization of rent seeking, monopoly, exploitation, and usury. As a result, inequalities may lead to further appropriations of the means of subsistence in the name of increased productivity. The liberalization of trade leads to further appropriation, penury, exploitation, and inequality in a vicious spiral of inequality. In a free market, exchange value represents appropriated usury; it represents the force of necessity. The overall effect is deeply ambivalent. In the first place, the liberalization of trade removes the regulations that protect precapitalist forms of social capital from appropriation. In the second place, it facilitates their replacement with the growth of capitalist forms of human and social capital, increasing productivity. And in the third place, most of the benefits of such productivity gains are extracted once more, leaving residual benefits as a substitute for pre-capitalist forms of life.[27]

4.2.3 Nutritional value is relative. It holds value not in itself but only in relation to some specific desire. Moreover, while forms of desire and relative nutrition may be unlimited, the quantity of each form of nutritional value is not. In addition, nutritional value is largely used, even if it is used only by microorganisms in a process of decay. Nutritional value cannot, strictly speaking, be hoarded and accumulated. It can simply be appropriated by certain circuits of consumption at the expense of other circuits. Nutritional value, unlike property, is in continual flow.

Time is similar to nutritional value. It is relative, finite, and spent. Time cannot be owned or hoarded; it gives itself in attention to something. Strictly speaking, time is not given or lent. It remains with the giver. While time itself cannot be taken, attention can be attracted or absorbed.

It can flow through broader or narrower circuits. Such payment of attention shapes the life of the source as well as the object of attention. Time, like nutrition, cannot be wasted. Yet nutrition can feed desires that do little to feed the wider ecology, and time can pay attention to expressions of values that do little to value the wider social sphere. The expenditure of time and nutrition are forms of economic entropy. Yet these very processes of continual expenditure provide opportunities for negentropic forms of desire and value to emerge that reconstitute nutrition and attention. Such economies of nutrition and attention operate by efflux and reflux. In an ecosystem, there is continual expenditure without guarantee of a return flow. Return, if it occurs, results from the action of complementary life forms that make the ecosystem into a sustainable cycle.

One may conceive of the economic institutions that produce a reflux of nutrition and attention in terms of social capital. Just as there are self-sustaining, negentropic life forms, so also are there self-sustaining, negentropic social forms. Such forms facilitate the creation of wealth through the accumulation, invention, and construction of capital. The formal economy in a contract society may be assessed as a mode of social capital.

Social capital directs the efflux and reflux of nutrition and attention. The formal economy does so through an entirely different representation: it aims to represent and capture the circular flow of value. Representing value on the basis of exchange, each economic agent functions as a center of accumulation that aims to order the circular flow of value through its possession toward an increase in rate and quantity. For exchange value, unlike the qualitatively differentiated nutritional value and time of attention, is a pure quantity without relation. It can only be accumulated and spent. Exchange value is appropriated by ensuring that it passes more rapidly through centers of accumulation. The measure of a rate of flow does not distinguish between a reduction in flow through other centers of accumulation and an enhanced flow through broader circuits.

Where accumulation of value through exchange provides an orientation for economic activity, the agreement of contracts specify the means. Contracts determine the nature of the nutrition provided, as well as the conduct and distribution of time. Contracts represent limits or conditions that must be met, although they need not specify in detail how these targets should be met. To promise to deliver a sum of money at a specified time is not to specify how time should be spent in acquiring such a sum. Contracts determine time but vary in the degree of freedom that they allow: to commit hours of labor to be commanded by another allows considerably less freedom than to promise the delivery of a sum of money. Freedom and power belong with the purchaser.

The effect of the formal economy, then, is to concentrate the distribution of social capital into circuits of formal contract. Instead of being dispersed through society, freedom and social capital is highly concentrated. For many, the priority of seeking the means of subsistence prevents the building of social capital in the form of relations of provision and care. If social capital is accumulated by those with access to credit and money, then this may occur at the expense of the formation of social capital elsewhere. By reducing opportunities for the accumulation, invention, and construction of capital, centers of accumulation impoverish much of society. When social capital is concentrated in the form of money, centers of efflux and reflux must grow to survive. Insofar as finite stocks of nutritional value and time follow the flows of money, then the accumulation of centers of nutritional value results in the deprivation of a vast periphery.

4.2.4 Since nutritional value and time are scarce and limited resources, the health of society is advanced by their dispersal. The adage of Francis Bacon is apposite here: money is like muck—no good unless it is spread.[28] Provision and care should take priority over the reflux of nutrition and attention; expenditure is more useful than accumulation. Social capital, by contrast, is not a finite resource. Its accumulation in one place may advance accumulation elsewhere. Yet social capital is initially produced in dispersal by successful relations of interdependence. Social capital is produced by acts of provision. It is a culture of care, trust, collaboration, and generosity. Social capital gives the capacity to extend networks of nutrition and attention.

In political economy, therefore, one cannot simply privilege dispersal or accumulation when considering forms of distribution. Dispersal of finite goods such as nutritional value and time may enhance the accumulation of the unlimited good of social capital. The accumulation of social capital may, in turn, enhance the dispersal of finite goods. Subject to differing political requirements, then, nutrition, time, and social capital require differing modes of representation. Where nutrition may be given, time is spent, and social capital accumulates. The equivocation arises when each is measured in terms of exchange, as though it could be represented as a commodity and subject to exchange. Such is the fundamental illusion engendered by the use of money.

Money itself has a triple nature: it participates in the spheres of nutrition, time, and social capital as a specific form of representation. Money represents nutritional value when it acts as a commodity that can be appropriated, alienated, and exchanged. Because of its liquidity, it acts as transferable wealth. It forms the basis for atemporal exchange value. Money represents time as a promise to pay, for a promise, like time, is inalienable. Money, like time, may be given and spent, yet as a promise it returns to its originator. Whereas an asset may be transferred, a liability remains; whereas an asset may be owned, a liability is contracted; whereas an asset represents accumulated wealth, a liability represents an enduring obligation. While assets may appear to balance liabilities on a balance sheet, such equivalence rests on an equivocation, imagining the completion of the circular flow and the redemption of the liability by the asset. Economic reality takes place, however, between such resolutions of the circular flow within the intervening intervals of asymmetry.

It is for this reason that money may also represent social capital. It does so in the form of debt. Liabilities need not be redeemed. Governments, corporations, and individuals have learned that debt can become a normal state of affairs, never to be repaid, maintained by perpetual refinancing. It is precisely such a condition that enables the existence of modern money. The circular flow is never completed when an economy functions as a spiral of debt. Social capital is reserved in a network of trust and guarantees. Credit embodies the wealth of society as a whole. For in credit, as history has proved, there are somewhat strange imbalances of power.[29] The threat of default may be as dangerous to the creditor as to the debtor. Default may either crush or release the debtor, depending on the network of interdependencies and trust. By contrast, a society in which all debts have been repaid and all contracts fulfilled returns to the abstraction of atomic individuals in a market society. Under such conditions, social capital is obliterated. Indeed, the entropic tendency to return to equilibrium is a tendency to annihilate social capital. Such an abstract society must begin over again to re-create social capital. Yet a society based on debt, by contrast, is already driven by its mutual obligations. The presence of indebtedness may indicate a healthy economy.[30]

The paradox of social capital is that accumulation enables accumulation. If interest is paid to banks that issue loans, then bank reserves become centers of accumulation. In one sense, they serve the common good insofar as these reserves function as the basis for fresh loans, enabling further mutual indebtedness. The presence of reserves makes the creation of money and the formation of social capital possible. Who owns the reserves or what form such reserves take may be less significant than that the reserves may be used for the creation of wealth. In another sense, the concentration of reserves in centers of accumulation directs time and nutrition toward the end of accumulating profits. It effectively results in the concentration of attention and nutrition. To serve society more effectively as a whole, it will be necessary to distinguish between the functions of nutrition, time, and capital as represented by money.

CLASS

4.3.1 Economic classes emerge from contractual appropriations of the underlying economic relations of nutrition, time, and social capital. The universal drive for nutritional value is the underlying motor of the entire economic process. A householder may be considered one who seeks nutritional value for himself or herself, for those in his or her care, and for the resources that provide diverse forms of nutritional value for the household. This relation of care and dependence is modified when it is represented under the form of private property, for once such relations of care and dependence are threatened, the drive for nutritional value may seek to preserve them. The represented claim to private property is such an expression of the will to survive. Such a *conatus*, a will to persevere in being, is a reactive formation. It responds to a potential threat.

The threat of the suspension of nutritive relations of care and dependence is an inevitable condition of temporal life. Moreover, it is inevitably realized in death. There are two contrasting ways to face such a threat: care of nutritive capital, which enhances life rather than resists death, and defense against external dangers, which resists death rather than enhances life. These form the basis for two different political strategies: an active politics that aims to create new bases for cooperation and production, so nourishing and enabling the emergence of forms of life, and a reactive politics that aims to defend what has been established against external threats.[31] Property, as opposed to nutrition, is reactive. Claims to appropriate private property appeal to the combined force of the social collective to resist external dangers. Threat is given a greater emphasis here than opportunity; it is also countered with threat. Yet it functions as a principle on which trust, credit, and social capital can emerge. This is an entirely different principle of the social order than trust in the opportunities afforded by nutritive capital as a basis for credit.

It is on the basis of this fundamental distinction between care and threat that class differences emerge. Where a householder may be primarily concerned with the care of nutritive capital, a proprietor is primarily concerned with the defense against threats. It matters little that the same individuals usually practice both strategies in differing respects; what matters is which strategy is dominant in their mutual relations. The householder expresses care for nutritive capital; the proprietor expresses a will to power. An inequality results from this contrast of strategy in their mutual relation. The proprietor aims to appropriate and so increase freedom of action; the householder aims to relate and nourish. Since progress in appropriation is protected at each stage by threats, the proprietor gains a greater access to the means of nutrition. While private property defends the opportunities provided by legitimate appropriation, it has the byproduct of maintaining its strategies of negation against external social formations and thus reducing significant amounts of nutritive and social capital. Eventually, the householder may have to become a proprietor to gain access to the means of nutrition and thus to continue to care for nutritive capital. Nevertheless, the relation between the householder and the proprietor is not one of strict mutual antagonism of interests. Conflict comes to define economic class only in the Hobbesian state of nature where private property is always acquired at the expense of another. Indeed, conflict signals the dissolution of differentiations of class, since all are now conceived as proprietors.

Proprietary classes may still be distinguished, however, by diverse modes of appropriation. While all modes of appropriation depend on the same three forces of the productive power of nutritive capital, the drive for nutritional value, and forms of social capital that mediate the relations between production and consumption, each has a particular relation to the productive process. A merchant appropriates nutritional value itself to provide social capital in the form of exchange. A capitalist appropriates labor time to provide social capital in the form of constructed and realized production. A banker appropriates social capital itself by recording and facilitating exchanges, assets, and debts. Nutrition, time, and social capital give way to differing means of appropriation. Each class appropriates from householders. Yet while the merchants, capitalists, and bankers compete within their own classes, each depends on the other classes. Class is defined by interdependence and complementarity rather than by competition. The threat of scarcity, or lack of nutrition, derives not from the other classes but, rather, from the prospect of either failure within the market or failure of economic society as a whole. All are united by resistance to the common threat of social and economic breakdown. Hence, as proprietors, each class has an interest in a strong state that protects private property, legitimizes appropriation, and guarantees the value of money. Indeed, to the extent that householders themselves become proprietors of property, labor, and money, they share an interest in a strong state. While, of course, state economic policy may be pursued in the primary interests of particular classes, and democratic opposition over policy choices might follow, there is no reason for such opposition to reach as far as violence and threaten the state itself. There are few circumstances in which economic classes may gain from seizing the monopoly of violence from the state.

4.3.2 The finitude of nutritional value and the finitude of time and labor prevent merchants and capitalists from escaping the reciprocal dependencies of the economic system. Only social capital, appropriated in the form of valuable assets or abstract wealth, is capable of unlimited increase. The principle that enables this is the creation of liabilities in excess of reserves. While the proprietors, merchants, capitalists, and governments who take out loans are now driven to increase their appropriations by the additional motive of debt, bankers who issue loans occupy the reciprocal position of this class relation. Bankers may be under an obligation to balance liabilities with assets, yet loans are neutral in this regard, since the liability (that the loan may now be spent) is perfectly balanced by the asset (that the loan must be repaid). On the one hand, bankers are placed in a position of power in relation to other classes, since they appropriate their property through interest. On the other hand, bankers remain susceptible to the fortunes of the other classes, since a default on a loan may lead to a loss of reserves and a contraction of credit.

A fundamental issue in the politics of money is the ability to issue liabilities in excess of reserves. It is the creation of credit as an active economic force. The monopoly of credit has largely been in the hands of the state or the clearing banks. While the state may hold the privilege of currency issue and taxation, banks hold the privilege of being financial intermediaries. The advantages of scale lead to most transactions between banks being canceled in the clearing house so that liabilities may far exceed reserves as long as the banks extend their positions cautiously and "in step."[32] Commercial credit, privately agreed between companies, is qualitatively different from money. Records of such debts do not circulate freely. Commercial credit may enable some limited circulation insofar as it serves as security for the issuing of further credit. It can only circulate, however, within a network of companies based on mutual recognition and trust. It is in some respects a regression to pre-market modes of exchange.

Banks, like governments, have limited resources to create money for use by themselves. Credit is a relation, not a possession, and banks are dependent on those who take out loans. The centralization of wealth in bank reserves is not a simple centralization of power. In particular, insofar as financial speculation is the most profitable of activities, banks may be dependent on the successes of speculators for the creation and repayment of money. Whether one speculates on real estate as the owner of property or one speculates on financial markets through trading in currencies, equities, bonds, and derivatives, and whether money is created as mortgage or as leverage, the effects are largely the same. A speculator, like the bank, may hold liabilities far in excess of reserves, since such liabilities are guaranteed by the value of the assets they have been used to acquire. Yet these assets hold a significant value because they have been inflated by speculation. As with bank money created by banks, there is no limit to the amount of exchange value created by speculators, provided they move forward together and in step. Banks are dependent on investors and speculators for the creation of money and the opportunity to acquire interest. Speculators may acquire reserves at the expense of the banks if the profits of speculation exceed the costs of commission and interest by a significant margin. While speculators may continue to hold their reserves in banks, the place where reserves are held is ultimately determined by the speculators. Speculation, as the most profitable of financial activities, holds the highest degree of class power. While speculators may in practice depend on merchants for nutrition, on capitalists for variable rates of profit, and on bankers for financial intermediation and leverage, they may profit even when the other classes are in decline. Speculators may therefore be taken to represent a distinct class from merchants, capitalists, and bankers: their interests are not the same. Yet for the speculator, the market is a site of wins and losses, opportunities and threats, greed and fear no longer protected by insurance and provision. It is a highly artificial "state of nature." Little creativity is possible, since all that can be made are profits. Otherwise, speculation is only a matter of information, strategy, discipline, and risk management. The speculator is more directly submitted to the authority of money and debt than anyone else.

A speculator, like a bank, may hold liabilities far in excess of reserves. A speculator is not simply in debt, however, for these liabilities are used to acquire assets. While the assets may vary in value according to market conditions, the liabilities do not. Hence, a speculator may make a significant profit from a highly leveraged investment in an asset that has a small increase in value. Misfortune can lead to significant losses. Yet such losses may be controlled and limited by an effective money-management strategy and automated stop orders. Since the risks can be limited in this way, it is possible to take out highly leveraged positions with limited risks. Speculators are subject to contracts and debts, yet they are liberated from debts by the correct predictions of prices. The dynamics of the market liberate speculators from debt by means of a new dependence — on the dynamics and predictability of the market. It is this new dependence and principle of dynamism that constitutes speculators as a separate economic class.

4.3.3 Speculators are intermediaries for flows of money rather than of goods. Their activities may superficially be taken to resemble those of merchants. From a synchronic perspective, a speculator makes profits from arbitrage: buying in one market to sell at a better price in another. The speculator would have to exploit advantages of information and mobility.

In practice, however, there is a time delay between buying and selling. Whereas commerce profits from transactions in distanced markets, speculation profits from price differences in markets separated in time. The creation of money as credit and debt is an alternative source of wealth to the production of goods and services.

Speculation attains this power of detachment from other economic processes by taking itself as its own object. As future conditions are unknown, speculation may involve less of an element of privileged knowledge (as in traditional strategies of investment) and more of an element of uncertainty. The profitability of speculation results largely from its own impact on prices. Speculation operates by imitation and herd behavior: it is a matter of guessing the direction in which the herd will move and staying ahead of a significant proportion. In this respect, all speculators compete with each other and win or lose out to each other. Yet such competition is merely superficial. The change in prices resulting from the herd is the main source of profits in the form of asset inflation. The wealth of speculators is created as a claim against bank reserves. The result of imitation is a positive feedback effect on prices: rising prices lead to further buying and further rises; falling prices lead to selling. Such positive feedback effects generate instabilities in price levels, leading to the significant swings up and down from which speculators profit. Such positive feedback effects are usually limited by the negative feedback effects resulting from uncertainty. Since no one knows when the herd will turn, it is in the speculator's interest to turn early. It is better to take a quick profit than risk a loss. This very uncertainty ensures that a turn will indeed take place. Such changes of direction spread by imitation. The oscillations generated by positive feedback are usually kept within bounds by a wider envelope of negative feedback. Overall, such wider envelopes may constitute self-confirming trend channels that speculators may use to predict probable outcomes. If probable predictions can be made, risks can be minimized through diversification, and small, quick profits can be amplified through leverage followed by reinvestment, leading to compound rates of growth.

Speculators may rely on events in the productive economy to have an impact on prices, leading to perpetual disequilibrium and readjustment. Speculative markets are enriched by investors' trading in the same markets. Yet whereas investors are concerned with the "fundamentals," or events in

the productive economy and their impact on prices, speculators are concerned with markets. Where small, rapid variations settle into trends and
overall patterns, then movements of price charts give a clearer indication
of the mood in the market among traders and investors, and techniques of
charting and technical analysis offer fair predictions of future behavior.

The creation of money through speculation is inflationary. It leads to
a general rise in prices of speculative assets. Such inflation is restricted to
markets in speculative assets, however, for money created as a loan for investment in speculative assets will have to be repaid in the form of money.
Thus, the inflation of speculative assets is the very reason for their profitability. Without contributing to production, speculative assets may inflate
much faster than consumer goods, leading to a differential in the level of
wealth. Inflation is always relative to particular markets. It is difficult to say
when any particular market has become over-inflated—indeed, there is no
reason in principle why any asset should not inflate indefinitely, acquiring
greater value the more constantly and predictably it ascends. There is no
reason why equities should be priced at a ratio to earnings of about 15:1 (fif-
teen years to recover the costs of investment) as a historical norm, rather
than any other value, apart from the self-fulfilling expectations of fundamental investors. In practice, however, all price trends come to an end. The
reason for this is simple: value acquired through speculative inflation is not
secured until it is converted back into money. All speculators will eventually have to sell and will seek to sell ahead of the majority of others. Crashes
are driven by attempts to realize profits or minimize losses. The preference
for liquidity is a preference for the realization of nominal value. Where
speculative inflation may be steady and continuous, speculative crashes are
sharp and sudden. Yet crashes are not driven simply by speculative bubbles.
Indeed, such "bubbles" may be stable for long periods. Instead, a crash is
caused by a coincidence of the activities of "bear" speculators and investors causing a break in a trend channel. Once the trend channel is broken,
traders diverge over the direction of the market, and the moments at which
they trade tend to divide, leading to distinct price rises and falls. The resultant instability undermines the confidence of speculative investors, leading
to some withdrawal from the market. The consequent selling generates the
crash.

Indeed, although the dominant trend of the market may be toward continual inflation, speculating on price falls may be equally profitable. For "bear traders" are capable of reversing time. By selling short, or selling an asset one does not possess in the expectation of delivering it later and in the meantime buying it when one wishes at a better price, one can make significant profits when the market is falling. Just as banks create money in excess of reserves, speculators who sell short may create assets in excess of reserves. Although such profits are made at the expense of others, and inexperienced traders can take significant losses, there may be profits overall for most participants. For most given prices at a particular moment in time, it is probable that there will be a later time at which the price is higher as well as a time at which the price is lower. All can therefore make some degree of profit from price fluctuations, even in a limited market where nothing is produced. For value is created by both asset fluctuations and bank loans. Such centers of accumulation drive the creation of profits; they also drive the accumulation of social capital. The impact of speculation on production and distribution is a subject of some complexity.

4.3.4 The creation of wealth is driven by three independent sources. In the first place, production is determined by the accumulation, invention, and construction of capital. There is no guarantee that such productive capacity will be used. With insufficient demand, productive capacity either will be under-utilized or will contribute to oversupply. In the second place, then, the presence of demand is necessary to bring productive capacity to utilization. There is no guarantee that the capacity for demand will be used. With insufficient money, demand will fail to become effective. Just as a healthy economy will seek to maximize its productive potential, it will also seek to maximize its effective demand. Credit, the power underlying money, is the power to enter into contracts. It is credit that facilitates the binding of nutritional value to time. It is credit that is the third source of wealth. Since credit, the power expressed by speculators, is unlimited, the dynamics of its appropriation may differ significantly from the appropriation of nutrition and time.

Capital, effective demand, and credit are subject to varying degrees of distribution. To be maximized, capital has to be assembled according to an invented form. In this respect, the concentration of capital may lead to an increase in wealth. The result of concentrating effective demand, by contrast, is to change its form from demand for common sources of nutrition to demand for luxury items and services, as well as for speculative or non-produced assets. The concentration of effective demand leads to an underutilization of capacity for demand in society as a whole, as well as oversupply and underutilization of productive capacity. Concentration of effective demand confines growth to narrower and narrower circuits, increasing inequality and turning the poor majority into servants of the wealthy minority. Concentration of effective demand restricts economic growth. It may have ambiguous effects on the environment: while it restricts overall levels of production and consumption, poverty may lead to practices with poor ecological sustainability through the necessity of immediate demands for subsistence. It may also contribute to population growth, which is closely correlated with poverty, leading to an increased burden on the environment. Overall, then, it is important that capital formation and effective demand be kept in balance to avoid the dangers of overproduction and inflation. It is also important that effective demand be widely distributed and not a mere function of ownership of the means of production, because the owners of the means of production are dependent on effective consumers. It is not production alone that is the creation of wealth. Effective demand is just as significant insofar as it determines what kind of wealth is needed and what is true wealth. The consumption of luxury goods by a minority, even if it is expressed as a large annual turnover, cannot be taken as a measure of wealth. Moreover, the condition for making demand effective is credit. Producers, consumers, bankers, and speculators all play a role in the creation of wealth.

It is by no means clear that private ownership of the means of production makes a positive contribution to the creation of wealth, for where wealth derives from the accumulation, invention, and construction of capital, owners of the means of production aim primarily for profits. Although the private sector produces goods and services, the criterion of profitability provides no defense against the consumption and depletion of natural, human, and institutional capital. The public sector, by contrast, may be regarded as primarily investing in environmental, human, and social capital. It accumulates resources that are later used, largely without individual contracts of exchange, by the private sector in bringing goods and services to the market. John Maynard Keynes's insight remains essential here: if a society wishes to avoid spending more than it earns, then it should prioritize public spending over private profits. Government spending, if funded from taxation, does not affect the quantity of money available in the economy. Government spending has a dual beneficial effect: it renews environmental, human, and social capital at the same time that it redistributes spending power to sectors beyond private circuits of investment, wages, interest, and profits. The private sector is only a partial contributor to wealth. It produces goods and services and performs some redistribution of money through wages and interest, but it contributes far less to the renewal of capital and the redistribution of wealth. Moreover, the money taken from the private sector in taxation is eventually returned to it through public spending and consumption. Since public spending does not aim directly at production, there is no danger or possibility of waste. Spending on welfare costs nothing to society as a whole when those who receive welfare spend their income on goods and services produced by the private sector. On the contrary, such spending may contribute to economic growth.

The difference between private investment and public spending lies in capacity utilization.[33] The labor of the unemployed is undisciplined: it may produce goods and services in an informal economy of provision and care; it may waste time in idleness. Private investment, by contrast, may at least find advantages in maximizing capacity utilization. Yet the distinction is by no means simple. Those who are employed for the sake of maximizing profits may not be effectively employed in the accumulation, invention, construction, and operation of capital. While their labor is disciplined, it may not be disciplined toward socially useful goals. There may be as much wastage of capacity and time from spending in the private sector as results from spending in the public sector. For just as an economy is not a single sphere of circulation but a network of markets where goods, services, assets, and money may circulate according to differing densities of accumulation, so the time of work is not an undifferentiated, productive whole but varies in proportion to natural, human, and social capital and has differing outcomes in respect to capital, goods and services, and money. A healthy economy requires a critique of the conduct of work, just as it needs a critique of the accumulation of wealth in narrow, self-replicating circuits.

When it comes to the distribution of credit, one may at first wish to distinguish between productive and unproductive forms of profit seeking:

between capital investment and financial speculation. The situation, in fact, is rather more complex. Money holds liquidity in virtue of its capacity to circulate through all markets. Where goods and services barely circulate at all, being rapidly produced and consumed, and assets recirculate within limited markets, money connects the network of markets. One cannot assume that its effects are geographically neutral, however. If investment is profitable, then the investment of money in a particular market or sphere of circulation may result in a greater quantity of value leaving that market through the repatriation of profits. As a result, it is likely that such a throughput will be increased so that greater profits may be realized. Regions of an economy may be either enriched or impoverished by investment. This is especially the case when poor regions are sold the necessities of life by multinational corporations at lower prices than they could produce locally. Their money leaves the local economy, resulting in the underutilization of their productive capacity. Given the concentration of money in tighter and tighter circuits of circulation, regions may be progressively impoverished through increased circulation when the overall effect is a depletion of wealth. Moreover, to the extent that money necessarily flows toward concentrations of wealth to realize profits and replenish reserves at interest, private profit operates as an effective drain on an economy. Capital investment and financial speculation can both reduce overall production.

Speculation has this economic effect of draining wealth. Asset-price inflation and increased profitability draw money away from the productive economy into ever tighter circuits of circulation. Yet the concentration of credit has somewhat more ambivalent effects, for credit may function as a reserve. The activity of speculation must be secured by underlying reserves, whether these are cash reserves held by speculators or bank reserves held against default on loans. Reserves to secure speculative assets are held in much less volatile forms of corporate and government bonds. Indeed, large concentrations of accumulated wealth are required to fund corporate investment and government borrowing. By means of accumulated reserves, speculators provide a service to both productive investment and public spending, even if they do not contribute directly to either. Unproductive profits, when held as reserves, may function effectively as the basis for credit and further production. Indeed, in the capitalist credit economy, production takes place only on the basis of non-productive reserves. Both corporate investment and government spending increase the money supply through the multiplier effect. Private investment stimulates capital formation while public spending stimulates effective demand. The extraordinary nature of debt money is that, even when it is hoarded and reserved, it may be in more than one place at a time, circulating through very different markets.

However, the concentration of credit in speculative assets may also have certain negative effects. Speculation leads to instability when it affects the price of a currency. Volatile price movements in speculative assets may affect the values of the currencies in which they are priced, since it is necessary to exchange currencies to buy or sell assets or bonds in differing currencies. Speculation applies its positive and negative feedback loops to inter-currency values, producing volatility. To counterbalance such volatility, it is necessary to hold reserves in a strong currency, and this in turn secures the value of strong currencies. Speculation, then, contributes to a hierarchy of currencies, with varying degrees of risk and volatility. Those who hold a weak currency are at the mercy of external economic forces. Similarly, speculation causes the risk of intermittent crashes. In a stock market or currency crash, banks become exposed to bad debts, negative reserve flows, liquidity problems, and instability. The dangers of such events can be mitigated by speculative instruments. If most major banks and investors have their positions effectively hedged, then a crash may harm small investors but may not be so severe for larger financial players. Indeed, the increased volatility of a crash is an ideal opportunity to generate more profits during periods of fall and recovery. In fact, the security provided by hedging may make a crash less likely in that there is less pressure to sell while confidence, risks taken, and speculative exposure are increased.

One cannot formulate simple rules regarding the effects of speculation and the concentration of credit, for concentration of credit is not opposed to its dispersal. Where wealth is driven by capital, demand, and credit, then it is increased by the distribution of all three. The wide distribution of capital and credit may be facilitated, however, by certain kinds of concentration of capital and credit. Equality, therefore, need not be the principal consideration for political economy. While the distribution of scarce resources of nutrition, time, and effective demand is beneficial, there are also other important concerns. The underlying tendencies orienting productive capacity and activity, orienting the flow of money between markets, and orienting credit and the availability of contracts are also highly significant. Such orientations are controlled in practice by the political economy of money.

MAXIMIZING WEALTH

4.4.1 All wealth derives from the accumulation, invention, and construction of capital: physical capital, both natural and artificial; human capital, in both health and education; and social capital, in both informal social bonds and formal institutional arrangements. A society will prosper to the extent that it directs nutrition and attention toward the maintenance and formation of such capital. It will also prosper to the extent that it develops a sustainable balance and relation between the various kinds of capital.

In this respect, just as it is traditional to distinguish between productive and unproductive labor, it is necessary to distinguish between degrees of prudence of investment of nutrition, attention, and credit in the formation of capital. Unproductive consumption of capital (in the form of war or enjoyment of luxury) is a greater threat to the wealth of a nation than unproductive labor. Unproductive investment of credit is more complex, since credit is not a finite resource, yet credit may be diverted from the formation of capital. Political economy should furnish a prudent and sustainable distribution of nutrition, attention, and credit. In practice, however, if an economy is disciplined by the need to repay debts, then an imprudent quest for profits may stimulate imprudent excess consumption from the class of skilled workers, without regard for prudent attention to capital. The illusion derives, as ever, from an inadequate representation of an economy in terms of market exchange.

The principal obstacle to the prudent investment of nutrition is the state's defense of the right to private property over and above demands for nutrition. The individual interests of those who have money and property are placed above all other interests. Similarly, the principal obstacle to the prudent distribution of attention is the moral legitimation of self-interest sustaining a wealth of cultural practices that reinforce the institution of the private individual. It is necessary to explore this moral basis for self-interest.

When society is regarded as the distribution and exchange of private property, all motivation for economic behavior is reduced to the alternative between self-interest and philanthropy, for property can only belong to self and other. It can only be acquired or given. Considered under the paradigm of property, relations with others are reduced to the dichotomy between self-interest and benevolence. Such is the origin of Adam Smith's famous deceptive maxim:

But man has almost constant occasion for the help of his brethren, and it is in vain for him to expect it from their benevolence only. He will be more likely to prevail if he can interest their self-love in his favour, and show them that it is for their own advantage to do for him what he requires of them. Whoever offers to another a bargain of any kind, proposes to do this. Give me that which I want, and you shall have this which you want, is the meaning of every such offer; and it is in this manner that we obtain from one another the far greater part of those good offices which we stand in need of. It is not from the benevolence of the butcher, the brewer, or the baker that we expect our dinner, but from their regard to their own interest. We address ourselves, not to their humanity but to their self-love, and never talk to them of our own necessities but of their advantages.[34]

It would be an inefficient and unsuccessful butcher, brewer, or baker who needed constant persuasion to perform his or her good offices. Payment may be regarded as a condition for such performance, but it need not be regarded as continual persuasion. In practice, only a limited amount of economic activity consists in such exchanges. Most labor does not arise from a two-way exchange, but payment is made by a third party. Whether the third party is an employer seeking profits and hoping to pay interest and dividends, or whether the third party is the state seeking to serve the common good on the basis of taxation, the individual worker is free to pursue excellence in performance of his or her role. Self-interest is only one of a number of motivations for work. It is compatible with an ethic of public service in the public sector and compatible with an ethic of excellence in the private sector. One works to achieve a good. Contracts need not be concluded solely on the basis of self-interest. Indeed, in a complex and wealthy society there may be many alternative ways to fulfill such interests. The deciding factor for contracts, then, may in practice be the pursuit of excellence or the pursuit of the common good. Humans are social and socialized animals, perceiving their interests to lie with the health and wealth of portions of society as a whole. The alternative between self-love and benevolence is therefore a false one.

When society is regarded in terms of contract rather than exchange, this false alternative evaporates. Once labor is regarded as an active pursuit of value rather than as a necessary sacrifice of ease, it becomes possible to conceive of the formation of contracts as a contribution to social capital. Contracts may enhance interdependence and cooperation; the fact that self-interest may be a necessary condition in the formation of contracts does not require that it be the overriding concern in the specific contracts chosen. Contracts always have dual dimensions: what is offered is time; what is received is nutrition. If contracts are regarded in terms of nutrition alone, then one may choose to enter those that maximize nutrition. If they are regarded in terms of time, then one may also choose to enter into contracts that improve time. Instead of being concerned with the output of work, one may be concerned with the experience of work. Whereas in terms of nutritional value the output of work is usually such that its benefiting of one excludes the benefiting of another, or such that it benefits some more than others, the experience of time is shared. It contributes to the formation of social capital. Contracts may be evaluated, then, on the basis of the nutritional value they produce, the quality of experience of time they require, and their contribution to the formation of enduring social bonds.

The pursuit of self-interest may have limits. Demands for nutritional value, when expressed through the voluntary capacity to enter contracts, appear to be motivated by self-interest. Yet such demands can be satisfied, leaving leisure for more complex demands. "Self-interest" in general obscures significant class differences and relations. The householder's struggle to survive, the capitalist's unlimited desire for profit, the debtor's obligation to repay, and the idealist's pursuit of the common good constitute differing motivators for economic activity. The justifications given for the motivation of self-interest depend on the hypothesis that the pursuit of profit is the creation of wealth. This, as we have seen, is mere illusion. For Adam Smith, labor and investment, rather than profit in the form of rent, interest, and monopoly prices, were the true source of wealth. Moreover, contracts between householders and traders who seek nutritional value and gain a mutual advantage differ in nature from contracts between capitalists and householders that profit from extortion and from contracts between speculators and debtors that profit from usury. That each involves some measure of self-interest is usually an effect of appropriation and lack of alternative access to nutrition, time, and credit.

4.4.2 The ethic of self-interest derives from the logic of money. The owner of property, including productive capital, can be liberated from the duties of care for productive capital only by exchange, by transforming capital into money. Only on this condition can the relation of reciprocal dependence on productive capital be replaced by a relation of apparent mastery over money. Money is the precondition of liberty. For the householder, dependent on productive capital rather than the market, care for the sources of nutrition is primary, since the self cannot be individuated and separated from relations of dependence. The individuation of an economic agent occurs through exchange: market relations may be substituted for prior relations of dependence. Detachment and appropriation occur through the mediation of money, for without the possibility of exchange for money, the relation to private property collapses from mastery into use and dependence.

The significant feature of money here is its triple nature as a measure of value, an object of exchange, and a promise of value. The primordial form of private property is money, for money demands no individual care or maintenance — even if the social institution of money itself does require continual maintenance. One has true mastery, rather than obligations and dependencies, only over money possessed as an asset. The individual maintains money only by accepting it and spending it. Yet separation from dependencies can occur only through new dependencies: the one who trades for money comes to depend on money instead of products. The distinctive feature of money as at once a measure of value, an object of appropriation, and a promise of value is the way money takes itself for its own object: money measures money and promises money. The condition for money to be able to measure itself and promise itself is that, through the mediation of exchange, it may substitute for itself. In a similar way, the modern subject takes itself as an object of reflection and an object of desire. The condition for the subject to turn to itself and reflect on itself alone is detachment from cares and demands that arise in the web of life. Reflection is a temporal suspension of relation in which the importance of the self is substituted for the importance of relations. The condition for demands for nutrition being comprehended as self-interest is detachment from mutually nutritive relations. Such detachment and temporal suspension is facilitated by the possession of money.

The absolute claim to private property, the absolute precedence of self-interest, and the absolute claim of the state to the monopoly of violence all derive from the structure of absolution embodied in money. Absolution, detachment, and the suspension of cares, demands, obligations, and responsibilities are essentially religious matters. The daily practice of piety involved in exchange and accumulation expresses credit as a hope for absolution from ongoing cares and demands. Ascetic detachment from the world, the justification of sinners, and financial speculation may express very different forms of piety; each, however, involves absolution from obligations to care for the maintenance, accumulation, invention, and construction of capital. Each is involved in the formation of a subject. Of course, history has demonstrated that each of these pieties may have the paradoxical effect of enhancing the formation of capital in certain respects. Production occurs on the basis of the unproductive. Each does so, however, by functioning as a condition that makes credit possible. Each may constitute a properly spiritual form of capital.

Just as economics is underpinned by political forces, so political forces themselves depend on credit, and credit is dependent on properly spiritual potencies. The institution of the market generates its own functions for the political in the form of the preservation of property and the enforcement of contract, the legitimation of claims to appropriate, and the maintenance of confidence in credit. Yet this very conception of the political expresses a very partial view of political economy. For the creation of wealth, property, and contract are of less significance than the formation of capital. The liberty to appropriate property is less significant than the distribution of nutrition and attention. The maintenance of confidence in money is less significant than the creative direction of credit. When the religious function of responsibility for the creation and direction of credit is delegated to institutions that manage money, an impoverished and unsustainable mode of political economy will result.

4.4.3 In practice, much of ecological and social existence remains outside the formal sphere of representation expressed in contract. Even if the whole world were divided into private property, flows of chemicals, seeds, and animals would still pass borders and interact. Even if all physical processes were shaped by technology, the natural invention of further processes and interactions would continually occur. Even if the whole of time were allocated to determinate tasks of work, different experiences of time would still emerge. Of course, in wasteland and leisure time, nothing ensures that productive processes will indeed occur. Nevertheless, a significant form of productive activity is the provision of a fertile environment in which growth and emergence can occur.

The same may be true in the social order. Productive processes are not entirely represented in contract. The provision of nutritional value, beyond the formal constraints of contract, may be a manifestation of care. Care provides a context in which social bonds may emerge as a response. Such a response, however, is not necessitated; it is merely facilitated by care. Care operates through nutrition and time. The spiritual requires the physical in the way that meaning requires spoken words or written language. The question of the maximization of nutritional value, while important, is less significant than the conduct of care, for care is a source that motivates the provision of nutritional value. It is a spiritual capital, the source of social capital.

The provision of a fertile environment is the provision of a kind of nutrition. Nutrition does not merely satiate desire. Nutrition feeds desires; it allows potential to grow. Forms of social capital, then, do not have a neutral effect on human desire. They call desire into being. Human nature has a variable range of potential that does not entirely pre-exist society. Instead, character is an evoked potential, called into being and nourished by particular social arrangements. In this respect, how a society represents itself to itself will have the utmost significance for its character. A society that imagines itself in the form of a market will have the effect of nourishing both self-love and philanthropy. It will evoke a quality of character concerned with the distribution of private property, leaving relatively undeveloped forms of social collaboration over the course of time.

Similarly, when work is reduced to labor to produce a surplus for an employer, it can become a toil and a sacrifice of ease. The exploited worker, unable to distribute his or her time freely, loses both his or her own health as well as the opportunity to contribute to the formation of social capital.

The efficiency gains in the production of surplus nutritional value in such organized labor should be offset against the loss of human and social capital. Huge inefficiencies and wastages are involved in the elimination of free space, free time, and free association.

4.4.4 A society lacking spiritual capital, the capacity to form social capital, remains deeply impoverished, whatever level of consumption it achieves. In such a society, interdependence increases vulnerability at the same time that it increases consumption. A society where wealth is measured in terms of money is such an impoverished society. For money, as a price differential, measures a profit opportunity, an opportunity for appropriation. It does not measure a difference in nutritional value directly, for contracts involve both time and nutrition. A price differential may indicate an efficiency saving in time just as much as it may indicate a gain in nutrition. Indeed, since each form of nutritional value is finite, efficiency savings in terms of time tend to substitute for gains of nutrition since these are more available to technological variation.

Efficiency in time may maintain the production of nutritional value. It does not measure such efficiency gains against the production of social capital, however, for each process is dual, involving both physical and social processes. Attending to efficiency of the production of nutrition alone leads to wastage of opportunities for the formation of social capital. Efficient labor is highly organized, with all moments that do not contribute directly to the production of nutritional value eliminated. It is time reduced to toil, where the experience and process of spending time is devalued in favor of the product. Excess consumption in leisure time, the complement of increasing production and profits, may be evoked to compensate for the lack of quality of experience in time at work. When work has no significant social meaning and workers are excluded from participation in the formation of social capital except via the medium of money, then society may need to be represented in the form of entertainment in leisure time. Such efficient use of work and leisure entails enormous amounts of wastage, both in terms of physical resources for the purpose of consumption and in terms of spiritual resources, which meet with minimal opportunities in commodified leisure time.

Measures of productivity or prudence vary significantly with the image of wealth conceived by society. If the wealth of a society is measured in terms of money, then the formation of social capital and the experience of time is devalued in favor of buying and investing power. Since money circulates and speculative values accumulate, it is difficult to measure the extent to which this enriches society as a whole. In such a society, the unequal distribution of wealth needs to be measured by the quantity and frequency of flows of money through particular nodes of ownership in excess of that required for the subsistence minimum for that society. The tendency of money is not to remain reserved or to distribute itself evenly, but to flow through a limited range of circuits in which it is strongly attracted to certain positions of wealth and power. Such a measure would need to be used in addition to the accumulated value of assets and a credit rating. If wealth, by contrast, is understood in terms of quality of time experienced by members of that society, then society will need to provide its own values in regard to the spending of time and meaningful social interaction. Alternatively, if wealth is regarded in terms of the accumulation, invention, and construction of physical, human, and social capital, then each of these will require its own measures. In short, the oversimplification of evaluation introduced by a monetary scale of evaluation reduces all values to a comparison with some imagined standard of external and future markets, evacuating significance from all existing forms of cultural self-representation and self-evaluation. What is required, above all else, is the liberation of other modes of representation and evaluation from their constraint under the forces of money in the forms of profit and debt.

Five

THEOLOGY OF MONEY

ACCOUNTING

5.1.1 WE HAVE EXAMINED MONEY in relation to productive capital as well as in relation to social powers expressed through the institutions of markets and contracts. It is now time to examine money in relation to its mode of representation and the belief that this inspires. For money is in itself nothing but a representation.

Money is normally treated as a representation of value. If money is regarded as a sign of value, the material basis used to signify value should not matter. The nature of money as a sign should remain unchanged when coinage substitutes for bullion, paper money substitutes for coinage, bank records substitute for paper money, and electronic records substitute for books. In each case, the value that is signified is supposed to be the same. In economics, therefore, one can quickly pass over the nature of money to explore the science of value. Only when it comes to determining the quantity of money in circulation does one face all the difficulties of determining what is to count as money. The insoluble problem of what in practice is to be counted as money testifies to an underlying philosophical problem that emerges from the nature of representation as such.

The extraordinary paradox we have to reckon with is that exchange value does not exist outside of its representation. Where representation normally reproduces a prior object or opinion, money engenders the very value that it appears to represent. Value is an abstraction. Only money is real, for value is only value in exchange, yet exchange values may only be determined by making comparisons with a sum of money. Comparison differs from barter exchange. Comparisons are made only when a neutral standard of measure already exists that determines in what respect commodities are to be compared. As we have seen, prices are determined in terms of money, yet the value of money is determined by its value in exchange. As a result, there are no absolute standards of value in economics. All exchange values are relative. Value is therefore a product of its representation for the purpose of exchange. It does not exist independently of exchange.

There is no external point of reference or comparison for value, except for vague expectations concerning exterior or future markets. There is no universal system of comparative or relative values as a whole, for the work of comparison is never completed. There is no true, just, or underlying price. There is merely a continual readjustment of expectations and comparisons in relation to money and its mode of bearing value. Individual agents cannot look at an economic system as a whole. They can merely make comparisons with current prices in accessible markets and recent price movements. There is no necessary relation between a given set of prices and the ultimate price of the item to be agreed. Pricing is an art rather than a science, proceeding by a combination of imitation of other market agents; calculation of costs, benefits, and rates of turnover and profit; and differentiation on the basis of specific differences to find a place in the market. It is not merely the case that no one knows where the equilibrium price is — there is no market equilibrium or true price. Yet the notion of a true, underlying, or equilibrium price is often a necessary postulate in the determination of prices. Each act of pricing is a guess, an estimate or approximation. Since there is nothing to which it approximates, then pricing is always an act of faith. It is inherently theological. Money records a transcendent value that does not exist outside of its recording.

5.1.2 A firm price is therefore always a somewhat arbitrary agreement. It marks the point where agreement has been achieved. When price is understood in terms of contract rather than exchange, one may make a temporal distinction between two kinds of price. It is necessary to distinguish between price quoted, an offer of a contract at a given value, and price agreed, the price recorded in the contract. While a price quoted reflects hopes and expectations, uncertainties and strategies, a price recorded simply reflects what has been done. While a price quoted depends on the credibility of the one who makes an offer, a contract depends on the credibility of public contracts within that society.

Where, then, is the standard against which contracts may be measured? What underwrites the value of the currency? In practice, currencies emerge from specific institutions, from states or banks. Although currencies have a market value, such a value is determined in relation to the credit of the institution that issues it—which is not independent of the credit of other institutions on which that institution depends. The value of money is not ultimately determined by economic behavior in society as a whole, for this never reaches consistent patterns or completion. Instead, the value of money must be determined by the credit of its issuing institution. In reality, therefore, it is not possible to conceive of money, prices, or exchange values as substantial goods. Neither is it possible to conceive them as relative to a determinate system taken as a whole. It is not even possible to conceive them as relative to some absolute standard of credit embodied in a state or bank. Even the credit of each state and bank is determined by a local and particular market. In each contract, the value of the contractual unit consists in anticipations concerning a network of other contracts. Money has no existence in itself. Money is merely the public accounting of contracts.

5.1.3 Monetary transactions are invariably shared fictions. There is nothing else to which such transactions can refer, apart from other, similar transactions. It makes all the difference in the world once a fiction becomes public. As every child knows, games of "let's pretend" are highly enriched when the pretence is shared; they are further enriched when they refer to other shared pretend games. As every religious adherent knows, religious beliefs are only credible when they are shared with a community of believers. With money, one cannot say the price agreed refers to anything other than itself and the network of assets and liabilities directly affected by the transaction. Money does not designate.

Exchange value is simply composed of records in public account books. Money is simply composed of public records held by banks. There is no sharp dividing line between money and exchange value. There are only assets and liabilities, credits and debts, with differing levels of liquidity. Moreover, while specific transactions recorded in accounts may designate the contracts agreed, the balances brought forward and totals do not designate anything beyond the books. A contract for exchange merely links one book to another. Indeed, since money is added to and subtracted from balances, it would be more accurate to say that contracts for exchange designate proportions of balances rather than claim that balances designate a sum of contracts for exchange.

There is, of course, a significant difference between a contract and a balance. A contract specifies a determination of time, even if it is simply to deliver a sum of money at a determinate time. The balance of an account, by contrast, must represent all time as already complete. Ongoing temporal contracts such as debts and credits are recorded in the atemporal form of assets and liabilities, as if the contract were already complete and the value delivered. Account books assume that contracts will be honored and debts and credits will be paid in full, even if those who use them do not. Account books designate possible futures as if they had already occurred. Account books therefore contain reasonable fictions.

5.1.4 It is a category mistake to suppose that account books contain the facts about an enterprise or that statistics represent evidence of the state of an economy. Since money has merely a residual status as a collective fiction represented through account books and bank records, there is nothing to which accounting can refer. Instead, account books belong within the categories of ethics and law. They are concerned with credits, debts, obligations, and contracts. While the contracts themselves stipulate the legally binding obligations, the need to count and balance such obligations is a moral duty. Account books operate with a moral conception of social obligation in order to direct economic behavior.

Account books are no less binding and regulating for being non-referential. As a first moral principle, income and expenditure have to balance according to the model of a circular flow. It is not normal to allow debts to increase at the expense of credits, for creditors will not allow debts to expand without seeing some evidence that such debts may eventually be repaid. Yet in certain circumstances, it is possible to allow the debts of powerful and credible economic agents, such as governments and large corporations, to increase indefinitely, being refinanced out of further loans, for so long as creditors are willing to receive the interest and can, if necessary, transfer such investments to others. This demonstrates once more that levels of debt and credit are shared fictions, yet they remain costly fictions, and the cost of maintaining their credibility is interest.

As a second moral principle, accounts, instead of merely designating sums of money, make economic conduct visible. When it comes to credit, it matters much less how much money one has recorded than how credit-worthy one's accounts are. Above all, account books make economic conduct visible, open to minute scrutiny. They maintain the credibility of the enterprise through auditing and publication. The necessity that the books balance is above all an ethical necessity. It is public proof of honorable conduct as the habit of discharging obligations and debts.

As a third moral principle, presupposed by the previous two, accounts enable self-disciplined conduct. They enable one to keep a record and a balance between income and expenditure, credits and debts. An enterprise maintains public credibility only if it maintains private self-discipline. Accounts enable budgeting, a limited distribution of scarce resources. They allow one to avoid excessive borrowing, spending, speculation, or concentration. Accountancy guides and demonstrates sober, moral, prudent, and judicious behavior. Far from being a mere description of facts in the real world or a record of contracts, accountancy is a system of moral self-discipline. For if accounts refer to contractual conduct in relation to others, then what they record is the outcome of such contracts. Accounts belong wholly to the moral sphere of social interaction.[1]

5.1.5 There is a further reason for regarding accounts as shared fictions. While accounts may balance income and expenditure, they may also balance debts and credits, treating debts and credits as though the time of their contracts had expired. If a credit is treated as a current asset, then its value may be used as a basis for further borrowing. During the time taken for the original credit to be paid, its value may already be spent once more. It is as though the same money exists in two places at once. Indeed, if this is the basis for fractional reserve banking as well as for the issuing of paper money, then most money has already multiplied in this way before further credit is issued.

The common-sense protest is that such fiat money is fictional, speculative money since it is not backed by reserves of solid value.[2] In truth, the fiction is that there is such a thing as "solid value," embodied in gold. Gold is merely another medium for the representation of value; it is a primitive technology for accounting. What gold fails to achieve is accomplished by coinage: the separation of its face value and substantial value. The separation may go further when the means of recording no longer reserves value. In double-entry bookkeeping, each sum is split into a credit and a debt. The essence of money is that it can be in two places at once, functioning as a reserve for itself. More precisely, money enables the coordination of simultaneous durations of time by means of contracts. Money does not exist outside of accounts. What money saves through its multiplication, then, is not mere value or time itself, since the same duration will be lived through, but the directing of attention.

Money has no present being. It merely has a past value that is recorded and a future value that is anticipated. Money only exists in memory or anticipation as a record in account books. One never sees money come and go. Even with live electronic access to markets, a change in value occurs instantaneously when a price is marked up or down. One never sees money make money; one never watches it breed. One has to send it away first, so that it may return at a profit. Money always breeds elsewhere, outside possession, beyond the limits of attention. The power, force, and activity of money always escapes attention. It leaves when it is invested and returns already changed, for profit or loss.

Money substitutes for attending directly to a process. Instead of waiting for a debt to be repaid, and instead of engaging in the work of production or renegotiating a contract, money maintains a supervising eye. A credit, when taken for granted as an asset, is excluded from attention that may be more profitably directed elsewhere. Contracts, once agreed, may be taken for granted. Contracts, as agreements covering future conduct, give security and freedom. Accounting, in addition to enabling one to balance out credits and debts, allows one to enter into profitable liabilities to the full extent of one's credits. On the one hand, accounting serves the need for balance and prudence; on the other hand, it serves the need to maximize growth and investment. It conserves the expenditure of attention on what has already been agreed so that attention can be directed to the forging of further contracts. Accounting enables the multiplication of contract, security, and credit. It measures the weight of each contractual obligation so that obligations can be balanced, guaranteed, and fulfilled.

Paradoxically, then, accounting measures that which no longer demands attention. It measures contracts, promises, and commitments that can be effectively relied on. It does not measure risk or uncertainty. It does not measure the arising of opportunities. It does not measure quality of experience. It does not measure that which provides no expectation of a return. It does not measure that which seems to have ultimate importance. Accounting is the measure of that which can be taken for granted.

A curious phenomenon develops, then, when accounting is taken as the ultimate guide in daily moral practice as a system for directing attention — as it is in global capitalism. Such is the outcome whenever the making of profits or the repayment of debts becomes the primary motive for action. Once attention is absorbed by prices, balances, and profits, a simple moral error has occurred, because accounting should facilitate the freeing of attention to focus on the immediate demands of that which matters. Accounting should facilitate the saving of time. Once accounting absorbs attention, then prudent behavior, concerned with that which can no longer be taken for granted, becomes impossible. There is no time left for it. It is therefore an error to suppose that money, accounting, or statistics can give a full representation of the world. What truly matters always exceeds representation, even in terms of money.

5.1.6 When money is largely composed of figures recorded by banks, accounting has replaced coinage as the material basis of money. Moreover, just as coinage functions as a token of value, and the metallic value of the coinage is less significant than the coin's acceptability in exchange, so accounting itself becomes the bearer of value, and it becomes irrelevant to ask about the truth of the prices or transactions recorded. All that matters is that such records are not seriously disputed.

Accounting, then, forms the basis for credibility and credit. Decisions concerning credibility depend on the evidence presented in accounts. Yet such evidence does not exist outside of the contracts that it records. Accounting gives the appearance of producing reliable evidence by means of the consistency with which it is used. Moreover, accounting presents a hypothetical vision as if time were complete, eliminating risk, uncertainty, and strategy from recording. It presents a world that has been mastered, a set of contracts that have been fulfilled, as though each term recorded were established as property rather than merely promised as contract. If accounting provides evidence of the health of an enterprise, such evidence simply presents the effect of prudence and self-mastery, as well as mastery over a determinate field of activity from which profits may be extracted. The fiction constructed by accounting, then, is of the mastery and independence of an enterprise, as if it were not dependent for its existence on a variety of ongoing contracts and as if it were not exposed to all the vulnerabilities of its contractual partners, as well as of the wider economy. In short, accounting generates an illusion of security because it records life as though it has been mastered and accomplished.

Accounting does not record all salient details. In particular, contracts have implications beyond the exchange of obligations between contracting parties. Externalities, the costs not recorded in the contract, are costs not incurred by either party. They express relations that extend in practice far beyond the details that are formalized in contracts. Then accounting, as the measure of that which can be taken for granted, has the effect of securing an illusion of mastery, saving the need for due care and attention to relations that are not recorded as costs or benefits.

The knowledge produced by accounting is highly selective and very limited. It is merely a partial knowledge of the balancing of debts and credits between contracts. As a system of moral discipline, giving guidance for prudent behavior, it has its limitations. Far from being concerned with the facts alone and neutral in relation to value, money and accounting have determinate moral effects and should be evaluated on moral grounds. Accountancy is an exercise in collective imagination, enhancing the intensity, precision, and security of ideas. It achieves balance and precision, however, by eliminating time, uncertainty, and externalities. It locks attention up within a closed system of thought. It produces an artificial illusion of mastery. As such, it exposes dangerous vulnerabilities.

MORALS OF ACCOUNTING

5.2.1 The acquisition of money leads to freedom and mastery. One can only effectively become a sovereign individual through appropriation of money. Accounting, as a system of self-regulation or a practical philosophy, instills the habits of discipline through which such freedom and mastery can be obtained. It attends to the balance of obligations so that one can practice honesty, temperance, fortitude, and justice. One masters oneself before one can master the world. Nevertheless, it is impossible that all should be sovereign individuals possessed of wealth. It is necessary that some will work to produce the goods and services that others will buy. Accounting does more than provide a guide through which freedom and mastery can be obtained. It represents action as though such mastery already exists. By managing accounts as if they designate property, an enterprise can appear to be in complete control of its business. This fiction requires further investigation.

In reality, those who enter into contracts are under a number of constraints that belie the fiction of self-mastery. In the first place, while it may be a relatively free decision to enter a contract, such contracts become binding once entered. While it may be an indication of economic strength to be able to enter into a range of liabilities with confidence, it is not an indication of freedom. Obligations bind, and an ability to fulfill contracts depends on the ability of partners to fulfill them also. One is only as strong as one's debtors.

In the second place, many factors influence or constrain which contracts are entered. When faced with a decision, one appears to have a free choice; with hindsight, one may observe the influences and constraints that determine that decisions that were taken. Indeed, free behavior can operate so consistently that one can hypothesize social and historical laws or processes that determine free decisions. Moreover, it is the very predictability of such patterns of choice that enables economic behavior to be studied and successful business strategies to be formulated. Freedom in theory, then, is combined with strong influences in practice. People enter into contracts on the basis of need, persuasion, imitation, and speculative aspiration. Contracting is not independent of a human sphere of mutual influence. So-called rational actors may not be able to perceive which course of action will maximize their self-interest and so will be subject to social influences and persuasion. Even when they do perceive, they can do so only by mistaking accounting for knowledge. The economy is not independent of culture, even if it does also influence culture. Whereas in the ideal market society all that is bought and sold remains property and one can calculate determinate uses and outcomes, in a contract society human behavior results from agreement. The mutual influence over the conduct of time takes precedence over individual calculations concerning the benefits of property. Because they depend on human behavior, relations, and externalities, the outcomes cannot be properly understood in advance.

In the third place, this social sphere of human relations that determines the practices and habits of forming contracts is not independent of other constraints. Physical location, mobility, and capacities determine the range of available contracts. Cultural determination, including location in a class or culture, determines in practice the limits of confidence regarding available contractual relations. In addition to cultural and physical factors, there are also strong and predictable drives: for survival, for profit, and for power. Similarly, the obligation to honor existing contracts and repay debts compels the formation of further contracts that will facilitate this aim.

None of these constraints are represented in accounts, even though they have an ongoing influence on the possibilities and choices of further contracts. They are regarded as something separable from money or often as obstacles to be overcome. Nevertheless, their inescapability calls into question both the reality and the ideal of self-mastery that is the principal moral force of systems of accounting.

5.2.2 In addition to the social and cultural factors determining the formation of contracts, accounting itself, as a disciplinary system, imposes its own moral requirements and judgments on the conduct of economic agents.

Accounting commands assent. The evidence it offers is repeatable, exchangeable, and potentially public. The personal judgments of the individual who writes in the account book are in theory irrelevant, even if assumptions about what is to be counted under any particular heading make all the difference to the outcome. The individual perspective and singular case are excluded. Accounting records only that which falls within the range of a mutual agreement — or that which, by virtue of appearing within the account book, takes on the appearance of being a product of mutual agreement. It excludes the incommensurable. One cannot easily disagree about the figures when they have been fixed by contract. The temporal work of evaluation, of finding and fixing a price, is not recorded. The price, once agreed, cannot be changed without renegotiation. The world that is counted, then, expresses the utopian ideal of a market where all prices have already been fixed and where the books have been balanced by enacting all trades. Not only does this differ from the real world of continual negotiation where prices never come to rest, but it also imposes the utopian ideal of determinate prices as an ideal frame of reference.

In addition, accounting increases power by saving time. By balancing out a set of debts and credits, obligations and expectations, it multiplies the number of possible relations that can be entered. It minimizes the attention demanded by each one. It counts internalized costs and excludes externalized costs so that attention need only be paid to opportunities. While it multiplies obligations, it minimizes the attention that needs to be paid to each obligation so that a worldview may be constructed consisting entirely of freedom and opportunities for the self, constructed by obligations borne by others. Such is the significance of the imaginary, utopian world constructed by accounting. It is a world without the experience of time or social relation.

Such discounting of the future has notable effects. Determinate figures are entered for uncertain outcomes. At first sight, such a measure would appear to be entirely neutral in relation to conduct. The internal logic of such a substitution suggests otherwise. Since a rate can be fixed for all uncertainties, and an insurance premium paid, then accounting can appear to count all eventualities. As long as every relation is substitutable, and a figure for monetary compensation is derived, accounting becomes the most encompassing, inclusive, and appealing mode of practical philosophy.

Monetary outcomes have no uncertainty or problems with liquidity. Expressed in terms of money, a value without risk is substituted for risk. Just as there is a difference between an actual amount of credit and a degree of credibility, so also is there a difference between a monetary value and the value of a monetary evaluation. Monetary evaluation, discounting the future and fixing a price, posits itself as the most effective evaluation because it becomes the most certain on its own terms. Substituting certainty for uncertainty, money needs no discount. It appears to be supremely valuable because it is the very value through which values are evaluated.

The effectiveness of accounting in its own terms leads to the colonization of as much reality as possible by assigning it a potential exchange value. As soon as property and assets are given a nominal value, it is possible to borrow on them as security.[3] From such a perspective, the whole of reality becomes valued on the basis of its being alienated, lost and requiring replacement, for exchange values are costs of substitution. Relations between things and people acquire a nominal value only on the basis of that relation's being imagined as broken. Indeed, submitted as security, the relation to things may often be broken to meet contractual obligations. By giving a nominal value to property and assets, then, one turns the relation first into the mastery of the property owner who can dispose of such assets, and then into the mastery of the economic field that may require such disposal to discharge debts. In short, accounting achieves first a nominal and then a real subsumption of all relations under the form of the fiction of mastery over assets.

Discounting the future is, however, an ambiguous procedure. If it seems to cede control to the present economic agent, this is not achieved without the agent handing over in return some social power to the future. It is comparable to a religious sacrifice through which one attempts to discharge one's obligations to the gods. One hopes to receive their benefits without corresponding dangers. It is a process of splitting, separating out life and death, blessing and curse, fortune and misfortune, so that the destructive forces can be expelled and passed elsewhere while the creative forces can be enjoyed. Just as offering a sacrifice at the start of a venture may be interpreted in terms of an insurance policy, so taking out insurance can be interpreted in terms of sacrifice. Moreover, discounting the future is little more effective than sacrifice. It is an operation that separates values in representation only. Insurance offers no protection against real threats of fire, flood, and theft; it merely offers compensation and the opportunity for substitution. In practice, to discount the future, like sacrifice, is also to owe a debt to the future. If one assumes that an outcome will yield a profit and enters into liabilities on the basis of future income, then one enters an obligation to ensure that one's assumptions become true. Attention is drawn to making the books balance after all. So while accounts may minimize the expenditure by taking the success of contracts for granted, they also leave a bad conscience. Since such contracts cannot be taken entirely for granted, even though one behaves as though they can, one is under an obligation to ensure that the outcome is such that it is as though they could have been taken for granted. Such is the absorption of attention demanded by its sacrificial practices. Such is the demand that ensures that account books can never be taken for granted.

Accounting, then, promises the world, but it leaves an obligation to build a utopia where all that is not accountable or substitutable has been excluded. It promises freedom and mastery, yet it imposes an obligation to balance the books. It promises a determinate set of outcomes, yet it delivers uncertainty and risk. It promises to limit exposure to danger, yet it extends and intensifies the need to account for all to an unlimited degree. Accounting does not deliver what it promises.

5.2.3 Contracts differ from living relations as writing differs from speech and agreed prices differ from quoted prices. Whether or not contracts are written, they have the nature of writing. Writing differs from speech in that it may be separated from the attention of the author. Beyond the sphere of the author's intentions and attentions, writing carries its meaning to posterity. It is temporally distanced from the initial situation; it is available to others apart from the original addressee; it can enter into different contexts where it can acquire new meanings.

Money embodies and epitomizes these features of writing. It is a sign that does not signify, a detachable unit of value without meaning. It carries value across social and cultural distances and through time. It is a transferable debt that may never return to its point of origination. Moreover, when values are accounted without meanings then money leads to the progressive elimination of meaning from all perspectives that are counted.

Contracts embody a curious ambivalence. They express a degree of social power, but all are rendered powerless by such social power. The authors, separated from control over the contract that exists in the public domain, are now powerless and can do little to add meaning or value to the original inscription. Similarly, the public readers of the contract are also relatively powerless. Each piece of writing is a command, a will, a testament that endures after the death of the author. Indeed, in writing contracts, the powers of the authors must be sacrificed for the words to become writing. Even if the contract is ignored or disobeyed, even if its meaning changes through receiving a new context, the weight of obligation enshrined in the contract remains.

Whereas writing in general has a limited liquidity or transferability, money is a chameleon that adapts itself to the demands of its possessor. Whereas writing in general offers no proof of its truth or value, money is effective because it is transferable and flexible. It demonstrates its value through the purchases it achieves and the production it stimulates. Unlike other forms of writing, its power is given to the one whom it commands, while its power is taken from the one who chooses its command. Moreover, money demonstrates its value through the delivery of profits. Whereas the promises and proclamations of scripture require external witnesses for verification, money speaks on its own behalf by offering an advance. Unlike scripture, one does not need to believe in the promise or value of money; one merely needs to behave as though it held value in order to spend it and receive the offer it advances. For just as accounting enables the multiplication of contractual relations balancing debts and credits, money enables the multiplication of possible transactions by overlapping and encompassing any determinate form of demand.

5.2.4 Accounting, then, presents a strange moral ambivalence. Once success is measured in public and objective terms as quantifiable figures then technical means of maximizing profits through efficiency and rational management take precedence over more obviously moral concerns. Accounting apparently deals with the facts; it poses as morally neutral. It provides the data on which technical rationality can operate. All can agree on the benefits of the creation of wealth. Any moral or political concerns regarding the distribution of wealth must come afterward. It is pointless to aim for a just distribution of wealth if there is no wealth to distribute.

In practice, then, technical rationality is grounded on the practice of accounting that underwrites the distinction between fact and value.[4] Facts are recorded as evidence by mutual agreement. Expressed in terms of numbers, facts are units of accumulation or property. They are abstracted from the temporal and social relations that have generated them. They are collective fictions, grounded in a utopian ideal of a world composed entirely of completed facts, of everything that is the case. Moreover, taking out liabilities on the basis of such facts, one is under an unlimited obligation to demonstrate by means of technical rationality that such facts will indeed prove to be true and will participate in the utopia of true and complete facts. Accounting effects both a formal and a real subsumption of the world into rational and technical processes.

This masquerade of moral neutrality is itself grounded on a disavowed moral stance. For the facts recorded by money are contractual agreements. Moreover, when the future is discounted and figures are treated as property having a definite value, the subject is portrayed as having sovereign freedom and mastery over their property. The implicit moral stance of accounting, then, is that making a profit, achieving sovereign freedom, is the goal of economic behavior. Such freedom is an eschatological hope. It has never been effectively achieved. The freedom that would prove accounts to be true, once all contracts have been discharged, remains under threat by the continuing obligation enshrined in contracts. As has been noted, money is both a promise and a threat—a promise of freedom and a threat of exclusion. The aim of rational economic behavior thus is to split one's assets and liabilities so that assets are retained while liabilities are transferred to others. The aim is to appropriate the promise offered by money for itself while using the threat contained within money to discipline the economic behavior of others so that they will work for the creation of wealth.

Accounting and the forming of contracts, then, take place within a broader moral culture. They presuppose property with its correlate of the sovereign individual to represent values as finite sums. Each sovereign individual is regarded as bearing ultimate responsibility for their economic destiny. Each contract is freely entered on the basis of perceived individual benefit rather than social constraint and obligation. Economic failure is perceived as moral weakness, the result of idleness or foolish choices, rather than an absence of capital, opportunity, and credit. Accounting as a moral practice enhances the sense of rectitude of its own moral judgments. Those who are successful in business are necessarily the good and the just by the standards of accounting. They are attentive to their own accounts and demonstrate mastery over their field of activity. They honor contracts and avoid excessive expenditure. They are careful stewards of time and waste as little as possible, making the most of opportunities. They serve the genuine demands of others. They contribute to the creation of wealth. They therefore deserve whatever profits they make and are effectively motivated to moral improvement by means of the promise of further profits. As a consequence, those who fail to thrive in a society represented through accounting may be suspected of moral failings. They may be inattentive to their accounts or financial position or fail to master their field of activity. They may renege on contracts or engage in profligate spending. They may waste time in idleness and squander opportunities. They do not serve the genuine demands of others. They do not contribute to the creation of wealth. The resulting poverty is deserved, as well as being a helpful corrective force to ensure that moral improvement may take place. If accounting appeals to an eschatology, it is one of reward and punishment in response to individual responsibility. The eschatology of universal freedom is at odds with the reality of universal obligation. There is no credit without someone undertaking a liability. There is no money without promise and threat; there is no freedom without the labor of others.

The culture of modernity is one of universal threat. Since freedom is claimed by right, then any obligations are perceived as an encroachment on that freedom. Such threats may be averted by a sacrificial practice that transfers liabilities onto others. Any moral discourse that threatens the rights of the sovereign individual by restoring permanent reciprocal obligations must therefore be opposed. Far from accounting being morally and politically neutral, then, it calls into being a culture of individualism, of threat, and of righteous revenge. Such an eschatology is not a mere addition to economic practices. It is the very foundation on which credit is based. Money holds value because liabilities can be enforced on others. Money holds value because it remains scarce. Strong currencies hold value because other currencies are weak. The wealthy must be rewarded so that the poor are constrained to work; the poor are constrained to work so that the wealthy may be rewarded. The illusion of universal wealth and freedom requires a fundamental operation of splitting, of distinguishing between us and them, the saved and the damned. Such splitting is required because of its bad conscience, because threats of encroachment on freedom never truly subside. In the last analysis, money holds value because its value is enforced. It morals are underpinned by a theology of sovereign, eschatological judgment.

A REVALUATION OF VALUE

5.3.1 It will be necessary to invent a moral practice that expresses a very different mode of evaluation. A revaluation of all values may begin with a modification of practices of accounting. For if money is an expression of a practice of recording value, then new kinds of money can emerge from new methods of accounting value. There are strong reasons for skepticism concerning the values represented in current accounts. Price signals and accounts do not produce certain knowledge or accurate moral guidance for practical conduct. The fundamental misrepresentations we have noted are threefold. Prices and accounts emerge from a contract, a two-way relation, that treats all content and externalities as passive objects of manipulation rather than as active agents and bearers of cost; prices and accounts treat relations as already completed exchanges, as though contracts were not enduring relations; and prices and accounts can take no account of the conditions of credit that give them a unit of account as well as credibility. Accounting constructs an internal milieu of economic value formed between economic agents while excluding from consideration all non-market agents as environmental background, all experience of time as a means to be overcome, and all forms of faith as credit that make economic relations possible. In spite of appearances, in giving a market value to land, labor, and capital, the true significance of land, labor, and capital is not properly accounted. Contracts to pay for land, labor, and capital in the form of rent, wages, and interest interact directly with the environment, time, and credit. It is land, labor, and capital that count.

It will be necessary to invoke new ethical criteria for the evaluation of economic conduct: criteria assessing importance to evaluate the output of production; criteria assessing purpose to evaluate the process of labor; and criteria assessing credibility to evaluate the formation of social capital. It is not simply a matter of counting capital or counting life as that which supremely matters, whether this is conceived in terms of the health of the environment, population, or society. For capital and life escape representation. They cannot be counted. One cannot simply return from relative and arbitrary values, as measured in accounting, to absolute and intrinsic values. For this is to assume that matters can be isolated as independent of the contexts in which they arise. Instead, it is necessary to discover a temporal and relational mode of evaluation, where value is not encountered within either object or subject but in a relation that exceeds the bounds of mastery of the evaluating subject.

Money, as we know it, is not yet valuable. It does not bear a good, enduring, credible value. Yet history has proved the superior power of money to outflank all other modes of evaluation due to its intrinsic force. Any attempt to contrapose true values to monetary values will fall on the problem of representation. Instead of abandoning money and current modes of accounting, then, it will be necessary to subordinate them to a fuller and richer mode of evaluation, combining the power of money as a medium of value with the evaluative power of attention to that which matters.

To achieve this, it will be necessary to invert the distribution of values expressed in money. Money has been regarded as a store of value. Yet if true value cannot be represented or stored, then it will be necessary to suppose that value is external to money. Instead of value being represented as an object of accumulation, then, value may be indicated by the tendency of money to flow in a particular direction, should such flows be directed by evaluations. Money has been regarded as a unit of account. Yet money cannot measure true value. Instead of attempting to measure value by money, then, it will be necessary to measure money by value, by lending it a determinate degree of credit. Money has been regarded as a medium enabling the exchange of valued objects. Yet the values exchanged do not exist outside the practice of exchange. Instead of being an object of exchange, value may be regarded as a potency determining the formation of contracts.

If value is truly relational, it should never be confused with a property, a measure, or an object. Instead of relying on a fixed mode of representation, it is necessary to turn accounting into a temporal mode of thinking that rests on credit rather than on the illusion of evidence. This is a question of counting contracts as processes rather than possessions. It is a question of viewing accounting as an ongoing distribution of attention rather than as a record of what is taken for granted. It is a question of orienting economic behavior toward that which is taken as mattering rather than allowing economic behavior to determine what matters. Value may be regarded as a potency, a tendency, and an orientation embodied in the movement of money and expressed in the capacity to form contracts. Such is the revaluation of values that requires exploration.

Value is produced by capital. Yet, as has been noted, production alone is insufficient for the creation of value. It is necessary that production fulfill some need or desire. Value requires both production and an evaluation. Moreover, demand alone is insufficient to produce value, for demand itself may be produced for the sake of profit. Demand may be created for products that do not effectively fulfill any significant need or desire. Furthermore, social consensus on value expresses little more than that certain products are in demand, without determining their value or significance for the formation of capital or for the quality of experience. Nothing is

more complex and problematic than the production of value. Nevertheless, we should seek the emergence of value from the encounter of three
dimensions: capital, which arises from the production of order; demand,
which arises from the experience of time; and credit, which arises from a
determinate theology of evaluation.

5.3.2 The paradox of accounting is that the act of evaluation, the practice that matters most, becomes subordinated to the practice of making
money, a representation of evaluation. To liberate evaluation from its representation, it is necessary to assume that true value resists accounting. Far
from being represented by a price or possessed as a property, true value is
that which can never be mastered. Only in a culture governed by money
is it possible to imagine that there are no true values. In reality, there is no
need for skepticism regarding the existence of value, for thought itself lives
and moves in the element of value. Thought does not represent, project,
or sense value as something external to it; thought is concentrated attention and as such is attracted and distracted by that which seems to matter.
Value is not so much external to thought as it is the environment in which
thought orients itself. Indeed, when thought encounters resistance, problems, and obstacles, when it is attracted by what is significant and problematic, it meets a value for which it cannot account. For example, thought
is attracted by economic opportunities and misfortunes. These, the events
that feed economic life, cannot be generally taken into account, for they
have an unknowable value. They lack a publicly agreed price.

A new kind of economic value may be regarded as that which cannot
be evaluated yet demands to be evaluated. It is far from the equilibrium of
a fixed or agreed price. Economic opportunity, like capital, is worth more
than money. It is the source from which the values expressed in prices derive. Moreover, once economic opportunities find a market price, they are
subjected to the equilibrating forces of the market and lose their potential
as opportunities. The creation of value, therefore, always occurs outside the
market. Far from value being embodied in a price, value is that which exerts
pressure on prices to move insofar as they have not fully accounted for the
emergence of opportunities or threats. Value cannot even be measured by
the difference between a price and a hypothetical equilibrium position, for
such a difference is merely a guess or a representation. Once given a price,

all values adjust so that no economic opportunity remains. Instead, it is necessary to consider value as a force operating through expectations. It has intensity, not an extensive quantity.

Value, then, is to be understood as the very environment of evaluation. It expresses itself in anxiety and anticipation. Value is not determined by pricing; pricing is determined by value. The relation between accounting and value is no longer one of domination, where values are mastered by accounts, or one of representation, where prices are modeled on perceived values. It is more like a relation of symbiosis, where values provide the environment that feeds evaluation. Instead of accounting's aspiring to a public and universal determination of value in a market price, true evaluation is necessarily local, partial, and responsive, attending to that which has the most urgent impact on it. Instead of being computed by linear chains of calculation, value emerges from the resolution of multiple, complex forces into a consistent outcome. Instead of representing an overall state of wealth to be compared with others, accounting would favor adaptation to a particular economic niche.

The current system of accounting places all enterprises in universal competition for a single scarce resource: money. Nevertheless, all enterprises thrive through cooperation. Although money is not in reality scarce, economic opportunities and niches are scarce in the sense of being determinate locations. Instead of competing for limited economic opportunities, it may be more productive to invent additional sites and opportunities made possible by existing arrangements. Instead of competing for productive capacity through a more efficient use of time, it may be more productive to discover new productive capacities and to take more time. For economic growth does not mainly derive from a quantitative increase in production or the saving of time; it derives from capitalizing on economic opportunities as they emerge. Instead of being measured against time or expenditure, efficiency should be measured against truly scarce economic resources, such as energy, land, and materials. True efficiency is encountered in the conservation of capital; it is encountered in symbiosis with complementary forms of life and processes that provide nutrients and feed on waste. True efficiency comes not from saving time but from accumulating capital. True efficiency results from growth in social capital, enabling more economic relations and opportunities to arise. True efficiency is an increase in the diversity and complexity of processes of production within a given resource base.

5.3.3 The new kind of value may be regarded as that which has an impact on assessments, even though it remains external to evaluation. Value is that which is not yet represented in a price. Yet if value is that which forms prices, then instead of being directly represented, its effects can be observed in the movement of prices. Opportunities, orientations, and tendencies have an effect on rates of change, accelerations, continuities, points of inflection, vibrations, frequencies, and volatility. Value that is external to prices has an impact on prices in three ways. News of the opening and closing of opportunities in the economic environment provokes a set of reactions; the progress of time allows underlying tendencies to disclose themselves; and flows of confidence internal to evaluation mark reorientations of price movements.[5]

Pricing, therefore, already floats in a wider economic environment. While capital is the source of all production, credit is the source of both exchange value and money. Although credit operates through subjective evaluations, through psychological forces of anticipation and anxiety, it is not, for all that, any less real. It does not lie within the power of the will of the economic agent but imposes on this will, determining which choices are taken, for credit is formed from a resolution of diverse social expectations. Indeed, such expectations communicate with each other and solidify via the medium of prices. Markets thus have a dual function. They facilitate the exchange and distribution of products and services, but they also communicate intensities of credit. They can even perform the latter function without the exchange of anything simply by movements in prices. Faith itself, instead of being confined to the private beliefs of the individual, can be tested out and gain social solidity as credit.

In reality, then, the market is guided by an invisible hand. External forces shape the movements of prices, whether these are the effects of economic conditions in the external world, the force of the passage of time, or the force of socially constructed credit. When the hand moves to compensate for imbalances, its action is always unjustly distributed—too late to save and too excessive in force. The market is ruled by an incompetent providence. Instead of returning the market to equilibrium, the invisible hand's imbalance, tardiness, and excessiveness ensure that equilibrium is never attained. The market is always unjust. In an interdependent world where power is exercised through money, casualties result from the failings of others. No one can be fully responsible for himself or herself. All are exposed to risk; no one achieves mastery. Outcomes are rarely proportional to economic prudence.

The injustice of the invisible hand has a number of consequences for economic ethics. In the first place, market forces cannot be foreseen or represented. True prudence—attuning oneself to the movements of the market—remains impossible. Economic misfortune and failure cannot be conclusively attributed to imprudent conduct. They need not carry the double misfortune of responsibility for failure alongside failure itself. Those who cannot be blamed for their misfortune do not disqualify themselves from care and provision from others. Indeed, such provision and care may be regarded as maintenance of human and social capital. The welfare of all remains the responsibility of all, since all may contribute in some way to future production.

In the second place, mastery over one's economic fortunes remains an impossible ideal. In practice, people remain dependent on the fortunes of others to achieve their own success. Success in the current system may be less an indicator of one's own economic prudence than one's practice of profiting from others. Moreover, interdependence provides a motive for cooperation and for ensuring one's own good fortune through ensuring the good fortune of others. As a result, the wealth of all is increased.

In the third place, a clear representation of market forces would place the market in perpetual equilibrium. There would be no remaining economic opportunities and little remaining incentive for production. Market equilibrium has an entropic effect on the economy as a whole, reducing it to the steady state envisaged by some classical economists. Under such conditions, it is doubtful whether negentropic economic institutions could be developed at all. Economic life depends on the existence of opportunities.

The incompetence of the invisible hand of the market therefore turns out to be rather providential. Where the invisible hand fails to reward prudence and produce wealth, it leaves scope for social forces to reward prudence and produce wealth. Here again, society lives off its imperfections.

A perfectly transparent economic system would have the effect of a perfect providence. It would reduce opportunity and social capital. An imperfect economy, by contrast, presents imbalances of distribution, ignorance, destructive behavior, and exploitation as so many problems that require resolution. Such problems may motivate economic behavior. It is not that such problems could ever be sufficiently solved or that a utopian solution should ever be an object of aspiration. It is the case, however, that such imbalances, inequalities, and dangers demand continual attention and so renew economic life.

5.3.4 The effects of economic providence are not an object of faith alone. They are the object of speculative markets. Prices in speculative markets fluctuate in response to news, unfolding trends, and speculative confidence. The demand in such markets is always for a single good: reward measured against risk. Instead of being determined simply by supply and demand, therefore, as in other markets, speculative markets dramatize more clearly the social forces exerted on evaluation. A share-price graph is a history of forces of expectation. It shows periods of confidence and stability, periods of uncertainty and volatility, periods of anticipation and high activity, and periods of calm and continuity. In short, speculative traders deal not in the underlying asset but in fluctuations in confidence.

It is the very uncertainty of price movements that adds to their volatility. Speculators crave information concerning the current forces acting in the market. Imitation of others is often the only source of information available, leading to an oscillation of positive and negative feedback effects. Speculative bubbles and crashes need have no external cause. Yet speculative markets cannot operate in complete abstraction. They require an underlying object of confidence, as well as news from the productive economy, to stimulate disequilibria and opportunities.

Price is the only means of communication between diverse economic forces. The price, then, does not simply represent equilibrium between competing forces of expectation and anxiety. Such forces may be pulsed rather than continuous, emerging into consciousness when they succeed in attracting attention. Beneath the economy of prices lies an economy of attention that lends energy to what is granted significance. Similarly, markets respond to news, not only for its perceived intrinsic significance, but also to the extent that it is vividly portrayed and captures the imagination. An economy of prices operates on the basis of economies of attention and imagination.

For economic behavior to change fundamentally, it is necessary to develop new mechanisms for distributing attention and imagination. Excessive attention to prices and excessive imagination of economic opportunities and threats may lead to a mode of economic behavior that cannot be receptive to what matters. The generalized state of excitement, anxiety, and stress generated by the market, while intrinsically unhealthy when excessive, may also be destructive of social capital.

CREDIT

5.4.1 Accounting measures exchange values: it is solely concerned with the amount of money that can be substituted for a product or outcome. Accounting does not evaluate the product itself or the process of production. By means of a substitution, it produces the effect of an atemporal value, even if that value continually changes. In the same way, land, labor, and capital are evaluated in terms of the money required to pay for their usage. As ongoing temporal contracts, the amount of money paid for land, labor, and capital is proportional to the time required for their usage. They are treated solely as costs of production and thus as a drain on value. Since it is difficult to invent and produce additional value in the form of outcomes and products, economic activity is largely geared to reducing costs by saving time. Indeed, such a large proportion of economic activity and innovation is geared toward saving time that one may wonder whether more time is spent on saving time than time is saved. Similarly, the multiplication of contracts through debts and credits is aimed at saving time. If the aim of economic activity is to make money, then its principal aim is simply to save time.

The problem of spending time, by contrast, is relatively unexamined. There is enormous scope for wastage in the time of production, as well as in the time of consumption, for if the spending of time is measured against reducing costs and maximizing profits, priority is no longer given to the formation of capital and the enhancement of experience. In an economy geared solely toward profit and debt, much time is wasted on unproductive activities that are designed to ensure profits within a competitive environment rather than to contribute to the formation of capital or the enhancement of experience. There is at least as much scope for unproductive labor in a market economy as there is in one planned by the state. To achieve time that is of value, saving time should be subordinated to spending time.

A new mode of accounting must begin with the process of spending time rather than the outcome of spent time. This is a matter of constructing a worthwhile life rather than simply increasing production. A theology of money must draw attention to the issue of which ways of spending time actually matter. Value, far from being an object of accumulation or acquisition, holds value only in motion.

In reality, of course, time cannot be saved at all. It continues to pass. The effort to save time is merely an attempt to control the distribution of time, taking less time for those activities that are deemed to be less important so that more time can be spent elsewhere. If the outcome of time is held as more significant than the experience, then to make efficiency gains, the quality of time may be downgraded by eliminating all that is superfluous and inefficient in relation to production. As a result, more time is spent on less significant experience, and the time that is spent is downgraded in quality.

When work is evaluated by managers in relation to its output, then time is not properly evaluated at all. Labor is always a cost for employers; it is only an experience for employees. The exchange value of labor is not fixed by the time that must be sacrificed for it in toil unless labor has already been downgraded to the point of tiresome drudgery. Instead, it is fixed as a cost by the sacrifice of employers' profits. The dominant perspective in such accounting of work is that of the employer. Work is evaluated from the point of view of its product, not from the point of view of the experience of the worker or from the point of view of mobilizing, nourishing, and connecting physical, human, and social capital. For quality of time may emerge in undetermined moments of idleness.

Evaluation, in principle, may be removed from output and attached to experience. If accounts that evaluate output are themselves flawed fictions, then other fictions that are more responsive to the experience of time may also be devised. For human subjects endowed with memory, value is created, sensed, and recorded by spending time, not by saving time. There is no need for additional proof of value beyond the experience of those who encounter it. Experience itself is the true record of value. Even if experience overlooks significance, missing opportunities beyond the horizon of experience, it is still experience itself that may test such opportunities.

5.4.2 In the current system, evaluations, in practice, have no more social effectiveness than the money that is able to support them—the effective demand through which they are backed. All evaluations are valued externally, then, on the basis of their profitability or their symbiosis with profitable enterprises. While there is no shortage of evaluations, each evaluation is subordinated to an abstract system where it is evaluated from a purely external perspective that is held by no one. Such an abstract system causes a kind of leakage of value from the forms of life in which it emerges. Evaluations can endure and thrive only to the extent that they maintain themselves in some form of representation. In practice, this means that values endure and thrive only to the extent that they are profitable. The value of profit is substituted for all other values; there is a kind of entropy of value, a decay of all established values, as their effectiveness passes toward purely monetary effects.

It is this very process of decay that allows for fresh economic activity. Economic activity can gain a new meaning: it is the production of value as a negentropic process, acting against a broader decay of value. If all production becomes the production of exchange value, if all evaluation seeks to determine a price, then the social field of evaluation decays toward an equilibrium point of perfect consensus based on the primacy of money. This utopia of the perfect market is a kind of moral heat death, where value no longer needs to be created and all needs or demands become arbitrary whims. An equilibrium point is not merely a moment of balance, when supply meets demand. An equilibrium point is also a moment of maximum entropy, when information has been destroyed. There is no possibility of tracing a movement back from equilibrium to its initial conditions, for the information concerning initial conditions is progressively eliminated in the approach to equilibrium. The marketization of society effects the progressive annihilation of history, culture, and value.

The production of true value thus requires more than a process of production and more than the production of profit. Such processes reorganize matter, changing it from its normal state of entropy to a state in which it can be used. The value that is added in negentropic processes of production is simply information. This is the true output of production. More is required, however, than an increased information content. The information has to be useful to someone. Order becomes valuable only when it corresponds to desire. Valuable information does not simply consist in facts. It is not objective or individuated into units. Information holds value only when it is ordered to meet desire. It is this experience of time as entropy and perpetual decay of both capital and value that produces demand for the creation of order. The decay of value, then, is far from being something to be lamented. It is the very engine that drives evaluation, producing order and credit.

The question arises of whether desire itself is sufficient to produce value. Of course, desire can do nothing without a material that it is capable of ordering. Moreover, desire does not generate information concerning the matter to be ordered, for the intrinsic properties of matter, including its potential to correspond to desire, can be learned only by experimentation and experience. An excess remains on each side—an excess of potential ordering and its correspondence to desire, as well as an excess of desire beyond what can be ordered. Indeed, the production of value cannot take place without this excess on each side. In this respect, it is not simply the correspondence or meeting of desire and order that produces value but their asymmetry, their lack of correspondence, as a positive potential and opportunity. It is this asymmetry that is the true source of wealth. Since it exceeds representation, evidence, and accounts, it has to be given credit.

A further element is required to realize production beyond order and desire: credit. For the production of value to become a social reality, rather than a private reality, the meeting of desire and order must be made effective. It must be given credit. It must be treated as valuable in advance so that it may demonstrate that it is valuable in practice. The texture of society, then, is not constituted solely by order or structure; nor is it constituted by production or desire. It is constituted by credit as the ontological substance of all social bonds.

The production of value begins with credit. While the realization of value occurs when order meets desire, the motion of production begins with credit. The production of value therefore begins outside all circles of knowledge and desire, outside all circular motions, outside all adequate ideas. The production of value begins in risk and uncertainty. The curious conclusion to be drawn, then, is that value derives from speculation. Even financial speculators, although they might operate within a narrow domain of activity, are still concerned with what is essential in the production of value. In addition to producers who order material, and in addition to consumers who express demand, speculators or venture capitalists are required who guess at the emergence of economic opportunities.

5.4.3 Speculative ventures are, of course, often mistaken. Credit is not the sole source of value; value has to be implicit as a potential of the situation. While credit expresses a flow of speculative evaluation, demonstrable value derives from economic potential. Each economic opportunity has to be advanced credit, invested with desire, and effectively ordered. All contracts involve at least three parties: sellers of time, buyers of nutrition, and those who give credit to the contract.

The difficulty in assessing economic opportunities lies in the fact that such opportunities have to be proved in experience. Once proved, the opportunity no longer remains. There is thus no true science of economics, because the realization of economic value depends more on divination than it does on public evidence. In addition to the sciences of production and distribution that deal with order, and in addition to the sciences of anthropology and psychology that deal with desire, there is also a theology of credit. Such credit is grounded in a dim awareness of economic opportunities, whether in unrealized possibilities for order or in unachieved satisfactions of desire.

More significant, there is also the question of unrealized values. It is one thing for the realization of an economic opportunity to be profitable; it is another for it to be truly valuable for capital and for experience. The production of value is most valuable either when it contributes to the formation of physical, human, and social capital or when it contributes to the quality of experience. The true value of an economic opportunity, then, rests in its ultimate implications for the production of capital, for meeting desire, and for enhancing credit. The highest form of value to be produced is the capacity to evaluate economic opportunity.

5.4.4 Money, as has been discussed, consists in a contract combining an asset, a liability, and a reserve. Each is a promise of exchange value.

Together, they generate an advance of exchange value in the form of an asset. When money is treated as a representation of exchange value, then such exchange value is treated here as a passive object of exchange, of measure, and of preservation. It is apparently subordinated to the liberated will of the economic agent. Promises, liabilities, and securities, by contrast, impose regulatory practices on the handling of value. While exchange value may be freely transferred, promises, liabilities, and securities have a moral significance for participants. The moral nature of money is obscured when money is treated as an embodiment of exchange value. If the value of money were simply that of the goods and services that may be exchanged for it, then its value would depend on a substitution for money, a substitution that prevents one from considering the essence of money at all. Yet rent, wages, and interest in practice are paid only in the form of money. Moreover, since debts can be repaid only in money, the veil of perpetual substitution has at last to be discarded, leaving money in its naked state as promise, liability, and reserve. Money must eventually return to be assessed against its original promise.

As a debt, money has a tendency to flow in a particular direction. Without the return flow of money, money would become worthless. The promise is underwritten by the liability and the reserve. The value expressed in money is not created by production, exchange, or substitution. The value promised by money is created by the combination of a promise, a liability, and a reserve. Such a value is realized by the meeting of the production of order, the effective expression of desire, and the attribution of credit.

Credit is granted on the basis of the security of the reserve. Since credit is not a delayed purchase, the aim of credit is not to acquire the reserve. Such a security is required only when credit fails. Security, then, is not the proper object of credit. The exchange value of the reserve merely substitutes for the object of credit should credit fail. Credit is attributed to economic opportunity. Just as capital — the ability to produce wealth — cannot be reduced to the exchange value of accumulated stock, so also an economic opportunity cannot be reduced to the value advanced on the basis of the expectation it generates.

Credit therefore cannot be reduced to the value of the security that serves as a reserve or guarantee, to the value of the advance offered as credit, or to the value that is realized when the production of order meets desire. For even at the end of the process, the economic opportunity has evaporated, and a realized profit has taken its place. No determinate value can thus be substituted for credit; nor can credit be attributed to value. Credit is attributed to economic opportunity in the form of capital, therefore, rather than to the possibility of future value.

The paradox of credit is that there can be no public evidence for economic opportunities. If information concerning such opportunities were to become exchangeable and repeatable, agreed by consensus, then the opportunity would be taken into account in existing price levels, canceling the opportunity itself while leading to a loss if its productive possibilities are left unrealized. Economic opportunities arise, by contrast, from a lack of public consensus. They arise for those who are able to perceive the whole situation and its dominant trends more effectively than others. They derive from reading significant trends and possible futures. They can be made effective, bringing such futures into being, by being attributed credit. The value advanced enables the future to come about. Wealth does not derive from production or demand alone; it derives from the consequences of the interaction of current trends. Credit may be attributed most effectively to emergent economic niches rather than to existing strategies of production.

One does not produce wealth by mastering and controlling reality as a whole. One produces wealth by sensing and responding appropriately to economic opportunities. One produces wealth by creating order and information from the processes that are already under way. Unintended consequences may be external costs; they may also be economic opportunities. At any rate, the emergence of new economic niches as unintended consequences is the driving force of economic activity. In short, it is distance from equilibrium and inability to make accurate predictions that enables the emergence of new sites, new orders, and new negentropic processes that keep economic activity alive.

EVALUATION

5.5.1 Wealth may be considered capital, the ability to produce order. Yet while capital produces order in reality, it is desire that gives value to order—and thus to capital—in evaluation. The question arises, then, of what gives value to desire. This is a theological question concerning the value of values, the value of desires, and the value of evaluations.

To value such evaluations according to a consensus or the market is to substitute a purely extrinsic evaluation for the intrinsic value of evaluation. Evaluations, like economic opportunities, are external to such a market. One does not substitute for them without obscuring the very perspective or location that gives them value. Evaluations, like opportunities, are singular points that exceed all confirmed knowledge. Nevertheless, they do indeed operate within the mind to give value to values.

True wealth thus requires more than capital formation, just as it requires more than making profits. True wealth also requires the production of evaluations and their effective realization through desire. True wealth is the realization of true values. It is necessary that such values should orient desire and production; it is not necessary that such values should be represented or given an exchange value.

If society is based on contract rather than exchange, contract itself is insufficient to represent values and opportunities that act on and through the mind. Such economic forces may operate through the imagination. One is not faced with a false choice between the transparency of knowledge, where thinking represents reality, and complete uncertainty and ignorance. Values may not be known in themselves, yet they still act over the course of time, producing a tendency toward a destination. What is necessary for the divination of value is some kind of supple, imaginative body that is capable of being affected by and indicating the potency of forces of evaluation. What is also required for the verification of such divinations is an experimental method for the realization of value. This theology of evaluation underlies credit.

5.5.2 Values tend to be expressed in perspectives of evaluation. While such perspectives of evaluation often tend to attribute considerable importance to themselves, the value of such perspectives may appear to be very different from other perspectives. There are no demonstrably objective or universal criteria. In practice, such perspectives may seek consensus and agreement. The external value of values has been determined by the profitability of their associated enterprises. Market value substitutes in this way for a universal value.

The vital question, then, concerns how one can invest in values apart from a market system for their verification. It will be necessary to develop a social infrastructure for the imagination of value and mediation of credit that operates apart from market systems of exchange and substitution. It will be necessary for temporal relations to take a significant role in the emergence and testing of values.

Investment of money substitutes for an investment of attention. No true evaluation can take place without attention to the perceptions, forces, and tendencies that have a direct impact on a particular location. Changes in prices and profits occur outside the sphere of attention; they exclude all true measures of value. What is required, by contrast, is continuing attention to and evaluation of given perspectives of evaluation. It is a matter of stripping away the values produced by evaluative perspectives so that such evaluative perspectives can be evaluated in their own right.

5.5.3 The curious feature of liabilities, in contrast to assets, is their located nature. Assets have an exchange value; one must substitute for them to realize their value. Liabilities, by contrast, need to be repaid in kind. They are defined by their contracts.

One of the illusions produced by treating money as a universal equivalent or representative of exchange value is that money is regarded as a better or worse embodiment of a universal, abstract currency. In practice, there are no universal, abstract currencies. There are merely specific assets and liabilities denominated in specific currencies, where debts need to be repaid in the currency in which they are denominated. Money is always a liability of a determinate bank. This is the ultimate significance of the creation of money as debt. It is a fixed liability rather than a transferable asset. It is always attached to a determinate location and practice of recording. Banks are perspectives of evaluation from which the world is measured and recorded. It is such a practice of evaluation that demands to be evaluated itself.

There is no reason that liabilities should be restricted to money. It is possible to issue other kinds of liabilities. If one sells stocks short, for example, promising to deliver them at an agreed future price and date, one then has the option to buy at a better price in the meantime. Yet the original stock has to be delivered at some stage—unless such trades are canceled out by the dealer according to a similar principle that operates in the clearing house.

Liabilities, then, may be attached to determinate institutions reflecting determinate perspectives of evaluation. Just as money can be created as a division of assets and liabilities, so can virtual shares be created as promises to deliver. There are no limits to the range and kind of values that can be created, just as there are no limits to the range and kind of currencies that can be created.

Money indicates the effective desire attached to a contract. Another measure is required to indicate the effective value attached to a contract. Even though they are private agreements between producers and consumers, contracts have a public value. Honoring private contracts is a public good since it leads to trust in contracts and an increase in social capital. Beyond this, performance of the contract may often affect other common goods. Each contract, then, may be evaluated not only in terms of money by consumer desire but also by its public effects.

The evaluation of such public effects is not a straightforward matter. While the public interest is served as a whole by the honoring of contracts, so that it is easy for the state to take on itself a liability to enforce contracts, a more complete evaluation of the significance of each contract requires a diversity of perspectives. Yet without at least some external interest that values each contract, the public can have no confidence that any particular contract will be of value. The public interest requires not only that contracts be kept, but also that they serve the common good. Value is not produced by the meeting of order and desire, or producer and consumer, alone. Value requires also that such a contract be given credit.

Transactions always involve at least three parties—the producer, the consumer, the public whose interest is served—as well as a source of credit for each contract. Alongside production and demand, then, it is necessary to have evaluation. Just as there are enterprises for the production of order to meet demand, in a healthy economy there also need to be enterprises for the evaluation of contracts that assess demand. If money is the institution that alone serves this purpose, then the public can be confident that common interests will not be served. Indeed, in practice money does not serve this purpose alone in market capitalism. Dominant relations are supported by a moral discourse that defends their inherent goodness as sources of wealth. Such uncritical moral discourse is purveyed through the media. Since media prosper only if they attract attention to themselves, such moral discourse can be published only if it flatters or serves the self-interests of its consumers. In short, the work of evaluation is short-circuited once more by the rule of the market. If evaluations are assessed by the effective demand for them, via profitability, then they can express only the wishful thinking of a dominant majority. The subordination of evaluation to desire at personal, institutional, and systemic levels is the fundamental corruption of democratic capitalism.

The short circuit between desire, money, and evaluation must be cut in order to liberate attention to the crediting, critique, and creation of effective evaluations. In short, the ethical economy that coexists with the economy of order requires its own distinctive institutions whose primary purpose is evaluation, not production or profit. The creation, critique, and crediting of evaluation is the theological activity that guides the economic order.

OF THEOLOGY

A PARABLE—
ON THE DESIRE TO BE RICH

If one were only a true metaphysician, thinking nothing but being itself, relieved of the distractions of social intercourse and material need, enjoying the subtlest of truths, the profoundest states of awareness, the richest of revelations, freed from the need to think the Good, for thinking itself would be good, freed from the need to think the True, for thinking itself would be true, freed even from the need to think reality, for thinking itself would be life, until one dismissed metaphysics, for there needed no metaphysics, dismissed thinking, for there needed no thinking, until one renounced even the knowledge that one was a philosopher before setting out to seek wealth, friends, and lovers.

Six

METAPHYSICS AND CREDIT

Whenever you receive a letter from a creditor
write fifty lines on an extra-terrestrial subject,
and you will be saved.

CHARLES BAUDELAIRE

THIS STUDY BEGAN by noting the opposition between God and money
proclaimed by Jesus: "You cannot serve God and Mammon." Indeed, "It is
easier for a camel to go through the eye of a needle than for someone who
is rich to enter the kingdom of God" (Mark 10.24). As Jesus explained, "For
where your treasure is, there will your heart be also" (Matt. 6.21). For the
philosopher, such an opposition raises the most fundamental of problems.
What is the true nature of wealth? Can wealth be understood in terms
of the monetary value of assets or products? What is the difference between "treasure stored in heaven" and treasures on Earth? What makes
for a rich life, a life lived in all its fullness? Here we approach the central
task of theology: what is the source of the value of values? Jesus's opposition to wealth belongs within the tradition of renunciation of the ways of
the world, which are concerned with storing up treasure on Earth to seek
out the "kingdom of God" or the true source of all treasure. The religious
impulse, expressed diversely by the Taoist sages, the Indian renunciants,
the Buddhist monks and nuns, the gurus, the cynics, the Essenes, and the
desert fathers, has often been one of renunciation for the sake of attaining
true, spiritual wealth.

Jesus's opposition is distinctive, however. For the alternative between
God and wealth (personified as Mammon) is that between two masters.
In either case, it is a question of service. Wealth attracts time, attention,
and devotion; it constructs a perspective from which the world is to be

seen. There are differing principles of power here. For the philosopher, this opposition raises another most fundamental of problems: what is the true nature of power? Is power to be understood according to the sovereign power of Caesar or the executive power of the state? Is the messiah to be understood as a somewhat belated yet benign Caesar who will eventually rule through just decrees? What is the difference between the power of Caesar and the power of God? Here we approach a central dilemma for Christian theology: either theology takes the option of Constantinianism, whether it sanctifies sovereign power, imitates it, or reproduces it in fantasy by decreeing the true spiritual meanings according to which the world is to be judged, or else theology takes the option of a kenotic Christology, re- nouncing all power and taking the form of a servant. In both cases, the dan- ger lies in insufficiently distinguishing divine power from imperial power.

What is striking about Jesus's sayings is that the two problems, those of true wealth and true power, are treated as inseparable: wealth is service. Yet can one not use worldly power in the service of the good, of the wealth of all, or of true spiritual values? Can one not use worldly wealth in the service of the enrichment of life? Is there not the possibility of human mastery rather than service, so that wealth and power are subordinated to humane values? Is not the whole of modern politics based on such assumptions?

There are two clues as to why, for Jesus, this could not be the case. One lies in taxation. The power of the procurator of Judea and Herodian client rulers of Galilee did not simply derive from imperial decree or the threat of force. In practice, it derived from taxation. Roman coins gained their value from the fact that they could be used — and, indeed, had to be used — for the payment of taxes.[1] Money was issued by the imperial mint and even- tually would have to return to Rome. The people of Israel were servants of Rome insofar as they paid taxes, not merely insofar as they were occu- pied by Roman garrisons. Hence, if wealth was acquired through the use of money, and money belonged to Caesar, then mastery over wealth was at the same time service of Caesar. To accumulate wealth was to participate in a system of exploitation and extortion.

Yet while the reality of taxation was central to the lives of those described in the Gospels, there is little evidence of a clearly understood theory of money. The second clue is perhaps more telling. Jesus inverted the relation of mastery between people and wealth — your heart is where your treasure is; not your treasure is where your heart is—by inverting the normal relation between the eye and light: "The eye is the lamp of the body. So, if your eye is healthy, your whole body will be full of light; but if your eye is unhealthy, your whole body will be full of darkness. If then the light in you is darkness, how great is the darkness!" (Matt. 6.23). Service is enacted through time, attention, and devotion. The object of one's attention is used as the material for forming the perspective through which the world is to be seen. One forms a perspective expressed in a metaphysics. If one does not turn attention to God, the source of the value of values, then one's evaluations will be shaped by the world. True power consists here in a perspective of evaluation. Hence, the modern notion of autonomy is an illusion, since it is always a perspective, a source of evaluation, that one serves.

Jesus's opposition between God and wealth therefore leads to a conjunction of two fundamental problems: the true nature of wealth and the true nature of power. For modern thought, by contrast, evaluation belongs to the subjective sphere of freedom, while money and power belong to the objective sphere of actualization. Modern thought rests on a series of dichotomies between thought and existence, between value and being, between mind and body, and between reason and religion. These metaphysical dichotomies are called into question as soon as one raises the problem of how time, attention, and devotion are to be spent. This is a universal question affecting believer and unbeliever alike. It undermines the modern exclusion of the theological from critical thought, for if one's perspective is indeed formed by the way one spends one's time[2]—and I will show how this is indeed the case with money—then evaluations, decisions, organization, and production emerge from a practice that itself arises from commitments. To what will one devote one's life? What authority will one call on for one's decisions to bear credit?[3] These are inescapable theological questions. Moreover, the dichotomy between the religious and the secular does not merely prevent secular thought from engaging with the most significant problems, for insofar as theology accepts this division of labor and concerns itself with the realms of belief, meaning, individual faith, and ecclesial tradition, it concedes much effective social authority to purely secular relations mediated by money. Rediscovering the problem of the effective source of the value of values requires a reformation of secular and theological thought alike.[4]

To call into question the modern division between subject, object, and the knowledge that reunites them is to raise a further fundamental philosophical problem: what is the true nature of being? Are the metaphysical assumptions embedded in modern thought, and especially in modern politics and economics, still viable? Can one believe in the passive, material object; the free, evaluating subject; and the neutral truth as genuine metaphysical entities? To pursue a theology of money, it is now necessary to turn to problems of metaphysics, of power, and of wealth, for a perspective determines what one sees when one considers the world. What one seeks and sees is expressed most fully in metaphysics.

THEOLOGY AND METAPHYSICS

Parmenides bequeathed a peculiar problem to Western metaphysics in the form of a tautology: "being is." This can be taken to mean "truth is true" or "the same thing is for thinking and for being."[5] What is the thing that is the same for thinking and for being? The entire history of Western metaphysics may be regarded as a series of experiments with possible solutions to this problem, for a solution to this problem would liberate knowledge from the sway of opinion. Yet it is precisely here that one may discern the bad conscience of metaphysics. The thing that is the same for thinking and for being emerges only from a disciplined thinking, a rigorous practice of thought, or even a piety. The tautology "being is," like all tautologies, invokes belief. A subject is identified with a predicate, but a subject always differs from predicate grammatically as subject and predicate. If they are to be the same, they can be so only in regard to a third term, above and beyond grammar — the thing that is the same for thinking and for being. This thing is the philosopher's stone that defines the metaphysical quest.[6] Being is made an object of belief by a tautology that reduplicates and abstracts it, as when Aristotle defined metaphysics as the science of being qua being,[7] when Spinoza defined a substance as that which is in itself and is conceived through itself,[8] and when Heidegger translated Parmenides's meditation as, "It is useful: to let-lie-before-us and so the-taking-to-heart-also: beings-in-being."[9] The currency of any given metaphysical solution to this problem is determined by whether it is accepted that the same thing is for thinking and for being. It is here that the bad conscience of metaphysics can be disclosed, for is it not inevitable that at the metaphysical level of tautology, where subject is identified with predicate, one may simply invert subject and predicate? Then the currency of metaphysics becomes the metaphysics of currency.

Thomas Aquinas offered a solution to the metaphysical problem: God is his own essence and his own existence.[10] Thus, when God is identified as the True, the Good, and Life, this is somewhat paradoxical: all beings may be judged according to their truth, goodness, and life, but God alone is at once both ultimate criterion and eminent instance. God alone is his essence. This striking identity opens up a fateful ambivalence: is God true, or is truth divine? Is God good, or is goodness divine? Does God live, or is life divine? The problem becomes more acute when we turn to power and existence. If God is power, do we mean that might is right or that right is might? If God is being, do we mean that God exists or that existence is divine? We seem to be presented with a choice between transcendence and immanence. The divine is invoked either as a power of judgment or a criterion, in the case of transcendence, or as a power of affirmation or an instance, in the case of immanence.

For a Christian metaphysics, this ambivalence between transcendence and immanence may be regarded as a false problem resulting from the division of a prior identity. God is indistinguishable from the True, the Good, and Life. Divine simplicity, the identification of essence and existence, comes first. God is the same for thinking and for being. Unity constitutes God, just as it constitutes Parmenidean Being. God both affirms in creation and judges at the eschaton. This may be fine for an eternal God, but for us, the temporal interval between creation and judgment leaves ambivalence. Are we to make divine the True, the Good, and Life? If so, what is accomplished by attributing to them a "divine" status? Such an act exemplifies Ludwig Feuerbach's concept of projection, in which one's own orientation within the fields of knowledge, ethics, and temporal existence becomes sanctified. The alternative to this idolatry is to declare that God is the True, the Good, and Life. In this case, one takes one's orientation within the fields of knowledge, ethics, and temporal existence from God. Religion takes priority over reason and ethics. Belief determines metaphysics. Theology then claims to offer to the world a vision of life interpreted according to the richest of categories: categories of importance, of meaning, of personhood, of relationality, of community, of events, of narrative, and of experience, for example. In contrast to these, the highest transcendentals of philosophy, even the "eternal" and the "one," may come to seem relatively lifeless. Theology, by giving the richest depth of meaning, gives life and wealth to the world. Affirmation is no longer immanent affirmation but divine affirmation.

Theology, in its essence and vocation, therefore offers a radical metaphysics: it overturns the ways of thinking of the world. Nevertheless, it remains haunted by the bad conscience of metaphysics. Divine simplicity may be a utopian aspiration, but it may not yet be achieved in human thinking. In the meantime, the doctrine of simplicity may be invoked to divinize implicit presuppositions about the True, the Good, and Life, so identifying idolatrous presupposition with theological declaration. It short-circuits the work of enrichment of a vision of life. Then the radical force of theology, its attempt to determine the value of values on the basis of true, spiritual insight, becomes lost beneath its established teachings. Even if God is truly simple, the doctrine of simplicity may veil divinity itself.

While for God eminent instance may indeed be ultimate criterion, for us there is no such bridge between reality and thought. For us, in practice, a third category of mediation will remain between essence and existence, between thought and reality. We live in a time before the end, before the full revelation of God. In the meantime, prior to the Parousia, time continues to pass. Awaiting the completion of metaphysics, the meaning of beings has not yet been determined. If the divine identity of thinking and being has not been achieved, a more modest identity may be anticipated when existence is treated as entirely separate from thought and no longer regarded as a predicate. The modern concept of existence, which adds nothing to the essence of that which is thought, places existence entirely outside of thought.[11] As Kant remarked, "A hundred real dollars do not contain the least coin more than a hundred possible dollars."[12] What is real and what is thought are sharply distinguished. Thinking and being need to be mediated by a third term. If truth is the correspondence between the two, then it is truth that is the same for thinking and for being. Each being and each thought bears a metaphysical supplement: the truth of this being and of this thought. The modern metaphysical division is threefold: subject, object, and knowledge.

Yet such a metaphysics does not escape belief, for while truth remains true independently of whether it is actually thought or demonstrated, the truth of a truth can never be thought or demonstrated apart from thought. The modern, objective notion of existence remains an object of belief, for no existence is ever encountered apart from thought. The metaphysical problem becomes a dilemma. On the one hand, thinking must address being to escape from mere belief. On the other hand, the metaphysical criterion, the thing that is the same for thinking and for being, remains an object of belief, for neither being qua being nor truth qua truth is encountered independently of a discipline and orientation of thinking. Metaphysics cannot provide its own critique. One cannot live with metaphysics or without it; one cannot live with belief or without it.

In the meantime, awaiting a metaphysics that bears a universal currency, it may be necessary to substitute an interim measure for the supreme form and criterion of being and value. The most modest form and criterion of being and value that can be agreed is agreement itself. An agreement that is agreed as agreed is a contract. And while contracts may be taken as social or subjective phenomena, one distinctive kind of contract is the object of contracts, restoring subject, object, and knowledge to primordial metaphysical unity: money.

Let us therefore return to where we started in the introduction. Money, according to the economists, is at once an instrument of exchange, a measure of value, and a store of value. As an instrument of exchange, money is an objective tool, the material basis of social interactions dependent on markets or contracts. It can be handled, transferred, and estimated more easily than anything else. As a measure of value, money is the conceptual basis of the science of wealth, the metaphysical precondition for any knowledge of agreed value. As a store of value, money participates in the subjective sphere of belief, for money holds value as long as people are willing to trust in its value and accept it in exchange. Money holds value, measures value, and transfers value only as long as it bears credit. Then the modern form of objectivity, disclosed as being essentially a matter of manipulation, transfer, and agreement; the modern form of knowledge, disclosed as being essentially a matter of comparison, substitution, and counting; and the modern form of subjectivity, disclosed as being essentially a matter of credit are reunited in the single metaphysical form of money. Money is the philosopher's stone, the solution to the metaphysical problem of the unity of being and thought. It turns truth into gold and gold into truth. It is the thing that is the same for being and thinking, for it is what it says and says what it is. Money becomes the most significant object for meditation for both the philosopher and the theologian.

For if money is essentially credit—a promise or a contract—then its essence is its existence. It does not exist outside of its concept. Just as the metaphysics of one singular being, God, was imported to resolve the problems of metaphysics as a whole, so the metaphysics of another singular being, money, may come to our aid. If the metaphysics of God may fail to empower thought insofar as God can never become an object to be handled and thought, then the metaphysics of money may prove more profitable. For money has all of the advantages of immediacy, universality, tangibility, and utility. It can be created on demand. It offers an illusory sovereignty to the subject who may spend it.

Cases of solution to the Parmenidean problem, as we can see from the examples of God, truth, and money, may have explosive significance in world history. The contemporary world is largely shaped by religion, by science, and by capital. Metaphysics is no longer simply an abstract, intellectual problem. It concerns the core of subjectivity and the formation of desire. Concepts of God, of truth, or of money evoke unlimited submission and aspiration. A certain kind of subjectivity is called into being by the infinite promise implicit within such concepts. An unlimited desire can find satisfaction through God, truth, or money. Moreover, the infinite metaphysical promise is one that concerns objectivity. Concepts of God, truth, and money act as principles of realization and actualization. Human activity can proceed in faith that it has been promised the world. In each case, metaphysics is made possible by belief. In each case, a particular metaphysics gains currency. A representation of the ultimate relation between being and thought is substituted in advance of knowledge of the true relation to make an actual and practical relation between them possible. Metaphysics, then, should not be understood as the projection of a real world in opposition to the apparent one, for the dichotomy between real and apparent is founded on a modern metaphysics that takes truth as the solution to the Parmenidean problem. Thus, the Kantian and Nietzschean critiques of metaphysics presuppose that the subject has been divorced from object and existence has been reduced to a predicate. Similarly, belief should not be understood in the sense of a subjective commitment to an objective uncertainty. The Feuerbachian and Freudian critiques of belief as projection are possible only once subject has been divorced from object and existence has been reduced to a predicate. Instead, belief is a way to inhabit thinking and being so that the real relation between them—one that exists perfectly well without the assistance of our mental constructions—can take on a specific form of expression. In other words, theology is an ontological commitment, a perspective arising from a dim awareness of the actual nature of life. Theology creates a metaphysics.

The metaphysics of money bears an extraordinary ambivalence. On the one hand, it offers a metaphysical form that occludes the work of metaphysics itself. In modern thought, that which is real is that which can be represented, tested, and exchanged. Just as the value of the commodity can be tested only when it is offered for exchange in a market, when money may substitute for it, so the truth of the matter is substituted for the matter itself. Reality is that which can be represented in thought in abstraction from its own context, production, fertility, tendencies, and energy. Taking the form of money that may be substituted for it, reality may be represented in imagination as capital in the form of accumulated stocks, invented forms, and assembled parts. In each case, the energy that gives being to such a representation is the energy of the imagination that represents it, not that of the original matter. In short, the metaphysics of money prevents the same thing's being for being and for thinking. Thus, when the world is reproduced in imagination, it is no longer reproduced as active being but as passive image. Such is the source of the theology of the human subject as creator. Since the world is known only as represented, it must be supplemented by the transcendent decrees of a human subject. The paradox here is that the real is taken to be that which has no force, life, or existence of its own, so that existence can be attributed to it as a predicate—hence, the arising of the fantasy of sovereign power.

A reapplication of this modern metaphysics to the case of money produces the standard definitions of the economic textbooks: money is an instrument of exchange, a measure of value, and a store of value. Thus, the nature of money is fully obscured, for far from being simply a passive instrument of exchange, money is in reality a contract that makes markets and exchange possible. Far from being simply a store of accumulated value, money, when invested, is in reality the condition for the production of value. Far from being a measure of value, money, when created as credit, is in reality both the promise of value that has not been produced and the spiritual source of the agreed value itself. The true metaphysics of money therefore constitutes a metaphysical revelation. This revelation consists in a direct inversion of current metaphysical assumptions. To be real is not simply to be an accumulated stock, an invented form, or an assembly of parts; it is to accumulate stock, to invent form, to assemble parts, and to energize production. To be real is not simply to be actually present in time; it is to be committed to spending time. To be real is to promise and to affect what is actually present through such promise. One may even propose that to be real is not simply to be real. The Parmenidean tautology must be broken open and must remain in suspension. To be real is to be not yet real; it is not yet to have become what one is. Reality is invariably an object of credit. Such is the reality of the metaphysics of money; such is the reality of modern metaphysics — a metaphysics that promises far more than it delivers.

WEALTH AND POWER

Such metaphysical considerations can inform a critical perspective on wealth. Wealth is fundamentally misunderstood when it is delimited to that which can be exchanged for money. We have considered wealth in terms of the production of capital: the accumulation of stock, the invention of forms, the assembly of parts, the energizing of production, and the provision of care or nutrition. These are metaphysical categories — perhaps somewhat tentative and inadequate ones — that have the merit of delineating locality, materiality, specificity, and activity. What matters most, when considering the wealth of existence, is particularity, for each particular reality has conditions of production, networks of dependencies, and potentialities that are not captured by exchange or substitution. All of the particularities of place and time are discounted in the substitution of money for property, just as they are discounted when reality is represented in the mind in the form of ideas. It is capital itself that can be destroyed in the quest for profit. Nevertheless, it is not particularity alone that matters. Any metaphysics that concerns itself exclusively with the particularities of matter or the generalities of form will be deficient, for capital becomes productive only when it is energized, when it is affected by an indeterminate flow of potential extracted from other particularities. Similarly, the provision of care and nutrition, the expression of desire or evaluation, involve the affirmation of the particular by means of that which does not have its particularity delimited in the same way. Energy, desire, time, and evaluation are dimensions of capital that are surplus to structuration by means of form. They exceed simple representation in the imagination. Far from being objects of representation, they are what make representation possible.

Wealth is therefore made possible by physical energy, human capital, and social capital. It is insufficient to denounce the abstractions introduced by money in the name of the particularity of life, for life, in its particularity, lacks wealth without energy, desire, and credit. The problem with money is not its abstraction as such but the fact that it substitutes for particularity instead of investing in it and affirming it. I have noted that money and property do not constitute wealth in themselves, since they may quickly be spent or exhausted; capital is defined as the means of production that has itself been produced. Similarly, particularities do not constitute capital in themselves, since they may not prove to be productive. The source of wealth lies in physical energy, human capital, and social capital. Here again, physical energy is directed by human capital, human capital by social capital, and social capital by credit. Credit, a pure flow of belief detached from all particularity, is the indispensable source in the creation of wealth. At the heart of the generation of wealth, therefore, lies "spiritual" wealth, the capacity to determine what is true wealth. Theology, considered a science of the distribution of credit, retains an essential role in the creation of wealth.

God and money are competing sources of credit. Each seeks to determine the value of values. Yet where God is presumed to have created the world as it is, money presumes to transform the world by dismantling and exhausting it, if necessary, to generate profits and repay debts. Where God presides over a world understood in terms of being or eternal forms, money presides over a world understood in terms of becoming or perpetual creative destruction. Where God embodies the moral virtue of generosity or grace, money embodies the moral virtue of honoring one's contracts and paying one's dues.

The opposition between modern rationality and religion has been a

mainstay of modern thought. Indeed, the rejection of sacred rites and arti-
facts, of occult powers, and of traditional obligations is a precondition for
handling and transforming the world on the basis of evidence. While modern reason is economical, selecting only for consideration that which can
be mastered, religion is lavish, spending its time and energy directing attention beyond material recirculation through offerings, prayer, meditation,
worship, and renunciation. Indeed, the defining feature of evidence is its
recirculation, repeatability, and exchangeability. Where modern rationality
saves time, religion spends it. In saving time, modern rationality merely
postpones the religious question of spending time. Indeed, by spending
time in saving time, modern rationality makes an unexamined religious
commitment to money.

One achieves little, however, by restating the opposition between God
and money or between reason and religion, for what is excluded from consideration by such means is the extent to which political and economic
life depend on credit. It will be vital to explore the power that they have in
common. If economic production is supplemented and driven by credit,
and if sovereign power is supplemented by a political energy or authority,
then God and money both belong to a metaphysical category that is beyond existing structures of representation. We have named this category
political "energy" or "authority." It is the constitutive element of a political
theology.

The supreme embodiments of such energy in the contemporary world
are God, truth, and money. These are the supreme authorities. Anything
can be done in the name of God, truth, or money. In each case, however,
this authority is founded on a metaphysical illusion arising from the Parmenidean tautology. The structure of this illusion is that "the same thing
is for thinking and for being." If God is thought as the Supreme Being,
then God exceeds all possible thought.[13] If truth is thought as simply objective, then the objectivity of truth exceeds all possible thought. If money
is treated as the thought that says what it means and means what it says,
it excludes the significance of all other thought. Yet it is not enough to
turn from metaphysics to belief, grounding political energy in the subject
as opposed to the object, for the subject itself has no authority over its
own representations. The sovereign decrees issued by God, the beliefs or
decisions enacted by the subject, and the obligations to repay debts en-

forced by money are embodiments of political "authority" that operate in abstract isolation from the field of conditions in which they are present. The power of reason is not reducible to the power of belief. The autonomy of the sovereign power, like that of the subject, is an illusion that depends on the capacity to use money or some other form of credit to command cooperation. Money operates in the absence of belief. The essence of political authority, like the essence of metaphysics, lies beyond the categories of subject and object.

The common power held by God, truth, and money is, in part, a power of evocation. Belief in metaphysics, far from being a result of subjective decision or discernment of objective truth, is something that must be evoked. The use of money evokes a metaphysics. For one who seeks to spend or acquire money, all things are passive objects of exchange, capable of becoming goods and services. All people are sovereign subjects capable of entering into contracts at will. All knowledge is science, the capacity to effectively realize projects in the world. Similarly, the use of money evokes a politics. A sovereign state is required to ensure that contracts are honored by means of the use of force; there can be no private property and thus no money without public sovereignty. Moreover, any social formations that challenge the absolute right of individual sovereignty over property are enemies of freedom, democracy, and justice. The sovereign state that supports market relations of contract claims the right to make war on other social formations insofar as they threaten property and contracts. The use of money also evokes an ethics, for money may only be spent, invested, or given. In regard to spending, money evokes the question, "What do I desire?" In regard to investment, money evokes the question, "How can I ensure ongoing growth and security?" In regard to giving, money evokes the question, "Where are my sympathies?" An ethics of pleasures, anxieties, and sympathies is evoked. The use of money even evokes a theology. The market rewards the prudent, the self-disciplined, the honest, and the keepers of contracts, whereas it punishes the foolish, the profligate, the idle, the dishonest, and the disloyal. The "invisible hand" of the market fosters the flourishing of virtue at the expense of vice.[14]

In the case of money, such an evocation of a metaphysics, a politics, an ethics, and a theology goes beyond the formation of a perspective reinforced by daily practice. These evoked potentials do not simply emerge as the religion of the capitalist, for insofar as money is created as debt and people, businesses, and governments are enslaved to an increasing spiral of debt — or are dependent on others who are so enslaved — then all are under an obligation to seek profits to repay debts. All are under an obligation to spend or acquire money and to view the world from the perspective of one who seeks to spend or acquire money. All political demands must be subordinated to the obligation to preserve the stability of a fragile financial system. The evoked potential is underwritten by the demand for money itself. It is this demand for money that is the true "invisible hand" of the market. It is this demand that is the manifestation of the political theology of money.

Emancipation from global servitude to the financial system can come only through some reorganization of the institution of money. It may indeed be essential that there is some form of political theology, some form of distribution of credit. It may not be essential that this is embodied in the form of money created as debt in the way that we have known it since the founding of the Bank of England. Nevertheless, it is not sufficient that one substitute alternative forms of money for the dominant form, for the dominant norm has indeed proved itself to be dominant by means of its own spiritual power.[15] What is required is not simply a new kind of money but an institution for the distribution of credit that evokes its own metaphysics, politics, ethics, and theology.

The Achilles heel of the current financial system lies in its own metaphysical failure, for the metaphysics evoked by the use of money fails to disclose the nature of money itself. Money does not say what it does or do what it says. The same thing is not for being and for thinking. Of course, it is not enough to declare the truth about money to be set free, for the spiritual power of truth may not be as strong as the spiritual power of money. Truth does not exist in a vacuum without a metaphysics that gives it determinate form. Metaphysics does not take on coherence and consistency without a form of life in which it may be embodied. Nevertheless, the critique of the institution of money may give some guidance as to the kind of institution that may embody a new and effective political theology.

The logic of money therefore inverts the normal relation between thought and existence. Money is apparently defined as a tool, an object of human control. At the same time it imposes a demand: the demand for money itself. Those who believe money can do anything for them are the ones who may be suspected of doing anything for money. Money evokes the spirit of capitalism, expressed in a metaphysics, politics, ethics, and theology. Yet although the spirit of capitalism reinforces and intensifies both the power of money and the demand for money, it does not by itself constitute the source of its power. Similarly, money operates through a constitutive illusion: money manifests itself, according to its own evoked metaphysics, as an instrument of exchange, unit of account, and store of value. It is because money is so lifeless, without power of its own, that its power is so great. Nevertheless, this dissimulation does not by itself constitute the sole source of its power. Lacking an alternative political theology, an alternative source of authority, the force of money continues to operate in the absence of belief.

Such a dissimulation does, however, place money in a somewhat paradoxical position. In regard to its own evoked metaphysics, money is not what it appears. The same thing is not for thinking and for being. In regard to credit, however, money is exactly what it appears—the same thing for thinking and for being—for money is itself the promise of money, and the promise of money counts as money itself. Nevertheless, it is important to distinguish between the promise of value and the power and authority of that promise. A promise bears no authority unless it is capable of evoking trust. There is a difference between relative purchasing power, the value that is promised, and absolute purchasing power, the power to make promises. A rise or fall in absolute purchasing power will, of course, be accompanied by a rise or fall in the value of that currency relative to others. Nevertheless, the two remain distinct. An ontological difference remains between money as an object of thought and credit that bears its own intrinsic power. Since the same thing is not for thinking and being, then the power of money lies in the mediation between thinking and being.

Wherein, therefore, lies the authority of money? Such authority can be distinguished into three dimensions. A first dimension is entirely exterior to the promise of money itself. The promise of money bears authority because value can indeed be realized through the use of money. The world is shaped through science, technology, and rational management. Yet it will only be effectively shaped in this way if money is invested. So not only is it necessary that science, technology, and rational management have a bearing on reality; it is also vital that money has a bearing on them. We should note the significance here of measuring sources of energy such as fossil fuels by means of the meter, measuring sources of labor by means of the clock, and measuring sources of value by means of bookkeeping. The meter, the clock, and the account book are three crucial inventions that mediate the promise of money in the modern world.

A second dimension of the power of money is internal to human behavior. Money, as we have seen, erodes the authority of other social formations. The promise of money introduces an interval between the acts of buying and selling, just as it introduces an interval into reciprocal obligations. Then the one possessed of money appears to enjoy a sovereign freedom of self-determination over how money may be spent. The time between receiving and spending money is a moment of absolute irresponsibility, a moment of reprieve from social obligations, a moment of forgiveness or absolution. The promise of money brings justification by faith. There is no necessary authority that determines how money is to be spent.

It is here that the second dimension of the power of money appears, for the moment of sovereign freedom is not without all determination. It is a finite interval: as soon as the money is spent, it is gone. Moreover, since the moment of absolution has eroded the force of prior social obligations, then the network of social interdependencies to which one returns when money is spent is somewhat weaker. Money exercises an entropic force on non-market systems of social capital. Hence, the moment of sovereign freedom is exposed to the threat of lack of provision once it is all over. The promise of wealth is accompanied by the threat of poverty. The second dimension of the power of money is therefore encountered in the form of internal drives: the drive for survival and the drive for power that extends the sovereign moment of freedom as far as possible. There is also a transfer of trust and dependencies from those mediated by other social formations to those mediated by the market. Hence, the drive for power may be manifested both as an individual desire for the prolongation of freedom and as a social force of marketization, extending market relations to all sectors of existence. Similarly, there is the social form of the drive for survival: the need to preserve market relations, including the stability of the currency. The individual correlate of this is the need to repay debt to maintain one's credit rating and one's place in the market.

The third dimension of the power of money belongs within the internal structure of money itself. The promise of money counts as money itself. The promise of money evokes credit. It is, of course, within the nature of a promise to evoke a certain tendency toward trust, especially if the contents of the promise can be portrayed vividly in the imagination. Yet the evocative power of money goes beyond other promises in that it bears its own authority. Such authority consists, first, in the way in which the promise of money counts as money, for although money is a promise of value, of satisfied demands, the promise of money does not merely repeat the promise at one stage removed. It actually advances the sum promised but advances it in the form of money. So while money promises to satisfy demands, the actual demand it satisfies first of all is the demand for money itself. In imagination, money can promise all things; in reality, money delivers itself. Hence, on the one hand, it appears as though the authority of money is grounded in either the endogenous demand for money of the market or the exogenous demand for money in the form of taxation required by the state. On the other hand, there is an intrinsic demand for money belonging to money itself. Money may be advanced as an asset in the form of credit, a promise of value, as long as that advance is matched by a liability in the form of a debt, a promise of money. It is notable that while credit, the promise of money, may easily circulate as a means of exchange, debt, the liability to pay money, does not circulate in such a way.

Money also consists in a perspective, a determinate act of accounting. A second intrinsic dimension to the authority of money lies in the authority of such a perspective. In accounting, an equivalence can be established between an asset and a sum of money. An asset is a promise of money; money is the promise of an asset. Yet money is not merely the unit of account but also the means of payment. To possess or realize the value of an asset, it is necessary first to possess money. So from the synchronic perspective of exchange value, the asset and the money are equivalent; from the diachronic perspective of acts of contracting and trade, money takes priority. In absolute terms, money is the universal means for the realization of all other values. So while in relative terms, the demand for the asset and the demand for money are equivalent, in absolute terms, the demand for money is always more urgent. Moreover, the device of accounting regards all things in terms of their exchange value, substituting money in advance as if an exchange has already taken place. To make money, it is necessary to balance the books and so regard all things as the promise of money. If money promises all things, it is only because all things promise money. The demand for money imposes an evaluating perspective on the world.

The authority of money also rests ultimately within the intrinsic nature of its authority as a contract. There are endogenous reasons for demanding money to pay debts: it is necessary to balance the books and maintain a credit rating. There are also exogenous reasons, embodied in the power to enforce contracts. Yet such agreement on the authority of money is facilitated because money bears its own authority. Contracts are enforced by culture and state because contracts are deemed to be valuable. If all contracts are measured in terms of money, then money is the conceptual and evaluative basis of all other contracts. It is essential to preserve the value and power of money to preserve all other contracts. Moreover, money measures a value that has been agreed by market forces. Since money is involved in all transactions, the pricing of money should be the most secure of all prices. Money therefore introduces an evaluative perspective that treats money itself as the most secure and valuable standard of comparison. Money is the supreme object of credit at the same time that it is the vehicle for the transmission of credit. The authority of money ultimately consists in the conjunction between metaphysics, wealth, and power. As credit, money is what it says and says what it is—it is the foundation for a perspective. As credit, money values money as the supreme value. As credit, money possesses the authority of an evaluative perspective that effectively realizes its aims. Money replaces God as the metaphysical source of truth, value, and power.

THEOLOGY AND CREDIT

Money is therefore inherently theological because it is a source of the value of values. Money is the source of prosperity and freedom. Money has its own implicit theology: it is the promise of value on which actual value may be advanced; it is the supreme value against which all other values may be measured; it is a speculative value whose intrinsic worth awaits demonstration; and it is a social obligation demanding that social interaction be ordered in accordance with profit and the repayment of debt.

The purpose of this study has been to assess whether money is a successful candidate for such a source of evaluation. It has been discovered that the theology of money expresses an extraordinary ambivalence. Money has been assessed against a wider field of interactions in which it participates. In relation to ecological criteria, a concept of capital has been formulated as the means of production that has itself been produced. The value promised by money opens up possibilities for new capital investment, leading to the transformation of modes of production as well as of the ecology of the planet. Money does indeed lead to the generation of wealth. Yet the cycle of investment is completed by trade—money is substituted for products, resources, and capital. Once debt, interest, and profit determine the flows of money, then it is only money itself that is counted rather than products, capital assets, or resources. Money promises the world but delivers only itself. Indeed, the very survival of ecological relations of production is sacrificed to the accumulation of money.

In relation to political criteria, money promises freedom. Those who possess wealth may be empowered to do as they please; they are emancipated from the constraints of natural necessities and social dependencies. Indeed, the promise of such empowerment may enable the provision of all kinds of services in exchange, for whoever spends money in the service of his or her freedom requires others who are willing to work and serve for money. For each empowerment there is also a corresponding servitude, whether of workers, of animals, or of productive resources. Moreover, wealth, as we have seen, has an intimate relation with democracy. Those who possess wealth are liberated from the constraints of necessity to be able to express personal opinions and preferences. At the same time, however, democracy rests in service to the creation of wealth, for once there is no common vision of the good around which society is to be structured, the common will concurs on the commonwealth itself. There is no higher political priority than the provision of economic and monetary stability for the purpose of creating wealth. Indeed, the political will of the masses must be subordinated to the demands of a fragile monetary system. Money promises freedom and democracy but delivers only itself. Indeed, political freedom is sacrificed to the accumulation of money.

In relation to theology, money must be assessed against criteria of spiritual wealth. Money possesses an extraordinary power of realization. Where

God is thought to create and maintain the world through his divine power, people are able to adapt and transform the world through money. Where God requires submission of the soul to his will, money submits itself to the will of the soul. Where God may serve as a basis for common consent and action only for those who truly believe, money may serve as a basis for common consent and action for those who share no belief apart from the efficacy of money. As the means of access to all other goals produced by collective action, money posits itself as the supreme value. It therefore evacuates all other values of significance and effectiveness. The opposition between the religion of money and traditional religions is not necessarily a direct opposition within the sphere of meaning. Religious devotion is widely regarded as being compatible with the creation of financial wealth. What money discloses, however, is the power of credit itself. If traditional religions have found themselves impotent in the face of money, whether they endorse it or condemn it, this is because money has a superior power of attracting credit. Money surpasses other religions through the power of effectiveness itself.

As a consequence, therefore, the implicit theology present in the religion of money cannot simply be judged and condemned in the name of true spiritual wealth. Money calls prior understandings of such wealth into question, for there is a theological model of power implicit in such understandings of wealth: it is assumed that an understanding of spiritual wealth can simply be actualized by the sovereign decrees of the divine being or by the sovereign decrees of human subjects devoted to such a vision of spiritual wealth. Yet the effectiveness of money has surpassed such sovereign power without claiming any power for itself. Similarly, the power of money cannot simply be curbed by state legislation, for money is the source of the prosperity and power of any state. The modern state could not exist without money. The sovereignty of the state, like the sovereignty of the democratic subject, is an illusion borne of selectivity in representation. It is necessary to respond to prevailing conditions, including conditions for the maintenance and enhancement of credit. Likewise, it is insufficient to denounce the illusions of global capitalism in the name of values grounded in life, health, and sustainability, for the very conditions of life are no longer grounded in resources alone. Material capital must be supplemented by physical energy, human capital, and social capital. Credit is an irreducible power present in production, in politics, and even in religion.

The significance of the theology of money, therefore, goes far beyond that of assessing the underlying infrastructure of global capitalism. Traditional theology, politics, and common sense have clashed with global capitalism and been found wanting in effective power. Nevertheless, one should not capitulate before the predatory, destructive, and nihilistic force of unfettered global capital. By contrast, it will be necessary to draw on the theology of money to revise and deepen our understanding of theology, of politics, and even of reason itself, for in somewhat diverse ways, modern theology, politics, and reason have been dependent on a notion of power that is now called into question by the theology of money. According to a dominant theological conception of power, power resides in the realm of ideas. Such ideas are actualized by an act of sovereign will. To shape reality appropriately, therefore, humans are understood by analogy with this model of the divine creator. It is essential to formulate the correct ideas before attempting to actualize them. All ongoing processes may be critically assessed in relation to ideas thought to be true. Power results from the apparent mastery that the subject holds over ideas represented in the mind. Yet the power of money is not of this nature. For any idea to be actualized in a determinate process, it is not sufficient that it be submitted to sovereign decree. Instead, the cooperation of a diverse range of material and social processes must be invoked, including supplies of physical energy and credit. The appearance of mastery within the mind results from selectivity, from the direction of attention to certain representations. In reality, far from this adding to the power of the mind and granting it sovereignty, selectivity is merely an expression of the mind's impotence. The source for a broader conception of the mind's power does not come from inside the mind itself but from the very basis that makes cooperation possible. Money, as a political body, possesses this spiritual power in the form of credit. It will be necessary to determine the nature of such spiritual power.

The ambivalence of the theology of money comes down to this: on the one hand, money expresses an extraordinary power of effectiveness; on the other hand, money institutes an autonomous financial system of debt and credit that effectively drives economic behavior without leaving any scope for real evaluations. The system of profits and debts seems independent of any evaluations about how one may wish the world to be. Accounting is a moral practice that lacks all moral compass. Economics is divorced from theology. As a result, the generation of profits is accompanied by the generation of debts; the creation of new productive capital is accompanied by the consumption and destruction of existing resources. Social cooperation is established through money at the expense of existing structures of social dependence, provision, and care.

In constructing the collective framework of trust in which economic activity can take place, religion makes an indispensable contribution to the production of capital in the rare and specific form of credit. It is the nature and function of money that discloses this social role at the same time that money itself comes to occupy it. There is no need to oppose the projected world of religion and metaphysics to the immanent world of material particularity. The object and source of credit, in the form of time, attention, and devotion, belongs to this world just as much as money does. Indeed, in a strange way, money is not only in opposition to God; it also discloses the significance and role of a source of the value of values. Perhaps one may reach a more complete understanding of what theology is and can be after considering a theology of money.

A revolution is required in the fields of religion, politics, and reason or metaphysics. The essence of the divine, of the political, and of being needs to be rethought apart from the categories of objectivity, in terms of an exchangeable product, as well as apart from the categories of subjectivity, in terms of freedom or desire. While it would be vain to imagine that a true and perfect ontology can ever be attained in human thought, it is possible to begin to build a more adequate ontology from the oversights embodied within the theology of money. Being has ecological dimensions: the essence of a thing is conditioned by a set of exterior relations. Being also has temporal dimensions: the essence of a thing is determined by its transformation and orientation during the course of time. In addition, being has a spiritual dimension: the essence of a thing is dependent on the degree of credit that is invested within it and that it, in turn, may invest elsewhere. Similarly, a political will is only as significant as the powers that cooperate with it. Its nature is determined by its orientation in time. The will to continue in existence, to accumulate power, or to pay back debt are fundamentally different orientations in time. Moreover, political wills are not autonomous, but they are effectively called into being by the conditions that make them possible. The desire for God is given by revelation; the desire for truth is given by science; and the desire for money is given by the possibility of trade, investment, or speculation.

It is precisely such dimensions that are obscured by the institution of money. Money calls into being an objectivist epistemology as well as an unfettered desire for freedom. As the universal representation of value, money substitutes itself for real relations of dependence and production, replacing existing ecological relations with purely economic ones mediated by money. As the objectification of contract, money naturalizes the sovereign power to treat one's property as one pleases, neglecting external relations and dependencies. As the unit of accounting, money counts only those values that have an agreed market price, neglecting to measure the surplus of credit that attaches to economic opportunities.

The metaphysics of money, constructed from exchange value, contract, and accounting, may be replaced by a metaphysics of credit. Credit gives a better account not only of the nature of money, but also of the nature of being, of politics, and of religion, for credit is always invested. It only has exterior relations. Moreover, credit is invested not in what something is, but in what it may become. Credit is a temporal orientation. Furthermore, credit does not have its power within itself; credit granted is only as valuable as the credit that is invested in the source of credit.

It will be necessary to separate money as the instrument of contracts from credit as the bearer of evaluation, for money may only be spent, invested, or given away. Each of these uses is in competition with the others. Money evokes an ethics grounded in rivalry between desires, anxieties, and sympathies. As such, the institution of money breeds individualism. An effective evaluation is displaced by the more emotive consideration of pleasures, security, and demands. With credit as a bearer of evaluation, by contrast, the subject is placed in an entirely different position. What is worthy of investment that is, at present, undervalued? What has the potential to emerge as a powerful source of value? How can I advance my reputation and influence as a judicious, responsible, and careful investor? The question of the value of values comes to take priority over immediate self-interest.

Such a distribution of credit may function as a fusion of the economic and the political. True political power is not an object to be accumulated or possessed, like money, but a spiritual culture or environment in which one may dwell. Where the freedom purchased by money is always relative, since one person's power to demand is always another person's need to serve, true political authority is a measure of cooperation. Such cooperation may function in independence of consensus or agreement.

It is beyond the scope of this study to construct an entirely new epistemology, metaphysics, or politics based on credit. I have merely indicated that these are necessary. It is possible, however, to bring to mind the commitments of time, attention, and devotion required by determinate practices involving credit. The questions "What is money?" and "What is credit?" remain premature, since the problems of metaphysics are as yet unresolved. The theological questions are much simpler. What is the price of credit? What must be given to foster a culture of credit that will evoke a new metaphysics, politics, and ethics? Answering these questions is the task for the future.

Seven

THE PRICE OF CREDIT

ST. FRANCIS OF PAOLA, who attempted to restore the Franciscan order to its life of voluntary poverty, was once offered a bag of gold by King Ferdinand I for his traveling expenses in Naples. He refused, claiming it was the price of the blood of the king's subjects. To demonstrate his point, he broke one of the gold pieces in half. Several drops of blood fell from the broken coin.[1]

The association between money and blood derives from the Gospel of Matthew. The chief priests refused Judas Iscariot's return offering of the thirty pieces of silver, the price of Christ's betrayal, thrown down in the temple. The coins were too impure to be placed in the treasury and were used instead to purchase a burial ground for foreigners. John Ruskin was later to reflect: "We do great injustice to Iscariot, in thinking him wicked above all common wickedness. He was only a common money-lover, and, like all money-lovers, did not understand Christ; — could not make out the worth of Him or the meaning of Him. He never thought He would be killed. He was horror-struck when he found that Christ would be killed; threw his money away instantly, and hanged himself. How many of our present money-seekers, think you, would have the grace to hang themselves, whoever was killed?"[2]

THE MERCHANT OF VENICE

Bassanio has run up numerous debts through living beyond his means. He conceives a speculative venture to clear his debts: to marry the fair and wealthy heiress Portia. Yet he needs to borrow even more to give himself the appearance of wealth to be in a position to press his suit. He turns to his chief creditor, Antonio, for a further loan that, if his suit is successful, may lead to the repayment of all his debts. Because Bassanio is obligated by debt, one suspects that nothing is sincere about his love, whether for Portia or Antonio. Surprisingly, Antonio places his purse, person, and "extremest means" at Bassanio's service. Is this Antonio's only hope to recover his money? Does he have faith in Bassanio's plan?

Antonio's means are temporarily tied up in seafaring ventures. Yet he, unlike Bassanio, has good credit. He will stand surety for a loan from some other source. Shylock will lend the money, but only at interest. Yet Shylock hates Antonio for regularly lending money without interest, bringing down the rate of interest in Venice. Antonio, in turn, despises Shylock for his practice of usury. Given this dispute over usury, the bond agreed is one between enemies: the forfeit of a pound of flesh, to be taken from the heart. Bassanio hesitates, but Antonio willingly agrees. Does he wish to teach his friend the price of love?

Shylock's ducats are derived from usury. For Antonio, they already contain the price of blood. Yet whenever money is lent on credit, there is always a Bassanio, an Antonio, and a Shylock.[3] There is always one who appropriates an asset to be spent, one who is liable for the return of the loan, and one who provides the loan from reserves. Whenever money is created as debt, there is one who spends, one who is obligated, and one to whom an obligation is due. Antonio indulges Bassanio in a speculative venture, an affair of the heart. What friend or parent would begrudge the same? Yet if Bassanio's money embodies desire and liberty, Antonio's bond is also an affair of the heart — a pound of its flesh. Antonio himself is mortgaged, pledged to death. Shylock, in turn, may have confidence in his enemy because of this power he exercises over his flesh. If Antonio refuses Shylock's friendship, cooperation can still be ensured by means of their bond. Bassanio will spend that very bond of Antonio's heart. It is the same the world over. Whenever money is created as debt, such money is the pledge of someone's life and liberty. If credit money is frozen desire and coined liberty, it is also contracted servitude. Who, then, is the cruelest: Shylock, in demanding justice from an enemy, or Bassanio, in so using the loyalty of a friend in an amorous adventure?

Portia's hand and love are to be won by the artifice of selecting one of three chests that contains her likeness. Each is inscribed with a motto expressing a principle of selection or a motive for love. On the gold chest is inscribed, "Who chooseth me, shall gain what many men desire." If gold symbolizes money, the inscription expresses the principle of mimesis by which money retains its value—money is valued because others also value it and accept it in exchange. This is a poor principle to serve as a basis for love. If one merely desires what others desire, one's love is likely to be fickle. On the silver chest is inscribed, "Who chooseth me, shall get as much as he deserves." If silver symbolizes money, the inscription expresses the value of justice by which money retains its value—money holds value if a fair price is given in exchange. This is once more a poor principle to serve as a basis for love. Why desire that which has equivalent worth to what one already has? On the lead chest, chosen not by any rich suitor but only by the indebted Bassanio, is inscribed, "Who chooseth me, must give and hazard all he has." Such is the risk to be undertaken in marriage; such is the risk undertaken by Portia herself. Such, also, is the nature of the bond Antonio undertakes for Bassanio. Such is the nature of money created on credit. Nevertheless, an important distinction can be made here. It is one thing to risk one's death, like Antonio, in a heroic gesture of self-sacrifice made in a rash instant of decision. It is another to give one's life to someone in an ongoing act of commitment that is renewed daily. Perhaps here lies the greater hazard: to risk one's life, as do Bassanio and Portia, rather than to risk one's death. Perhaps Bassanio's speculative venture is a more serious matter than Antonio's brush with death.

Hobbes's analogy of money as the blood of the body politic was perhaps more apt than he knew.[4] The circulation of such a currency in flesh and blood—whether as love or money—is expressed no more poignantly than in Bassanio's insight into the true significance of the letter announcing the wreck of all of Antonio's ships:

> Here is a letter, lady,
> The paper as the body of my friend,
> And every word in it a gaping wound,
> Issuing lifeblood.[5]

Once the "veil of money" is removed, there stands not mere imitation or barter exchange or private property but a sacrament of flesh and blood. Credit, contract, law, sacrifice, and love are theological matters. Each note of paper money, each electronic bank record, distributes the sacrificial power of the pledged flesh and blood on which it is written.

So to the dénouement. The loan not repaid, Shylock demands his pound of flesh. The duke is powerless to overrule the bond. To do so would set a precedent that would undermine all future contracts in the city and so undermines its entire wealth. Sovereign power becomes dependent on credit. The duke, like Antonio, can only appeal to the merits of mercy. Shylock refuses offers from the quickly wed and newly rich Bassanio of twice or thrice the original sum. It is no longer a matter of money; it is a personal affair of the heart. It has been said that Shylock acts irrationally, rejecting the modern calculus of utility.[6] It has been said that Shylock belongs within the ancient social structure of gift and vendetta rather than the modern social structure of money and exchange.[7] Yet perhaps Shylock is more modern than he appears, for he chooses to demonstrate the superior power of impersonal contract over the personal relation of mercy. Despised and excluded from the bonds of friendship (Antonio has refused amicable terms prior to the agreement of the bond, whether from motives of objections to usury, anti-Judaism, or anti-Semitism), Shylock has to appeal to the one power — that of contract and justice — that preserves his place in society. As a despised Jew and usurer, he cannot place his faith in mercy. He, like the duke, is bound. Only public justice based on written law can protect him, so he chooses to place his faith in enactment of the letter of the law.

Portia, disguised as a doctor of the law, proclaims the theological merits of Christian mercy over against Jewish justice. In the course of justice, no one would see salvation, so Christians pray for mercy. Portia proceeds to demonstrate this point by appealing to the letter of the law herself: in cutting a pound of flesh from Antonio's heart, Shylock is to take no more or less or to spill any drop of blood. Moreover, in seeking his pound of flesh, Shylock is found guilty of seeking the life of a citizen. Framed for seeking justice, Shylock is then treated to a display of Christian mercy and forced to convert. In triumphalist Christian supersessionism, the law is upheld at the same time that the bond is abrogated. The Christian polity is defended against the threat of Jewish usury, as well as against the threat of modernity. Forgiveness is proclaimed as the supreme virtue of theological sovereignty:

'Tis mightiest in the mightiest, it becomes
The thronèd monarch better than his crown.
His sceptre shows the force of temporal power,
The attribute to awe and majesty,
Wherein doth sit the dread and fear of kings;
But mercy is above this sceptred sway,
It is enthroned in the hearts of kings,
It is an attribute to God himself,
And earthly power doth then show likest God's
When mercy seasons justice.[8]

Mercy is what the duke longs for yet cannot achieve, for mercy dissolves the credibility of sovereignty. It is not simply the duke's own credibility that is at stake; it is the credibility of sovereignty as such, the credit of the political body, the principle on which all contract is based. If Portia praises the divinity of mercy, such mercy is the prerogative of an absolute sovereign whose credibility knows no bounds. When mercy is enthroned in the heart of sovereignty, the scepter of sovereign power holds unbounded sway.

The figure who may be contrasted most sharply with Shylock, therefore, is not the duke or Portia or Antonio, for each insists on the letter of the law. Portia's mercy toward her new husband, Bassanio, in forgiving him the gift of their wedding ring to the doctor of the law, is matched equally with her cruelty in demanding from Bassanio, when disguised as the doctor of the law, the wedding ring that she has forced him to promise never to give away. One figure external to the play itself who contrasts sharply with Shylock is holy Judas Iscariot, who willingly gives up what is his by right—his money and his life. It is Iscariot who renounces the power of contract. It is Iscariot who sacrifices all credibility, along with his money and life, in a futile and uneconomic gesture that achieves nothing. It is Iscariot who knows the true meaning of mercy. He sacrifices all for some vague sense of honor and justice. What Iscariot finds intolerable is the condition of moral debt. He would rather die than live on in shame. Yet in the sacrifice of sovereign power, of credibility, of money, and of life, may one catch a glimpse of a different power of credit?

From the play, it is Bassanio who ventures all that he has. It is Bassanio whose debts solicit the care of his creditor, Antonio. It is Bassanio who instigates the forming of bonds. It is Bassanio who, lacking credit in himself, inspires credit in others. It is Bassanio who offers multiples of the sum of the original bond to save Antonio. It is Bassanio who betrays the bond of his promise never to part with Portia's ring. Might it not be Bassanio who understands the truly divine power of mercy? Might mercy not be manifest in the taking on of debt?

THE BANK OF ENGLAND

The problem of the creation of capitalist credit money is that of how private contracts of credit and debt may come to circulate freely, apart from their authors, as public money. It is, of course, essential that oral contracts, as agreed before a notary and witnesses, be replaced by written contracts containing all the agreed details. Alternatively, circulation can occur at the same place that the contract is agreed by means of a transfer between bank accounts. The merchant's bill of exchange was designed to fulfill such requirements. The bank note achieves the same aim. The problem, then, is how one can guarantee that a bank has sufficient reserves to meet all such liabilities. Money is worth only as much as the bank that guarantees its value. As the early economist Charles Davenant explained in 1682:

> Of all beings that have existence in the minds of men, nothing is more fantastical and nice than Credit; it is never to be forced; it hangs upon opinion, it depends upon our passions of hope and fear; it comes many times unsought for, and often goes away without reason, and when once lost, is hardly to be quite recovered. . . . [And] no trading nation ever did subsist and carry on its business by real stock; . . . trust and confidence in each other are as necessary to link and hold people together as obedience, love, friendship, or the intercourse of speech.[9]

The network of private credit is always a fragile business. Most early attempts to issue banknotes ended in failure. A loss of confidence can lead to a run on the bank; default on a loan may lead to other defaults farther down the chain. Moreover, since credit is always an anticipation of wealth, there is never enough wealth present to repay all loans in a network of private credit. Anyone, however prudent or prosperous, may be caught with cash-flow problems in a network of private credit. In England in the 1580s, litigations for default on contracts are believed to have numbered in excess of one million per year — one for each family in the country.[10] The remains of the feudal network of personal loyalties and obligations must have collapsed in the rancor of default and litigation. Such dissolution of the social order paved the way for the revolutions of the following century and the eventual advent of capitalism and globalization.

Given the interdependence of credit, its circulation depends ultimately on the presence of a reliable debtor of last resort. Such is the manifestation of a rather different kind of sovereignty: it is the power of an Antonio rather than the power of a duke. If the Bank of England took the role of lender of last resort, this was possible only because the newly emerging nation-state took on the role of debtor.[11] The English monarch seemed especially ill-suited to such a role. Deriving income from essentially private obligations, patronage, and demesne revenues, the monarch was also charged with the expensive public business of waging war. The interests of Parliament, given the authority to raise extraordinary taxes for war, were not always consonant with those of the monarchy. Indeed, the history of the seventeenth century was a story of the opposition and compromise of the king and Parliament. When Charles II threatened an unpopular war against the Protestant Dutch in 1672, insufficient financial support from Parliament led to the Stop on the Exchequer and default on existing loans. This was sufficient to deter potential lenders, so weakening the monarchy and culminating in the Glorious Revolution of 1688, in which Parliament effectively seized power once more and deposed James II. The newly appointed sovereign, William of Orange, was deliberately awarded insufficient revenue by Parliament so that his debt would become public and national and his actions would be kept under Parliament's control.

More than a hundred schemes were proposed to manage public finances in the seventeenth century. The scheme adopted was the Bank of England.[12] A permanent loan of 1.2 million pounds was raised by public subscription, with the promise of a return in interest of 8 percent per annum. In return, this private bank was given a monopoly on bills of exchange that formerly had been heavily regulated and taxed. Since the reserves of the bank were guaranteed by future taxation, the bank itself became the lender of last resort. The most sought-after promise to pay was that of the state to its creditors. The Bank held good credit because its income stream could be derived from taxation.[13] The threat of default was over.[14] The terms of the settlement were regulated by Parliament. While the state was financially indebted to its creditors, the creditors were politically indebted to the state: they had a vested interest in its health and continuation.[15] England was able to establish its military and trading predominance, in competition principally with France, by means of the financial revolution.[16] The state could enforce the payment of taxes; the Bank's creditors were given a secure income stream; and merchants could increase trade by means of reliable bills of exchange. While the institutional nexus was a four-way social relation, consisting of taxpayers, state, rentiers and merchants,[17] it was overseen by Parliament, which represented the interests of the landowning and merchant classes. If the national debt became public at the same time as the nation-state and paper currency, this is because the "public" consisted of the trading classes and their concern for mutual class interest. It was their self-regulation that constituted their sovereignty.

The move toward trustworthiness and self-regulation as public and communal virtues, rather than private commitments in which one distinguishes between friend and stranger, were cultural innovations. No doubt they were aided by the individualist Puritan ethic in which personal conduct became the site of self-examination in place of personal relations, bonds, and obligations. No doubt such a culture was fostered by public representation through drama, ballads, and poetry:[18] The Merchant of Venice itself, in which the show of commitment, loyalty, and honor is converted into the actuality of commitment, loyalty, and honor, may have been both agent and signal of such a cultural shift. The play turns the Christian virtues of mercy, self-sacrifice, and fidelity into public virtues. No doubt, the increasing use of practices of bookkeeping also fostered a public culture of self-regulation and probity.

It is therefore a matter of little surprise that contemporary Bank of England notes may contain, on the reverse side to the head of the monarch, the head of William Shakespeare; or Isaac Newton, master of the Royal Mint for twenty-six years; or Adam Smith; or Charles Darwin, whose theory of natural selection was heavily influenced by Thomas Malthus and the character of economic life in eighteenth-century and nineteenth-century Britain. Such notes represent a fusion of sovereignty with the economic power of credit. The bearer of such a note may command sovereign power over those who are willing to serve the bearer's needs. People become willing servants in return for a brief chance to exercise such power. Credit may be the supreme sovereign power, but it can be exercised only insofar as it circulates. Money is the blood of the body politic.

Nevertheless, there is one respect in which the Glorious Revolution remains incomplete: distributed sovereignty is partial. The fragility of the relations of credit, even when secured by a central bank in a prosperous economy, admits little mercy. Credit is inherently a public, not a private, matter. One person's default may lead to a collapse of the entire system. With the public interest to be upheld, the sovereign power of mercy is held by no one. The regulators of the economic system have to act as the duke, awarding a pound of flesh to any Shylock who rightfully demands it. Sovereignty is bound in chains. Economics becomes divorced from ethics in the very act of considering the commonwealth. The divorce between politics and theology, typified by Martin Luther's distinction between the two kingdoms and John Locke's distinction between the public commonwealth and the private and voluntary worship of God,[19] is a necessary effect of the sovereignty of public credit. Ultimately, we all become Shylock, demanding our pound of flesh.

SOVEREIGNTY

The significance of the Glorious Revolution and its subsequent dispersal of sovereignty via the Bank of England can be grasped only when the nature of such sovereignty itself is clarified. Medieval sovereignty emerged not from social contract but from war. War can be considered in physical terms of force and violence; war can also be considered in legal terms as the declaration of a suspension of peace due to the presence of a named and identified enemy. Yet war can also be considered in theological terms: for what cause is it worth pledging one's own flesh and blood? One fights and dies for "king and country." This pledge of ultimate commitment to a cause that exceeds life and death in significance may be considered the defining gesture of the religious.[20] Here one stands on ground that is beyond the merely moral. In the act of self-sacrifice, one gives more than one receives. All equity, reciprocity, or justice is excluded. We can, in this way, understand sovereignty as an essentially theological concept. Where fundamental political divisions derive from the real possibility of actually killing,[21] fundamental theological commitments are expressed in the real possibility of actually dying.

The sovereign, of course, is charged with executing law and justice. Conflict may be mediated by moderation and measurement, in the exercise of justice, to establish the possibility of cooperation. The sovereign's word is law not merely because it is enforced by the threat of violence,[22] or because the sovereign may risk his life in the prosecution of war for the sake of the people, but because the soldiers and servants of the monarch are willing to risk their lives to preserve and enhance the authority of the monarchy. Such authority consists in the flesh and blood that may be given for it. The energy of the political is a sacred—indeed, sacrificial—energy.

It is therefore important to regard sovereignty as an institutional form that resolves a range of fundamental problems. There is the theological problem: what is worth the pledging of one's flesh and blood? There is the political problem: how is conflict—the real possibility of violence that is made all the more dangerous by the pledging of flesh and blood—to be mediated to become cooperation? How may potential opponents be incorporated into the same body? There is also an economic problem: how is wealth, the benefits accrued through cooperation achieved through the pledging of flesh and blood, to be distributed? What is worthy of credit and investment, in other words: the pledging of time, attention, and devotion or the pledging of flesh and blood? Here the economic problem fuses with the theological problem. Life may be valued only through a pledge of life; all such pledges are ultimately a pledge to the death. If such questions are not addressed, then the whole of economic and political conflict, whether historical or contemporary, becomes incomprehensible. More fundamental than the division of labor or the conflict of class or ethnic interests is the conflict of religious commitments. Any attempt to comprehend human life in terms drawn purely from within the sphere of life, whether the rational calculus of ends or the raging of the passions, whether production and exchange or the conflict of interests, whether biological conditions or the development of cultures, is doomed to failure. For *homo religiosus* will sacrifice reason and passion, wealth and politics, nature and culture for the sake of what stands in place of the divine.

The question then emerges of what happens to sovereignty and political theology when it is dispersed and democratized.[23] The original subscribers to the Bank of England in 1694 were willing to risk a portion of their substance or wealth for the sake of a secure income. Since the investment was managed by the Bank, there was little real sacrifice of life and time. King

William III had to stake the credibility of the monarchy on its ability to claim and collect taxes. This, again, is hardly a matter of hazarding his flesh and blood. By contrast, it was the citizens who gave a portion of their working lives, their income, and their pleasures in the form of taxes. While the payment of taxes may not always be a matter of life and death, comparable to the commitment of military service, it remains a matter of flesh and blood insofar as the fruits of inheritance, trade, or labor are devoted to paying taxes.

The situation is little changed when we consider money created as debt. According to Georg Friedrich Knapp's state theory of the origins of money, the value of money is assured by the decree that money is acceptable for the payment of taxes.[24] In a similar way, the value of credit money is assured by the fact that it is acceptable for the payment of interest and the repayment of debt. The Bank of England succeeded in forming a hybrid of two separate means of payment: the coin of the realm, acceptable as payment for taxes and in use as a unit of account for the measure of prices, and the bill of exchange, acceptable for the payment of merchants' debts and so an instrument of credit.[25] The coin of the realm, like the bill of exchange, was merely a token of value, whether that value was reserved in the metallic content of the coin, the vault of a bank, or the promise of some future undertaking. Of course, the assets of a central bank have to be secured by a rate of interest, by the security of borrowers from the bank, and by its reserves.[26] Yet beneath such contractual claims to property, the value of the reserves is ultimately guaranteed by the sacrificial pledge by the state of the lives of its citizens. The value of the Bank of England note, guaranteed by future taxation, consisted in its power as a promise. On the one hand, its value was bought by the sacrifices of taxpayers. On the other hand, its value was bought by all those who borrowed from the Bank for their merchant ventures. The same duality is to be observed in Antonio's bond: on the one hand, the pound of his flesh; on the other hand, the security of his seafaring ventures, in which the flesh and blood of his sailors was staked against the risk of possible shipwreck. When one comes to consider who ultimately staked their flesh and blood to ensure the profitability of the ventures undertaken by the eighteenth-century English merchants who profited most from the new credit economy, one quickly comes to sailors, Irish navvies, and African slaves.

The credit economy is a network of contracted servitude. It may not always be the case that flesh and blood is sacrificed for sovereign, for nation, or for religion, although such sacrifices show few signs of abating. The contemporary call may be to sacrifice one's life for freedom, democracy, civilization, and development. Such values are often treated uncritically because they are regarded with a religious awe. While taxation remains a major dynamic force in the contemporary economy, contributing to profit in order to pay debts is accelerating in magnitude. Contracted servitude is the condition of all borrowers, whether householders, corporations, governments, or highly leveraged speculators. Whenever one spends money, one spends a portion of the substance, wealth, and life of those who have undertaken loans. Yet the value of money is also backed by profitability, including the drudge of labor in sweatshops and factories, the exclusion from the formal economy of those who are not employed profitably, the consumption of natural resources, and the erosion of ecosystems and societies. The value of money is still paid for in flesh and blood.

What, then, is flesh and blood sacrificed for in the global economy? It is hardly the case that one willingly gives one's life so that interest may accrue to the banks. Instead, one gives one's life to enjoy that sovereign moment of freedom, that moment when circulation stops, when one has money in one's pocket, one's bank account, or behind one's credit card. One gives one's life to others so that one may, in turn, hold that sacred, sovereign power in one's hand. It is a power that causes others to provide for one's needs and desires with goods and services. Money exercises the sovereign power of command. The one who offers money, whether as a consumer or as an employer, exercises sovereignty. Just as people, regardless of political opinions or personal preferences, used to serve the monarch out of religious obligation to the divine right of kings, one serves customers or employers not through any belief in their merits but because of the religious obligation to money. In the final analysis, it is only debt itself that exercises sovereign power. Yet those who undertake debts, who underwrite the value of money in their own flesh and blood, are those who exercise the divine power of credit.

Democracy, then, remains an illusion. While the sacred authority of money may pass through anyone's hands, its presence rarely lasts. It is contract and debt that endure. Time, attention, and devotion are committed to fulfilling contracts, keeping accounts, and maintaining the value of money.

The physical expression of worship and devotion has mutated from the offering, through the tithe and the tax, to the interest payment. One offers one's life and death for the sake of money—whether the chance to one day possess it or to guarantee its continued authority. The modern age is by no means impious. It has a political theology of money.[27]

POSING THE PROBLEM

The current global economic system is based on concepts of property, liberty, and money. Economic activity, moral and legal evaluation, and credit and aspiration are founded on these concepts. Such concepts are abstractions, cut off from ecological networks of capital, political forces of obligation, and religious networks of credit. Each functions as a support in the composition of the others. Taken together, they obscure and obstruct the effective distribution of nutrition, attention, and devotion.

The founding principles of economic life can no longer be considered to be the preservation of property and the enforcement of contract. More significant than these is the underlying principle from which property and contract derive. The founding principle of economic life is the maintenance, accumulation, invention, and construction of capital. Capital is conceived here apart from property, liberty, and money as the means of production that has itself been produced. It includes physical capital, human capital, social capital, and dynamic capital.

The founding principle of political life can no longer be considered to be liberty. More significant than this is the underlying principle from which liberty derives. It matters above all else that evaluations are truly valuable and actually effective. Desire is conceived here apart from property, liberty, and money as the expression of an evaluation that must itself be evaluated.

The founding principles of spiritual life can no longer be considered to be the accumulation of profits or the repayment of debts. More significant than these is the underlying principle from which profit and debt arise. The founding principle of spiritual life is the investment of credit in that which deserves credit. Credit is conceived here apart from property, liberty, and money as the investment of nutrition, attention, and devotion that itself demands nutrition, attention, and devotion.

It is such investment that has not been effectively accounted in modernity. It is such investment that is an object of theology. At the end of modernity one confronts a peculiar paradox, for the dream of a secular order based on property, liberty, and money is merely an abstraction. In abstract representation, one accounts all as wholly positive because one counts only the money or ideas that may be substituted for produced realities. One does not count the conditions of production. One does not count the investment of nutrition, attention, and devotion. One does not count the flesh and blood that is given to make credit, cooperation, and production possible. Thus, the cost of such a bloodless ideal is paid for immeasurably in uncounted flesh and blood. The dream of liberty ends in tyranny. Furthermore, little is achieved by denouncing the abstractions of the formal economy in the name of values grounded in subsistence, sustainability, and life, because such values remain abstractions that demand the total commitment of flesh and blood. Life itself inescapably involves sacrifice, cruelty, exploitation, incorporation, and consumption. It is not necessary to agree with Nietzsche that all life is will to power. "Power" is always a relative and composite notion, a product, and a later quantification. It is never a primitive or essential concept.[28] It is, however, possible to agree with the Buddha that all life is suffering while making the opposite, Nietzschean judgment:

You want if possible—and there is no madder "if possible"—to abolish suffering; and we?—it really does seem that we would rather increase it and make it worse than it has ever been! Wellbeing as you understand it—that is no goal, that seems to us an end!... The discipline of suffering, of great suffering—do you not know that it is this discipline alone which has created every elevation of mankind hitherto? That tension of the soul in misfortune which cultivates its strength, its terror at the sight of great destruction, its inventiveness and bravery in undergoing, enduring, interpreting, exploiting misfortune, and whatever of depth, mystery, mask, spirit, cunning and greatness has been bestowed upon it—has it not been bestowed upon it through suffering, through the discipline of great suffering?[29]

The fundamental theological problem we face at the end of modernity is neither that of abolishing suffering nor that of increasing and profiting from it. To ask who will suffer for us so that we do not have to is the implicit theology of the pursuit of money. It is to seek to end the meaning of life, whether for those who suffer or for those who profit, for life itself is suffering, the distribution of nutrition, attention, and devotion. To refuse the responsibility of committing flesh and blood is to refuse the responsibility of living. The aim is not to make a judgment for or against life, for or against suffering, but to respond to it in such a way as to create true health and wealth. Such creation only occurs when life itself is committed. The fundamental theological problem is that of how one distributes time, attention, and devotion. To disavow devotion is to demand devotion from others in the form of the sacrifice of flesh and blood. To refuse theology is to practice a cruel and unreflective theology. The fundamental problem is this: what is worth the sacrifice of flesh and blood, of time, attention, and devotion?

All solutions to such a problem, whether nominally religious or political, become institutions for the facilitation of credit so that effective cooperation can be achieved. We have to ask: is money worth the sacrifice of flesh and blood? Are there better institutions for facilitating credit and cooperation that more effectively distribute health and wealth? True revolution occurs through institutional innovation. It is not a question of seizing existing powers, whether those of the state, of corporations, of banks, or of financial speculators. It is a matter of inventing a new kind of power embodied in a new institution that will interact with old institutions to endow them with a new form, function, and purpose. There is nothing necessary about the existing institution of capitalist credit money. There is nothing to prevent the invention of new forms of credit, contract, and exchange, for the current system, institutionalized effectively in the Bank of England and copied around the world, was constructed to resolve a set of theological, political, and economic problems. At the end of modernity, our problems have changed.

Any effective innovation must successfully resolve these fundamental problems:

1 Credit must be given to that which is worthy of credit. The divorce between evaluation and currency, between ethics and economics, must be overcome. The flow of money must be directed by effective evaluations; effective evaluations must not be directed by the flow of money.
2 The conflicting needs of sustainability and profit must be reconciled. The divorce between capital, understood as the means of production that has itself been produced, and profit, the reflux of credit to its focus of origination, must be overcome. An increase in profit must effectively symbolize an increase in wealth.

3   The divorce between the secular and the religious, between attending to
treasure on Earth and attending to treasure in heaven, must be overcome, for
the commonwealth will always be founded on the commitment of flesh and
blood. The problem of that for which one will give one's life as time, attention, and devotion is one that faces us all, believer and non-believer alike. It
is a matter of developing a system of accounting and recording that directs
attention to that which matters. Both material conditions of production and
spiritual conditions of credit must replace the sovereignty of the self-reflective
subject as the focus for reflection.

The new millennium requires the invention of a hundred schemes of
institutional innovation that resolve the competing forces of these fundamental problems. Such schemes may perhaps best be developed and enacted within indigenous communities, developing nations, international
religious organizations, and internationalist movements. Those closer to
the apex of power in dominant nations, corporations, financial institutions,
and universities may have less interest in finding alternatives to the current
system, for the urgency of experimenting with new kinds of credit is felt
most keenly by those whose lives are oppressed by debt.

Eight

A MODEST PROPOSAL

Evaluative Credit

PROPOSALS FOR ECONOMIC REFORM have to be evaluated against the following criteria:

1 Whether they do indeed achieve effective reform that changes the entire nature of the global economic system.
2 Whether they can achieve effective reform without severely disrupting normal economic processes that provide the necessities of life.
3 Whether they achieve a better outcome in terms of prosperity and health for all.
4 Whether they are designed in line with the true principles that shape economic life.

While there is much to be learned from existing proposals for radical reform, most seek either to repair the existing system or to transform money into the ideological object described by the classical economists. None is based on the understanding of ecology, politics, and the theology of money explored here. Much further creative work is necessary.

The invention of new institutions does not come naturally to a philosopher's mind; a mind that is more familiar with concepts and principles is somewhat stretched when it comes to considering institutions. The following suggestions should be regarded as highly tentative. The primary aim is to illustrate how one may begin to apply the theology of money to the invention of institutions. One cannot be confident that these suggestions will not ultimately turn out badly. Nevertheless, one has to admit that the influence of philosophers over political life has been immense, and even if such influence has often had deeply destructive consequences, it need not prevent us from perpetually striving for improvements. While it is possible to outline the concepts and principles through which new institutions may be invented, such concepts and principles need to be subjected to continual critique. It is therefore to be hoped that imaginative and critical engagement with the problems outlined in this study and with the following sketchy proposal may contribute to the invention of an alternative to the capitalist credit-money system.

The fundamental aim is to enable flows of credit and investment to be directed toward that which matters the most. The contemporary world does not lack institutions for making evaluations. The media, think tanks, civil society organizations, charities, religious organizations, pressure groups, political bodies, and universities all play such a role. The problem with such evaluations is not simply lack of consensus. After all, diverse needs could be met by a diversity of evaluations. The problem that hinders the directing of credit by evaluation is the lack of authority or social effectiveness attached to such evaluations. The democratic solution usually involves attempting to ground the authority of evaluations on reason. Yet since the objectivity of objective truth can never be definitively manifested within thought, and the value of values does not meet with universal respect, one has to make do with representation, argument, and persuasion. Social authority is simply grounded in consensus. Yet a consensus can be formed in accordance with a particular perspective more easily than it can be found in the flux of opinion. The process of forming a consensus is disrupted, however, by a range of extraneous forces. In the first place, inquiries find the answers only to the questions they explicitly pose. The formation of problems and inquiries is regulated by culture, tradition, and political interests. Dominant political norms affect the consensus that is produced. In the second place, internal rules of virtue, merit, and prestige emerge within any kind of evaluative inquiry. The goal of gaining respect within the eyes of one's peers may take over from attributing attention to that which matters. In intellectual life, the aims of innovation, taking up a stance, achieving recognition, or following acceptable fashion take precedence over considering carefully what matters most. In the third place, research tends to follow the flow of money; money does not tend to follow the flow of research. Evaluation becomes subordinate to profit rather than investment being subordinate to evaluation. In short, the democratic solution of appeal to a rational consensus has failed and will always do so, to a greater or lesser extent.[1]

Instead, evaluations should no longer be regarded as universal. Indeed, if evaluations are local, partial, and responsive, then they may address more effectively the most urgent and local needs. Consensus need only be achieved at the most local level. The division of labor must be complemented by the division of evaluation. Just as it is grossly inefficient to have the same worker perform a multitude of tasks requiring differing skills, knowledge, tools, facilities, and conditions, so is it grossly inefficient to expect the democratic subject to hold informed, balanced, and sensitive views on each issue. If such is indeed already much the case, then it is vital to detach social authority that renders evaluations effective from both consensus and debt money.

Evaluations, like commodities, are produced. Moreover, the production of evaluations is a delicate activity that requires knowledge, expertise, character, sensitivity, culture, and training. Furthermore, the production of evaluations is just as important in contributing to health and wealth as the production of goods and the provision of services. My proposal is this: *there needs to be a secondary tier of the economy concerned solely with the production and distribution of effective evaluations.* Demand has to be managed as carefully as production. In principle, such a secondary tier already exists in the institutions of civil society. In practice, such institutions fail to make their evaluations effective insofar as they are constrained by the flow of money. The secondary tier of evaluation therefore requires a new mode of intermediation apart from discourse and apart from money.

Institutional innovation is therefore required at a further level: one of evaluative intermediation. By analogy with banks and financial institutions that mediate the flow of money in the production of goods and services, it will be necessary to mediate the flow of credit to evaluative institutions to grant them social effectiveness. Just as commerce and development are difficult with insufficient money or credit in circulation, so too is the effectiveness of evaluations held back if those evaluations lack authority. In short, something like money is required to enable diverse and local evaluations to become effective. The new form of evaluative credit must synthesize the functions of currency, credit, and evaluation. I therefore propose that evaluative credits should circulate alongside money, goods, and services.

Just as the Bank of England was able to fuse the functions of currency and credit, doing so in such a way that currency became subordinate to credit, it will be necessary to construct a new fusion of credit and evaluation, doing so in such a way that credit is subordinated to evaluation. The following conditions need to be met:

1 Evaluations need to have a causal impact on the flow of money to orient and direct it. Some kind of institutional arrangement is required that directs credit to the objects of evaluation.

2 The capacity to make effective evaluations is an intrinsic good that all should desire. This capacity appears to be present already in the form of money. Some kind of demand for evaluative credits is needed that makes their use possible alongside money.

3 Evaluative credits need to flow in a way different from that of money. Monetary power is achieved through cycles of investment and reflux of profit, short-circuiting the work of evaluation. The opposite must occur with evaluative credits. Rate of return should be replaced by care in investment as the criterion that determines evaluative power.

Evaluative credits, unlike money, are not inherently transferable. Each act of social evaluation may be regarded as a contract between four parties:

1 the one who makes the evaluation;

2 the one who receives the evaluation and carries out the investment in a means of production that is deemed to be worthwhile;

3 the institution that offers expertise in the making of an evaluation, termed an "evaluative institution"; and

4 the institution that attributes social effectiveness to such evaluations, termed a "bank of evaluative credit."

This is the inherent structure of the distribution of credit. Credit is neither an instantaneous exchange nor a permanent obligation. It is an act of investment that endures over time. The seriousness with which an evaluation is regarded is measured by the amount of time devoted to it. One may therefore propose either that evaluative contracts endure for a minimum period of time or that such credits carry maximum rates of investment and withdrawal. Alternatively, one could combine both features: the value of evaluative credits may depend on the duration or rate of investment. Such a system would sacrifice efficiency in terms of time in order to gain a greater degree of gravity.

The power to make effective evaluations, or to issue evaluative credits, does not reside within all people as a natural or human right. It is, by contrast, a privilege conferred by social authority. It will therefore be necessary to have a bank of evaluative credit that issues the power to make evaluations to all its members. The principles for qualification for membership, comparable to the principles by which one qualifies to vote in a democratic organization, will be subject to a wide range of political, moral, and, indeed, theological differences. What qualifies one to count as an evaluative member? Should all be invited to join? Should all members have an equal power of evaluation? Should it be possible to buy the power to make evaluations by investing money in the evaluative bank that regulates credits? Should evaluative power be measured in terms of the proportion of an individual's wealth that is to be invested in the bank?

It is unlikely that such differences can be easily resolved. One may therefore envisage a range of evaluative banks, each expressing its own political, moral, and theological perspective on inclusion, exclusion, and the distribution of evaluative power. Individuals would subscribe to the bank that best expressed their beliefs and preferences. While such banks could be international in scope, related to each other through clearing transactions, enabling the transmission of the effectiveness of evaluation across large distances, the institutions that produce evaluations would have a more localized perspective, drawing on an international fund of knowledge, technique, and experience to apply toward meeting urgent local needs.

The secondary tier of the evaluative economy would therefore require that these two new kinds of institutions correspond to the roles played by existing businesses and banks in the conventional economy. To prevent short circuits in the flows of credit, it will be essential for the division between the two to be carefully regulated. Instead of differentiating between the political and the religious, between state and church, between the power of force and the power of faith, it will be vital to differentiate between the power of evaluation and the power to make evaluations effective, for any short-circuiting of these two would lead straight back into the situation in which an evaluative authority gives authority to its own evaluations. This is precisely the problem with money, for just as the nature of time is that it should be spent or given, the nature of evaluation is that credit should be invested. Only heterogeneity opens scope for adaptation, flexibility, and critique. The narcissistic circle of self-affirmation always becomes blind and cancerous.

The process should work as shown in Figure 1. At the local level, the system works through evaluators and enterprises for investment. Investment is always dual. On the one hand, an evaluation is made that an enterprise is worth investment; on the other hand, credit or effective demand is granted to the object of investment. There is no reflux from enterprises to investors to prevent short circuits. The duality of credit and evaluation is expressed in the single act of a credit contract. Its evaluative dimension, however, is supported by evaluative institutions, while the effectiveness of credit is supported by the bank of evaluative credit.

Since this is a secondary tier within the existing economy, banks of evaluative credit will have to guarantee the effectiveness of invested credits by means drawn from the money economy. It will be necessary to issue loans, which may return to the banks in the form of interest. Now, while some worthwhile enterprises may be profitable in monetary terms, others will not be directly profitable, only leading to the profitability of others. Yet if enterprises remain worthwhile, they may continue to attract credit and so may continue to be funded by ever-increasing permanent "loans." The ability to command a permanent loan should not be restricted to states and large corporations; it should be possible for any enterprise that is genuinely worthwhile. As the loans increase in size, such enterprises may feel the weight of the responsibility to fulfill their obligations. Yet the worst effects of debt are avoided, since such loans need never to be repaid. Even a loss of credit and a default on the loan leading to the end of the enterprise need not be catastrophic, since it should occur only when the service is no longer deemed worthwhile. Of course, money spent by such worthwhile enterprises does not immediately flow back to the bank. It may circulate throughout the global economy. It may not be necessary for a bank to recover its "bad" loans directly if they contribute to economic growth else-

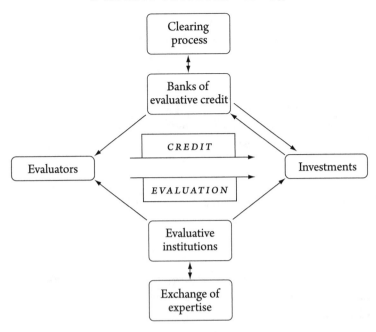

1 A system of evaluative credit.

where and if the bank has the capacity to profit or draw money back in from economic growth.

Several outstanding problems remain to be addressed in such a system. How are evaluative institutions themselves to be funded? They may also be treated as nonprofitable enterprises for investment. It should be ensured that evaluative institutions can recommend investment in each other but cannot recommend investment in themselves. The credit granted to evaluative institutions must always come from another. Moreover, any completion of a circuit of evaluation of the form A→B→C→D→A should be sufficient to negate the credit of the whole chain.

Here we come to a further consideration: each evaluator may have a determinate number of credits to invest. Yet such credits, once invested, may vary in terms of social effectiveness or monetary value. The possibility of negating credits leads to a variation in their value, giving, in the first instance, the possibility of full value or zero. Yet the gravity of monetary value may also vary further, according to principles laid down by the bank of evaluative credit, to foster a healthy environment for investment. Such principles may include the following:

1   To ensure the viability of the entire process, the value of credits may vary uniformly with the monetary reserves of the bank of evaluative credit, just as currencies float in value in relation to each other.

2   To ensure the localization and diversification of credit, credits should increase in relative value in inverse proportion to the number of investors. In other words, individual evaluations are more effective than large, collective evaluations.

3   To ensure that credits are invested in enterprises that are genuinely valuable, the number of credits permitted to an investor (or the value of subsequent credits) should rise in proportion to the number of subsequent investors in an enterprise. This may appear to contradict the preceding principle, but it differs in respect to time. It enables greater power to be given to investors who are capable of finding economic and evaluative opportunities. Of course, it is not ideal in that it still appeals to some degree of consensus, albeit a somewhat delayed one.

4   To ensure the diversification of credit, credits should increase in relative value the more widely they are dispersed by any single evaluator.

5   To ensure effective cross-fertilization, credits should increase in relative value in proportion to the number of different evaluative institutions that recommend the same investment.

6   To ensure that the power to make evaluations is itself valued, the power to issue evaluative credits may be borrowed. Repayment of evaluative credits issued in such a way can be achieved only through reneging on the use of credits of a determinate value at a particular time in the future.

It is likely that such principles will lead to further problems, including ways to work the system to one's own advantage. These would have to be regulated by technical means. It is also likely that such principles will be subject to a high degree of technical development. At this stage, they are merely suggestions or illustrations to provoke further consideration. It is important, when designing an evaluative economy, to note the contrast between the emergence of complexity, diversity, negentropy, and ecological balance in natural systems and the monocultures, entropy, and imbalance of existing economic systems. Principles for constructing a renewed, healthy economic order may be created by means of an analogy with successful principles found in ecological and physiological orders.

The devising of alternative credit systems is relatively easy. In principle, given the power of computing and virtual modeling, any kind of economic force can be engineered.[2] The entire system surrounding a bank of evaluative credit should be designed to act as a filter that removes the harmful social forces of the monetary economy to foster healthy social forces of care and provision. While relations between enterprises will remain monetary and economic, flows of money should become primarily driven by flows of credit and evaluation. Moreover, such a system should be intrinsically attractive. On the one hand, the power to issue evaluative credits is more significant than the power to vote. The system of evaluative credit may therefore be regarded as a further stage in the evolution of economic democracy. Once the principal exercise of power within sovereign states consists not simply of the exercise of force or the enactment of regulation, but of acts of executive decision empowered by selective funding, then true participation in sovereign power goes beyond the right to vote and extends into the capacity to issue effective evaluations. On the other hand, if credit is invested in enterprises that are genuinely worthwhile, then it should lead to an increase in environmental, human, and social capital, so improving the wealth of nations.

The principal problem for such a system, however, is that it needs to be viable and to grow within the existing economic and political climate. In practice, there has to be a reflux of money to the banks of evaluative credit. In some ways, such a bank takes on some of the functions of the existing nation-state in terms of enabling the funding of public services and care for the common good. Unlike the state, however, it separates out the functions of making evaluations and giving effectiveness to those evaluations. Rather like the contemporary central bank that is concerned with the provision of monetary stability independent of political concerns, the bank of evaluative credit is concerned solely with the provision of an effective climate for evaluation while the task of making evaluations is devolved to institutions and individuals.

There are two approaches to ensuring a reflux of money to banks of evaluative credit. A bank of evaluative credit could, in principle, become a matter of national policy, funded by the state via taxation. Indeed, if the system were to work effectively, it would foster economic development and enhance the proceeds from taxation in a virtuous circle. Difficulties in implementing such a policy may arise, however, from constraints imposed by international economic orthodoxy and finance capital on autonomy in national policy.

There is, however, a second source of funding. A bank of evaluative credit must participate in both the conventional economy and the evaluative economy at once. Like any normal bank, it should be able to receive deposits, make loans, and disperse profits in conventional money. It is vital that such a bank is either privately owned or owned by the state so that it is not subject to hostile takeovers or market forces. Profits, instead of being dispersed to shareholders, would be used to fund evaluative credits. Such a bank would have to be highly profitable in the conventional economy and would have to earn most of its profits in the same way as other banks: by speculation on financial markets and currency transactions. Instead of feeding parasitically on the conventional economy by means of taxation, it would feed on it parasitically by means of speculation. Indeed, the most secure and profitable assets for speculation are precisely those that express the centralization of vast flows of wealth in the global economy. To speculate on the strongest currencies is to extract once more a portion of the credit that is extracted from the global economy as a whole. This may seem to compromise the ethics of the entire system; nevertheless, credit can be issued only on a guarantee written in flesh and blood. While the growth of an alternative economic system should be grounded in increased productivity and the power to make effective evaluations, wealth and attractiveness are insufficient by themselves to guarantee success. Monetary income has to be assured either by taxation or by speculation. The issue is not whether sacrifices can be avoided in the utopian ideal of a bloodless society, but for what it is worth making sacrifices. If the power to make effective evaluations is endowed once more on those whose sacrifices underpin the global economy, only then does the circuit of evaluation come full circle. Justice occurs only when sacrifices of time, attention, and devotion are effectively counted. Whether the evaluative economy is funded by taxation or by speculation, it is vital to ensure that the intrinsic violence that makes the entire system possible does not compromise internal relations of evaluation. Moreover, just as contemporary currencies float freely with-

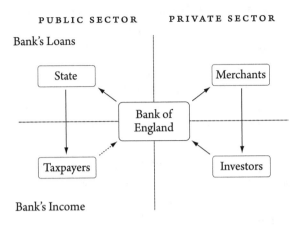

PUBLIC SECTOR   **PRIVATE SECTOR**

Bank's Loans

Bank's Income

2 Social structure of the Bank of England.

out the backing of gold, it is possible to conceive of a time when evaluative credits will bear sufficient credit to count on their own merits, without being backed by a determinate reserve of hard monetary income.

A bank of evaluative credit may take its structural model from the social forces resolved by the Bank of England, as shown in Figure 2. The Bank of England formed a nexus between public and private circulation in which each depended on the success of the other. A finite reserve was used as a basis for circulation through public spending that recirculated through taxation. At the same time, the reserve was used as a basis for private borrowing that recirculated through profits and interest repayments. Increased public spending leads to increased demand, increased production, and increased profit. At the same time, increased investment led to increased economic growth and increased revenue from taxation. Such is the institutional heart of the global economic system.

The result is an effective alliance between taxpayers, investors, banks, and state, as depicted in the money cycle in Figure 3. While money flows in one direction, goods and services return in the opposite direction. The quantity and velocity of money in circulation increases in line with economic growth, even if this money is effectively underwritten by an increasing quantity of debt. A bank of evaluative credit has a similar structure. It forms a nexus between the money cycle and the credit cycle. Evaluative credits, although not directly transferable, hold their value from their convertibility on investment. The dual circuit of evaluation can be represented as in Figure 4. The key to the virtuous circle, here, is that evaluative investment should lead to effective capital growth, while effective capital growth should, via either taxation or speculation, lead to a growth in evaluative investment.

There is, however, a further virtuous circle to be considered, for credit is a negentropic form of capital. The more credit that is given, the more credit there is in circulation. Rather like the Buddhist notion of merit, a moral quantity acquired through generosity, morality, and meditation that increases when it is transferred to others, so credit increases when credit is given, for credit itself cannot be reduced to its material representation in contracts for evaluative credit. There is a reflux of credit to sources of social authority that effectively issue credit. The more effectively a system for evaluative credit operates, the higher the renown in which it is held. Just as a market is enabled by a dealer, a reserve, and a reputation, so a bank of evaluative credit is a dealer, backed by a reserve, with a reputation. Indeed, it may acquire its reserves by means of its reputation. Just as large worthwhile institutions, whether religious or otherwise, have generally been funded by large endowments, so may banks of evaluative credit, if they appear worthwhile, be initiated and expanded by endowments. Endowments, however, may be less significant than choosing to participate in the evaluative economy, whether as an individual evaluator; as a worker at an evaluative institution; or as an investor who seeks support from the evaluative economy. In short, the more the evaluative economy grows, the higher its reputation and the greater its degree of credit. Then withdrawing from evaluation to provide the conditions that make evaluation once more possible becomes a supremely meritorious act comparable to ascetic acts of renunciation.

To issue an evaluative credit is at once to invest in worthwhile production, to express provision and care, and to invoke an authority that gives effective power to evaluations. To be granted the power to issue an evaluative credit is to be faced with the most fundamental of questions: what is true wealth? What is worth spending time on? Where is the effective source of power? Such questions are no longer posed in an abstract, philosophical

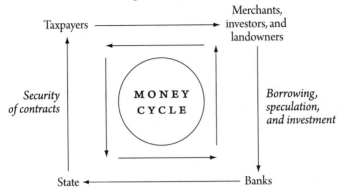

3 The money cycle.

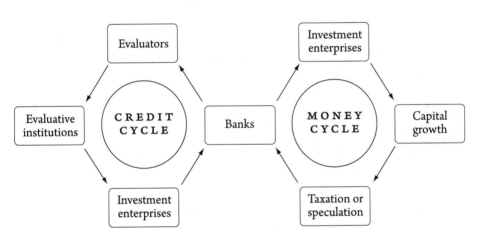

4 Integration of credit and money cycles.

sense. Responses to such questions need be neither universal nor conceptual. The question is not one of identifying what matters more than anything that can be conceived. It is merely one of identifying what urgently demands time, attention, and devotion. Such evaluations are partial, local, and responsive. Indeed, the system of evaluative credit thrives on diversity, on the division of evaluative labor. There is, of course, no guarantee that urgent demands will be met. But there should, of course, be some means of investing credits in urgent demands as they are identified. Nevertheless, although evaluations may be local and partial, the entire system of evaluative credit evokes a particular subjectivity. It may even evoke particular technologies and a particular theology.

There are three great errors in evaluation evoked by the money system. First, by means of the meter, the clock, and the account book, the world is reinscribed in terms of money. The money system evokes a perspective that pays no attention to that which matters most. It considers all things insofar as they promise money. The system of evaluative credit, by contrast, turns its attention outside itself, toward that which matters. That which matters is assessed according to what it may become. The value of that which matters consists in what it may promise. The system of evaluative credit evokes a perspective that cares for what is outside itself.

The second great error of the money system is that it evokes a subjectivity that imagines its own sovereign power. The world is examined from the perspective of what can be purchased, what can lead to profitable investments, and what can be an object of charity. Desires, anxieties, and sympathies form the perspective from which the world is seen. Yet in the play of desires, anxieties, and sympathies, urgent demand, careful consideration, and rational distribution may be subverted by internal pressure. The system of evaluative credit, by contrast, takes the burden of evaluation away from the individual and the present moment, for instead of responding immediately to emotional pressures and formulating a decision, decision makers can be educated by evaluative institutions that are based on traditions and disciplines of care in evaluation. The system of evaluative credit evokes a perspective that aims to take due care in the distribution of attention.

The third great error of the money system is that it evokes its own political theology of the authority of money. Money becomes the supreme object of credit as well as the source of credit. Money promises all things to those who devote themselves to it while delivering only itself. By positing itself as the supreme value, money devalues other values. The system of evaluative credit may also be threatened by such an error. It may seem as though a bank of evaluative credit demands supreme devotion as the source of all credit. It is for this reason that there should always be a plurality of such systems for evaluative credit. Only the ongoing problems of clearing and comparison between such banks maintain the differences that avoid such an error. For in the last analysis, a bank of evaluative credit is merely a constructed institution. Any authority it bears has to be lent to it by those who commit themselves to participating in its system and practices. The credit or authority of an institution is like a ghost in the machine, the spirit that accompanies any determinate organization of time. Such spirits are objective possibilities, genuine potencies enabling cooperation and interaction that otherwise would be impossible. Yet they only come to life when they are invested in an institutional body, a determinate form. The error consists not in invoking a spirit but in the subsequent assumption that the spirit is the only divine form, for in this life, credit, like time, attention, and devotion, has to be distributed.

OF REDEMPTION

MODERN REASON, modern politics, and modern economics have been founded on the ideal of autonomy. The individual was to be released from superstition, from tyranny, and from traditional duties and obligations. If the individual was threatened by external powers, enlightenment and emancipation could be achieved by seizing the same sovereign power that threatened from without and using it to defend the autonomy of the individual. Such an emancipation could only ever be partial and ideal, for if there is to be one who commands, even if that person commands only himself, there is also one who serves, even if that servant is only oneself. Power is a relation, not a possession. Liberty can never belong to the human subject. If the subject exercises power, the physically effective force of that power has to be borrowed from physical means; one has only as much power as that to which one can give organization and orientation. Similarly, if the subject exercises power, the socially effective force of that power has to be borrowed from spiritual means; one only has as much power as the credit invested in one's person. The exercise of sovereign power in a moment of decision draws on whatever physical force and credit is available. Such decisions are, of course, a necessary part of life. Yet they cannot be taken as an end in themselves, for to do so is to close the questions of how power may be enhanced, how the means of production can be produced, how true wealth can be generated. It is also to close the questions of where credit should be placed and how values should be evaluated. There is, of course, a time when such questions have to be temporarily closed. Yet when a society is founded on the principle of their closure, then sovereign liberty becomes disoriented.

The modern rejection of political theology consists in the ideal of autonomy: instead of asking how one may serve nature, society, or God, one asks how nature and society may be made to serve oneself. The disavowed spiritual energy that gives authority to such an autonomous subject is embodied in money. Money has replaced God. In its pure form, such energy is in fact the power of credit. Credit cannot exist without a commitment of time, attention, and devotion. To rephrase Marx, credit is the spiritual aroma of life, the general illumination that bathes all the other colors. Credit is the general theory of the world, its logic in a popular form, its enthusiasm, its moral sanction, and its solemn complement. It is the treasure from heaven that is realized on Earth. It is pure wealth, pure power, and pure promise. It is at once faith, hope, and charity. It is at once the driving force of history and the object of religious aspiration.

The modern rejection of political theology is not a problem merely for secular thought, for modern religious thought, insofar as it confines itself to narrating history or myth, interpreting the world, advising the individual subject, explaining the religious community, or even commenting on sovereign power, remains broadly humanistic. Theological notions can become truly embodied and meaningful only when nature, society, and God are thought together. Such a unity is not to be found in the atemporal realm of Greek metaphysics or in the modern metaphysics of change and process. Such a unity is to be found in promise and credit.

A revolution in theology, politics, metaphysics, epistemology, and economics is required that explores the place of credit and commitment in the constitution of the world. Such a revolution can occur only when it is fully embodied in institutional practices and in the daily life of commitment of time, attention, and devotion. The politics of credit must become the central concern for a theology of the future. The principal problem with the contemporary organization of credit by means of the capitalist debt-money system is not its unreflected nature but its delimitation of evaluation. True emancipation is not that of human knowledge or will but that of the human capacity to evaluate. It is an emancipation of time, attention, and devotion. It is the subordination of credit to evaluation.

The proposals of this study are intended to pose the problem of the emancipation of evaluation. We have sought to see beyond the oppositions of God and money, Christ and Antichrist, the theological and the secular, the spiritual and the material to be able to address the most fundamental problem posed by each. I do not envisage that any of the institutional proposals contained here could solve all of the crises of the end of modernity. In particular, the effective accounting of the ecosystems and lives wasted by the modern economic system is still to be addressed. An effective curbing of rates of consumption may not immediately spring from a liberation of evaluation. The actual costs to be attached to effective evaluation and credit are not yet apparent. Yet in an age of approaching crisis and the tyranny of debt, little can be done until the spectral power of money is addressed. It is urgent, above all else, that time, attention, and devotion be committed to developing new institutions of credit that make effective evaluations once more possible.

The theology of money poses an extraordinary challenge to any future theology. Does money promise value in such a way that value may be advanced? If so, then any effective theology must do likewise. It is not sufficient to promise a glorious future or explain the true meaning of value. Indeed, for a promise to be credible, it is important not to promise too much. Instead, an effective promise is one that identifies the true potential of a situation and enables it to be realized. While money identifies potential in terms of profit, the promise of more money, an effective theology must identify potential in terms of capital, the means of production that can itself be produced.

Is money the supreme value against which all other values may be measured? If so, then any effective theology must do likewise: it must become capable of measuring all other values. It is a matter of assessing, recognizing, and acknowledging the value of potential wherever it may be found. When money substitutes a single form or quantity for such values, it fails to make the most of potential, since it fails to acknowledge the actual values that are present. Instead, an effective theology has the task of acknowledging the intrinsic value of all things.

Is money a speculative value whose intrinsic worth awaits demonstration? If so, then any effective theology must be likewise. Theology belongs within the realm of the possible, the realm of "what if?" One cannot know in advance what the outcome of any particular theology will be. There is always an element of risk. Yet if money deals with speculative values, it quickly aims to convert speculation into certainty. Whether one counts only the realization of values that are certain or one counts possibilities as if they were certain, the speculative element of value is not effectively represented. Instead of a theology appealing solely to that which can be taken as certain (as in the worldview of naturalism) or appealing to that which is uncertain as if it were certain (as in the worldview of dogmatism), it is necessary that theology offer its speculations for experimental proof. What values are realized in practice by lending credit to any particular theology?

Is money a social obligation demanding that all interaction be ordered in accordance with the repayment of debt? If so, then any effective theology must do likewise. Theology need not hesitate to impose its own demands. Theology consists in the ordering of time, attention, and devotion. Yet if money imposes its spectral power as debt, it does not, for all that, demand that attention be given to the perspective evoked by debt from which the world is to be seen. As a consequence, while debt may ally itself with other powers and forces — such as those of productive energy or those of drives for survival, pleasure, or power — it does not recognize any spectral power other than itself. If debt has proved to be cancerous, this is because it can achieve cooperation with other powers and forces only on its own terms. As a spiritual perspective, debt cannot exist harmoniously in the world with other demands. It is ecologically illiterate.

Any effective theology, while imposing its own demands, must provide an effective basis for cooperation with other demands. Instead of attempting to possess all time, attention, and devotion, divine power consists in the coordination and orientation of other powers so that the same time may be used to attend to a range of demands. Such is the true meaning of efficiency. Such is also the true meaning of redemption. It matters little if time is subordinated to particular demands if the same time is effectively coordinated with higher demands.

Redemption from debt is not debt cancellation, for if debt takes on the role of constructive capital, then to cancel debt is to destroy productive potential. It is to dissolve the basis for trust and cooperation. Redemption from debt occurs, by contrast, through forgiveness. To forgive is to cease to oppose, resist, or exclude a harmful presence. All too often, forgiveness has been understood in terms of the sovereign power of judgment: it is treated as a matter of suspending revenge, punishment, or blame. Yet revenge, punishment, and blame are only matters for a sovereign power or a responsible subject who relates to life through representation. Alternatively, forgiveness has been conceived in terms of metaphysics as an assessment of deeds—what they are and what they should be. A truly theological approach to forgiveness, however, is concerned with the ordering of time, attention, and devotion. At this level, divine power has largely been conceived as the spiritual equivalent of Caesar. Idols are broken; demons are exorcized; and spectral powers are conquered. Divine ownership is proclaimed over time, attention, and devotion. Yet it is precisely this power that is exercised by the spiritual force of money. It is such opposition, resistance, exclusion, and conquering that prevent effective cooperation and coordination. What one takes to be God is Mammon in disguise.

True redemption occurs only through new creation. If the basis for cooperation with harmful spectral forces is not yet present, then it remains to be created. True forgiveness does not consist in the separation of the sin from the sinner or in the separation of the sinner from the spiritual power of sin. Sin, sinner, and spectral power are not conceivable without one another. That which God has joined cannot be put asunder. Instead, true forgiveness consists in cooperation with sin, sinner, and spectral power to create good out of evil. Forgiveness is not a matter of sovereign decision. It is not something that already lies within our power. Forgiveness is a matter of divine creation. It consists in creating or discovering a new basis for cooperation. It is a challenge to be achieved. Redemption from debt therefore consists in the creation of a new basis for cooperation with debt. It consists in a new ordering of time, attention, and devotion alongside debt so that the renewal of life in all of its fullness is once more possible.

NOTES

INTRODUCTION

1 All citations from the Bible are from the New Revised Standard Version.

2 Pelagius, "Of Riches," 7.2–3, in Bradstock and Rowland, *Radical Christian Writings*, 16–17.

3 Quoted in Jackson, *The Oxford Book of Money*, 312.

4 Note the Christian philosopher Robert Spaemann: "The phenomenon of attention and inattention is the best paradigm for what we call good and evil" (Spaemann, *Happiness and Benevolence*, 190).

5 Mitchell Innes, "The Credit Theory of Money," in Ingham, *Concepts of Money*, 355.

6 Galbraith, *Money*, 18–20.

7 See Ferguson, *The Cash Nexus*, for an account of the reasons for this and its historical implications.

8 Ingham, *The Nature of Money*, 121–31.

9 Galbraith, *Money*, 30.

10 See Ingham, *The Nature of Money*, 13, 151.

11 Schumpeter is cited in Richard Arena and Agnès Festré, "Banks, Credit and the Financial System in Schumpeter," in Ingham, *Concepts of Money*, 377.

12 Schumpeter, *A History of Economic Analysis*, 318.

13 Quoted in Arena and Festré, "Banks, Credit and the Financial System in Schumpeter," in Ingham, *Concepts of Money*, 376–79.

14 Quoted in Jackson, *The Oxford Book of Money*, 312.

15 Polanyi, *The Great Transformation*.

16 R. H. Tawney charts the history of this transformation in *Religion and the Rise of Capitalism*.

17 Quoted in Jackson, *The Oxford Book of Money*, 238.

18 Innes, "The Credit Theory of Money," in Ingham, *Concepts of Money*, 358.

19 See further Goodchild, *Capitalism and Religion*, 127–29.

20 It is clear that money meets some definitions of religion and is excluded from others. This is of little significance, since the separation of the religious from the secular is a defining gesture of a society organized around money. Definitions of religion are always constructed to play a role in a distinctive intellectual project, and are of little significance beyond those. My point is not that any inferences can be made from a description of money as "religious," but that money lends itself to a distinctive kind of theological inquiry—one that is constructed in the very work of studying money. For my views on defining "religion" and the role of the study of religion as a discipline, see Philip Goodchild, "On 'Religion': Speeches to Its Cultural Despisers," in Crossley and Karner, *Writing History, Constructing Religion*, 49–64.

21 It has been common to incorporate an essentialist conception into definitions of religion, so that it is defined in relation to a feature such as the supernatural, a belief in God or Gods, the holy or sacred, the transcendent, or a theory of salvation. No such conception is universally applicable to all cultures, even if rites of veneration are universally found. Such essentialist definitions cannot be maintained on anthropological grounds: see Fitzgerald, *The Ideology of Religious Studies*. The religious, in these conceptions, is positioned as the exotic other of modern reason and social life: see King, *Orientalism and Religion*. There is also, by contrast, a tradition of critical theory that aims to disclose the "fetishism" or exotic other as a presupposition of modern reason and practice itself, including the work of Karl Marx, Walter Benjamin, Max Horkheimer, Theodor Adorno, and Jacques Derrida. Like my earlier work, *Capitalism and Religion*, my theology of money is situated within this tradition.

22 Douglas, *Purity and Danger*, 70.

23 A recent exception is Doctrine Commission of the General Synod of the Church of England, *Being Human*.

24 Kant, *Critique of Pure Reason*, 505. "Thalers," the word from which "dollars" is derived, is used in the original.

25 By beginning his study of the philosophy of money with the distinction between being and value, Georg Simmel obscures what is distinctive about money. Objective value is reduced to a distance or delay in realizing subjective enjoyment: see Simmel, *The Philosophy of Money*.

26 For a more complete statement of this argument, see Philip Goodchild, "Truth and Utopia," *Telos* 134 (2006): 1–19.

27 For a derivation of this practice as the essence of theological reason, see idem, "Proslogion," in Benson and Wirzba, *The Phenomenology of Prayer*, 232–43.

28 Locke, *An Essay Concerning Human Understanding*; idem, *Two Treatises of Government*; idem, "A Letter on Toleration," in Yolton, *The Locke Reader*, 245–75.

29 Kelly, *Locke on Money*.

30 More, *Utopia*, 46.

31 For a description of this method in philosophy, see Bergson, *An Introduction to Metaphysics*; Deleuze, *Bergsonism*. For a more complete account of the conception of reason pursued here, see Goodchild, *Capitalism and Religion*.

32 Georg Simmel explains that a philosophy of money "can present the preconditions that, situated in mental states, in social relations and in the logical structure of reality and values, give money its meaning and its practical position": Simmel, *The Philosophy of Money*, 54. The task here, by contrast, is to explore how money itself can give meaning and practical position to mental states, social relations, and even the structure of reality and values.

33 Aglietta and Orléan, *La monnaie entre violence et confiance*; Altvater, *The Future of the Market*; Ingham, *The Nature of Money*; Mies and Bennholdt-Thomsen, *The Subsistence Perspective*.

34 Duchrow and Hinkelammert, *Property for People, Not for Profit*.

35 For me, money has displaced the pivotal concepts of twentieth-century European philosophy, such as being, time, difference, repetition, subjectivity, signifier, lack, void, and universality, as that which most demands thinking. Since money discloses its essence as credit, philosophy rejoins theology in a synthesis that modifies both.

ONE POWER

1 Schmitt, *The Concept of the Political*, 35.

2 Ibid., 33.

3 Ibid., 46.

4 Quoted in Ferguson, *The Cash Nexus*, 41.

5 Schmitt, *The Concept of the Political*, 38.

6 See the distinction between *auctoritas* and *potestas* in Agamben, *State of Exception*, 74–88.

7 Hence the emergence of social contract theory to replace theological ideas of a corporate body. While some kind of social contract makes sense in terms of Richard Hooker's Anglicanism, where the state is an ecclesiastical polity and people are joined by the religious authority that unites them, it loses all credible authority in Thomas Hobbes's writing and thereafter. From Hobbes to Schmitt, the authority of the social contract becomes a practical expedient when faced with the threat of violence. In practice, however, people remain united by the blood of the body politic rather than by its head: the material circulation of goods via money.

8 Schmitt, *The Concept of the Political*, 54.

9 Oliver O'Donovan argues that judgment is the essential political act: see O'Donovan, *The Way of Judgment*.

10 Manent, *An Intellectual History of Liberalism*.

11 Hume, *A Treatise of Human Nature*, 415.

12 Schmitt, *Political Theology*, 36.

13 In a strange way, therefore, modern philosophers of immanence such as Benedict de Spinoza, Karl Marx, Friedrich Nietzsche, Henri Bergson, and Gilles Deleuze may be regarded as faithful apostles and prophets of Christ insofar as they most successfully achieve the incarnation of thought.

14 On the body of the sovereign, see Kantorowicz, *The King's Two Bodies*. On money itself, see the forms of the socius discussed in Deleuze and Guattari, *Anti-Oedipus*, chap. 3.

15 Quoted in Jackson, *The Oxford Book of Money*, 16.

16 Lacan, *The Four Fundamental Concepts of Psychoanalysis*, 110.

17 In Jackson, *The Oxford Book of Money*, 22.

18 Buchan, *Frozen Desire*.

19 Jackson, *The Oxford Book of Money*, 23.

20 Marx, *Grundrisse*, 83–84.

21 Ibid., 95–99.

22 Heilbroner, *Twenty-First Century Capitalism*.

23 Marx, *Grundrisse*, 106–7.

24 This also calls into question whether it is appropriate to begin an analysis of the nature of money with its earlier forms, such as the use of tokens in religious sacrifice, the issuing of coinage by the state, or the use of a general equivalent in mercantile exchange. Marx's approach in the first volume of *Capital* is to derive money from the model of mercantile exchange. This subordinates money to an expression of the wishes of the free, trading subject. The implication of these comments in the *Grundrisse* is that it is necessary to begin an analysis of the nature of money from its specific power within capitalist society.

25 Marx, *Grundrisse*, 107.

26 Ibid.

TWO THE END OF MODERNITY

1 See Harvey, *Justice, Nature and the Geography of Difference*.

2 National Research Council, *Abrupt Climate Change*.

3 See Cox, *Climate Crash*.

4 Ibid., 119.

5 Ibid., 123.

6 Hadley Centre, *Modelling Climate Change*.

7 See http://news.independent.co.uk/environment.

8 Recent reports on the effects of climate change, including the *Stern Review of the Economics of Climate Change* (2006) and *Fourth Assessment Report 2007* (2007–2008) from the Intergovernmental Panel on Climate Change, are based on

models that assume stability and continuity with recent meteorological behavior. For all of their authority and their urgent warnings, the reports can hardly be used as a basis for confidence in ongoing stability. It is still unknown where the threshold or tipping point is that moves the climate system from a regime of anthropogenic forcing to a purely natural dynamism over which humans have no control. Current momentum behind the processes involved in anthropogenic forcing, however, suggests that crossing such a threshold is all but inevitable. The processes leading to the emission of carbon dioxide and methane are intimately tied into global economic and population growth; efficiency gains in energy production and use are likely to be offset by higher levels of consumption unless there is a major setback to economic growth.

9 Such as regulation of the gaseous composition of the atmosphere, protection of coastal zones, regulation of the hydrological cycle and climate, generation and conservation of fertile soils, dispersal and breakdown of wastes, pollination of many crops, and absorption of pollutants: see United Nations Environment Programme, *Global Environmental Outlook*, 120–21. See Mathis Wackernagel et al., "Tracking the Ecological Overshoot of the Human Economy," *Proceedings of the National Academy of Sciences* 99 (2002): 9266–71.

10 See the World Bank Development Indicators database at http://www.world bank.org.

11 Campbell, *The Essence of Oil and Gas Depletion*; Deffeyes, *Hubbert's Peak*; Heinberg, *The Party's Over*; idem, *Powerdown*; Leggett, *Half Gone*; McKillop, *The Final Energy Crisis*; Simmons, *Twilight in the Desert*; Strahan, *The Last Oil Shock*.

12 See Colin Campbell, "A Reply to 'Global Petroleum Reserves—A View to the Future,'" in McKillop, *The Final Energy Crisis*, chap. 17.

13 Idem, "The Assessment and Importance of Oil Depletion," in McKillop, *The Final Energy Crisis*, 54.

14 See Jacob Lund Fisker, "The Law of Energy," in McKillop, *The Final Energy Crisis*, 85.

15 Ross McLuney, "Population, Energy and Economic Growth," in McKillop, *The Final Energy Crisis*, 178.

16 Some estimates suggest that even France will be able to support less than half of its current population; Australia will be able to support less than 10 percent: see Sheila Newman, "Future Settings," in McKillop, *The Final Energy Crisis*, chap. 20. I cannot assess the plausibility of such estimates myself. The transfer of crop production to biofuels may mitigate some effects of the crisis, yet only for the comparatively wealthy.

17 Schmitt, *The Crisis of Parliamentary Democracy*, 15.

18 Ibid., 16.

19 Ibid., 28.

20 Ibid., 29.

21 Schumpeter, *Capitalism, Socialism and Democracy*, 252.

22 Schmitt, *The Crisis of Parliamentary Democracy*, 9.

23 Ibid., 24–25.

24 Plumwood, *Feminism and the Mastery of Nature*, 47–55.

25 Marx, *Grundrisse*, 165.

26 The World Bank reports that some sixty-nine countries have suffered from serious banking crises and eighty-seven have suffered from adverse currency speculation since 1975: Lietaer, *The Future of Money*, 321.

27 For an account of this process, see Harvey, *The New Imperialism*, chap. 4.

28 Historically, the most significant event of such deregulation occurred in the early 1970s under the regime of U.S. President Richard Nixon. It was the closing of the "gold window" underpinning the exchange rate of the dollar, followed by the removal of restrictions on the investment of foreign capital in the New York Stock Exchange. This event was no doubt a contingent political choice, although one that responded to the financial pressures of balance-of-payments deficits. The result has been admirably described by Peter Gowan as the "Dollar Wall Street Regime," in which the U.S. government enjoys the unique advantages of seigniorage, the ability to print money at will, and the ability to pursue economic warfare through its control of the international financial regime. Despite the enhancement of political activity that this entails, the U.S. government has engaged in a gamble by releasing financial forces that it cannot directly control: see Gowan, *The Global Gamble*. The turn from neoliberalism to neoconservatism signifies not so much a return to direct imperialism as a desperate bid for power when faced with imminent collapse of U.S. global dominance.

29 Aristotle, *Politics*, book I, 1257a-b, 12–13.

30 Smith, *The Wealth of Nations*, 117.

31 A fourth function of money as a standard for deferred payments is often included but may be regarded as complementary to its role as a measure of value or unit of account.

32 The Marxist view of money maintains a strict distinction between money and credit, since in a credit squeeze or market crash, there is a sudden rush for "real" money. (This point is emphasized in de Brunhoff, *Marx on Money*, 80–86.) Such a rush is generated by a positive feedback effect—the credit of the state is simply regarded as more stable than credit issued by other institutions. Marx's theory depends on the existence of a general equivalent, in the form of a monetized commodity such as gold; it is simply necessary, however, to substitute a particular representation as the measure of values in the absence of an actual general equivalent, as demonstrated by all the periods in history when currencies have functioned without a gold standard.

33 Geoffrey Ingham, "Fundamentals of a Theory of Money," in idem, *Concepts of Money*, 136.

34 One may question how such wealth and power of the speculator class are to be

"realized." Yet credit is no less real than products and property. Even if there is hyperinflation of luxury property and speculative assets, it is this very hyperinflation that drives speculative profits. The key differential remains between speculators and other classes, including traditional capitalist shareowners.

THREE A TREATISE ON MONEY

1   Georg Simmel founded his philosophy of money on a dichotomy between being and value. Value is conceived in terms of alienation from a prior subject. Thus:

> In the same way, we invest economic objects with a quantity of value as if it were an inherent quality, and then hand them over to the process of exchange, to a mechanism determined by those quantities, to an impersonal confrontation between values, from which they return multiplied and more enjoyable to the final purpose, which was also their point of origin: subjective experience. This is the basis and source of that valuation which finds its expression in economic life and whose consequences represent the meaning of money. (Simmel, *The Philosophy of Money*, 78–79)

2   One may think especially of the work of Spinoza, Nietzsche, Heidegger, and Wittgenstein, among many others.

3   The concept of "society" invented by Marx and the concept of "culture" invented by Simmel are designed to solve this problem of the objectivity of value. We need to explore whether such concepts are basic or an effect of relations involving money.

4   Gilles Deleuze and Félix Guattari explore this route to conclude that "desiring-production is everywhere": Deleuze and Guattari, *Anti-Oedipus*, 1.

5   See further Daly, *Beyond Growth*.

6   This has been pointed out in a number of popular works, such as McBurney, *Ecology into Economics Won't Go*. George Monbiot explained this clearly in "Deliver Us from Finity," *Guardian* (London), 31 December 2002.

7   This is known as the "Jevons paradox."

8   The multiplier effect is an important dynamic discussed in economics textbooks. It describes how increasing the supply of money by lowering central bank interest rates or increasing government borrowing and spending has a knock-on effect throughout the economy. If a government spends more, then it pays workers and suppliers more, and so they in turn have more to spend, and so on, throughout an integrated, localized economy. One should note that speculative profits have a multiplier effect, as well. If one sector of the stock market yields speculative profits, then those profits can be used to buy other stocks, which in turn raises prices, leading to further profits. This is one reason the stock market can outstrip growth in underlying values that results from dividends.

9   Hahnel, *The ABCs of Political Economy*, 100.

10   Ibid., 105.

11 Simmel, *The Philosophy of Money*, 79.

12 Ibid., 120.

13 See the examination of free choice in Nietzsche, *Daybreak*, 79, 129.

14 See Karl Menger, "On the Origin of Money," in Ingham, *Concepts of Money*, 3–17.

15 The fundamental difference, as argued by John Maynard Keynes, is that barter is always bilateral, whereas the use of money makes possible the use of price lists and comparisons in an extensive, multilateral, decentralized market: see Ingham, "Fundamentals of a Theory of Money," in idem, *Concepts of Money*, 133.

16 Bourdieu, *The Logic of Practice*.

17 Marcel Hénaff explains that a gift is distinguished from an economic exchange not by means of disinterestedness but because it aims at public recognition rather than the enjoyment of goods: see Hénaff, *Le prix de la vérité*, 154.

18 For a useful summary of views on the nature of money, see Ingham, *The Nature of Money*.

19 This problem is noticed in ibid., 23.

20 See Wray, *Understanding Modern Money*.

21 Cencini, *Money, Income and Time*.

22 The structure of money produced by the Bank of England makes interdependence between the state and civil society the basis for trust in the value of money.

23 This is known as the quantity theory; it is not borne out by empirical evidence. The assumption is that the quantity of money causes price movements, but not vice versa. Nevertheless, capital investment, made possible by an increased supply of money through loans, has a direct effect on prices and the quantity of goods in circulation. Moreover, increases in the money supply can circulate through restricted circuits of the economy without having a general impact on prices. Since loans determine deposits, and since deposits restrict loans, the money supply is variable apart from inflation.

24 The fact that commodities are actually given prices makes it appear as if such a comparison with the market as a whole has taken place, if one assumes that all prices result solely from comparison. If other factors are involved in pricing, however, they may be specific to localities in the market.

25 Hence, models of behavior in neoclassical economics based on Walrasian equilibrium have very little bearing on economic reality since they are premised on a model of exchange rather than contract.

26 Smith, *The Wealth of Nations*, 385.

27 See Davies, *A History of Money from Ancient Times to the Present Day*, 230.

28 Innes, "The Credit Theory of Money," in Ingham, *Concepts of Money*, 354.

29 The role of mimesis in the constitution of money is emphasized in Aglietta and Orléan, *La monnaie entre violence et confiance* .

30 Note that these considerations do not apply simply to fiat or debt money in the contemporary economy. They apply to all money as such. Thus, any currency re-

form that simply aims to turn money back into a token of legal tender or a valuable commodity will not succeed in neutralizing the power of money. Moreover, money coined by a state and distributed as legal tender, valid for the payment of taxation, is already created effectively as debt money, however valuable its intrinsic metal content.

31 The problem of the overaccumulation of capital has been a staple ingredient in Marxist explanations of the contradictions of capitalism. Excess money capital cannot find suitable vehicles for investment if there is a falling rate of profit: see Harvey, *The Limits to Capital*. While such a tendency is doubtful in itself, excess money capital can always be used for speculative investment in property or financial products rather than for capital investment. The creation of money as debt is more effective in explaining the engine of modernity. Geoffrey Ingham argues, by contrast, that the tension between the expansion of value through the elasticity of supply of credit money and the breakdown of monetary stability through loss of confidence is the central dynamic of the modern capitalist system: see Ingham, "Fundamentals of a Theory of Money," in idem, *Concepts of Money*, 142.32.

32 This point is emphasized in de Brunhoff, *Marx on Money*, 80–86.

33 Smith, *The Wealth of Nations*, 420.

34 Marx derives the essence of money as a universal equivalent from his analysis of the commodity form: see Marx, *Capital*, 1:124–77. This analysis presupposes that it is possible to move from a general equivalent, a commodity that may be exchanged for many others, to a universal equivalent, against which prices are measured. But a universal comparison of prices is a utopian ideal that is never completed. Instead, all commodities promise money, but money is the promise of a power of effective demand in different and future markets. In this sense, money is essentially a promise of the power to realize possible future demands. Its essence cannot be given as a relation between commodities. Money is local and temporal, not universal. Its value remains indeterminate and uncertain.

Speaking of exchange value or price, Marx famously explained:

The mysterious character of the commodity-form consists therefore simply in the fact that the commodity reflects the social characteristics of men's own labour as objective characteristics of the products of labour themselves, as the socio-natural properties of these things. . . . It is nothing but the definite social relation between men themselves which assumes here, for them, the fantastic form of a relation between things. In order, therefore, to find an analogy we must take flight into the misty realm of religion. There the products of the human brain appear as autonomous figures endowed with a life of their own, which enter into relations both with each other and with the human race. (Ibid., 164–65)

Yet money is a product of the human brain that becomes an autonomous figure endowed with a life of its own, just as music is the product of sound vibrations or speech is the product of the mouth. The instrument vibrates as it does because the music is written so; the mouth moves as it does because of the intention to speak; people enter contracts, buy and sell, to pay back debts. The "misty realm," in practice, is that of "definite social relations." Social relations are definite only with hindsight; in economic life, everything is uncertain.

35 For this dual pledging of securities on the part of creditor and debtor, see Gunnar Heinsohn and Otto Steiger, "The Property Theory of Interest and Money," in Smithin, *What Is Money?* 67–100. Note that I diverge from their theory insofar as I also attribute significance to the role of promise as the reason for undertaking the contract in the first place.

FOUR POLITICS OF MONEY

1 Smith, *The Wealth of Nations*, 134.

2 This formal equality of people is described by John Locke in terms of a gift of the world by God to people in common. It is notable that Locke, having attributed the right of private property to the act of joining labor with what is given, points out that people could only have as much as they could use were it not for the invention of money. Money enables value to keep without spoiling and so enables unequal possession. People have therefore, by "tacit and voluntary consent," agreed to the disproportionate and unequal possession of the Earth. Without money, the Earth would be used inefficiently, with great tracts lying waste. So those people who make use of land, and so have a greater right to its possession, are those who use money: see Locke, *Two Treatises of Government*, 286, 293, 299–300.

3 Hobbes, *Leviathan*, 125.

4 This is what Locke means by "freedom under government": anyone who transgresses the natural laws of private property places himself in a state of war against all others, and all have a duty to punish them (Locke, *Two Treatises of Government*, 272).

5 For more on the nature of such dependencies, see Mies and Bennholdt-Thomsen, *The Subsistence Perspective*.

6 See Brenner, *Merchants and Revolution*.

7 In the English Civil War, Parliament—composed very largely of agrarian capitalist landholders—effectively seized sovereignty from the monarchy. While this was reversed at the end of the Commonwealth, the Glorious Revolution of 1688 completed the process. Such a move was ideologically justified by Locke in his critique of patriarchy and discussion of the state of war.

8 See Heinsohn and Steiger, "The Property Theory of Interest and Money," in Smithin, *What Is Money?* 79, 81.

9 Locke's political theory is a defense of slavery and colonization: see the discussion in Duchrow and Hinkelammert, *Property for People, Not for Profit*, 44–70.

10 Jeanne L. Schroeder can celebrate contract (instead of gift) as "the true love relationship in its most rudimentary and primitive form," because it involves mutual recognition and thus the birth of subjectivity. "For a brief, shining moment, each party recognizes the other as a free, equal, legal subject, and therefore achieves her goal of becoming a subject. It is a moment of love": Schroeder, *Triumph of Venus*, 13, 54.

11 As John McMurtry remarks, "When people are then forced to obey 'value neutral' laws — as the indigenous peoples across the world have been over 500 years by invasion, mass murder, land clearances and criminal prosecution for resistance — their remainders are eventually forced to submit": McMurtry, *The Cancer Stage of Global Capitalism*, 14. See further idem, *Value Wars*.

12 Note the verdict of Joan Robinson: "Once we admit that an economy exists in time, that history goes one way, from the irreversible past into the unknown future, the conception of equilibrium based on the mechanical analogy of a pendulum swinging to and fro in space becomes untenable. The whole of traditional economics needs to be thought out afresh" (quoted in Altvater, *The Future of the Market*, 75).

13 Even Marx's analysis of money in terms of commodity fetishism falls into the same illusion that it criticizes: economic society cannot be analyzed in terms of exchange.

14 Note the judgment of Gunnar Heinsohn and Otto Steiger: "There is no economic theory worthy of the name because economists have never come to terms with property. . . . They resemble a fish which does not know of water before it is pulled out of it" (Heinsohn and Steiger, "The Property Theory of Interest and Money," in Smithin, *What Is Money?* 71–72). The relevant distinction between property and possession as use, for these authors, is that property can be encumbered and collateralized as a debt. Indeed, they regard money as deriving from a mutual pledge of property. The debtor issues a contract as a claim against his property to the creditor; the creditor issues a claim against his property to the debtor; and it is the latter claim that may then circulate as money. Money cannot be created out of nothing, therefore, because it requires the mutual pledging of property reserves. Our concern here, however, is with the social forces and expectations that invest and vivify such claims.

15 Smith, *The Wealth of Nations*, 136–40.

16 Ibid., 226.

17 Ibid., 462.

18 Ibid., 250.

19 Ibid., 182.

20 Ibid., 137–39.

21 Ibid., 138.

22 See Hutchinson et al., *The Politics of Money*, chap. 8.

23 See n. 2 in this chapter.

24 Smith, *The Wealth of Nations*, 198.

25 Ibid., 247.

26 More formal definitions of usury concerned money and interest on such obscure grounds as money representing appropriated time and time belonging to God.

27 It is notable that if a rate of interest or an average rate of profit is higher than the growth rate of the GDP, then more money overall is extracted from an economy than enters it through investment. As such, foreign direct investment can easily lead to an extraction of wealth from the economy into which it is invested.

28 Jackson, *The Oxford Book of Money*, 11.

29 See Kindleberger, *Manias, Panics and Crashes*.

30 Note the comments of Samuel Taylor Coleridge: "What evil results to this country, taken at large, from the National Debt? I never could get a plain and practical answer to that question. As to taxation to pay the interest, how can the country suffer by a process, under which money is never one minute out of the pockets of the people? You may just as well say that a man is weakened by the circulation of his blood. There may, certainly, be particular local evils and grievances resulting from the mode of taxation or collection; but how can that debt be in any proper sense a burden to the nation, which the nation owes to itself, and to no one but itself?" (quoted in Jackson, *The Oxford Book of Money*, 239).

31 For the difference between active and reactive forces, see Deleuze, *Nietzsche and Philosophy*, chap. 2.

32 Keynes, *A Treatise on Money*, 1:26.

33 For Adam Smith, "A man grows rich by employing a multitude of manufacturers: he grows poor by maintaining a multitude of menial servants": Smith, *The Wealth of Nations*, 430. He generalizes this to businesses, governments, and nations, providing an argument for keeping the "unproductive" public sector as small as possible. Nevertheless, this argument assumes that only those activities that yield profits are productive, whereas public services may be much more worthwhile and beneficial to a nation than private services. There is, however, a different way to read Smith's point: he comments that the rent of land and the profits of stock are the principal sources from which unproductive hands derive their subsistence: ibid., 433. Thus, landowners and capitalist investors are perhaps more significant than the state in causing the underutilization of capacity. The successors to the menial servants of the eighteenth century are those who are employed to provide leisure services for the rich, often as waiters or cleaners. Then one must ask whether the provision of luxury goods and services is truly productive. For Smith, "Parsimony, not industry, is the immediate cause of the increase of capital. . . . By what a frugal man annually saves, he not only affords maintenance to an additional number of productive hands, for that or the ensuing year, but, like the founder of a public workhouse, he establishes as it were a perpetual fund for the maintenance of an equal number in all times to come": ibid., 437–38. This is

the vital problem of capacity utilization: are the productive capacities of all set to work most effectively to ensure the maintenance and benefits of others?

34 Ibid., 119.

FIVE THEOLOGY OF MONEY

1 On bookkeeping as a moral self-discipline, see Poovey, *The History of the Modern Fact*, 11. James Aho has argued that the formal conventions of double-entry book-keeping were devised to defend against accusations of usury, "for every credit I am due, this double-entry declares, I owe just so much": quoted in ibid., 37–38. It is notable that in bookkeeping, value consists entirely in credits and debts. The same is true with paper money.

2 Thus, even John Maynard Keynes distinguishes between commodity money (in the form of coinage and fiat money or composed of tokens) and managed money (which has a determinate relation to an objective standard): see Keynes, *A Treatise on Money*, 1:7.

3 This is recommended by Hernando de Soto as a solution for world poverty: see de Soto, *The Mystery of Capital*.

4 This is the central argument in Poovey, *The History of the Modern Fact*.

5 It is important to note that in financial markets, value is not expressed in a price at any given time, for a price has discounted all economic opportunities. Instead, value is discerned through fundamental analyses of underlying conditions and technical analyses of price movements. Such value is not yet recorded in current prices.

SIX METAPHYSICS AND CREDIT

1 There are three principal reasons that a state introduces money for the sake of taxation. First, because money enables the transfer of wealth, it allows the insti-tution of taxes in forms other than on labor and nonperishable goods, such as poll taxes and customs duties. Second, it raises the demand for more money and thus increases the profit from seigniorage or money creation. And third, it forces taxpayers out of a non-monetary subsistence economy into a cash economy: see Charles A. E. Goodhart, "The Two Concepts of Money," in Ingham, *Concepts of Money*, 450. It is the third factor, combined with the profits obtained by local tax collectors, that seems to have been the cause of major social transformations during Jesus's lifetime and probably had an impact on his teaching on wealth.

2 The concept of habitus developed by the sociologist Pierre Bourdieu expresses such a determination of perspective by practice: see Bourdieu, *The Logic of Prac-tice*. It is also, perhaps, implicit in the premises of the materialist method outlined by Marx in *The German Ideology*: see Pierson, *The Marx Reader*, 94–95.

3 It is the consciousness of such a problem that explains the pre-modern fusion

of the religious and the political. The term "political theology" goes back to the pagan Marcus Terentius Varro (116–27 B.C.E.). It meant the correct and public interaction with the gods (Varro is cited in Augustine, *City of God*, 234). The sphere of the political is not confined to law and right, on the one hand, and sovereignty, agency, force, and subjectivity, on the other. It also consists in piety. The polis constituted itself in public through cult, sacrificial rituals, ceremonies, and festivals. It is such piety that has been replaced by money as the authority of credit.

4   See further Philip Goodchild, "The Babylonian Captivity of Theology," unpublished essay.

5   Parmenides, fragments 3 and 6, translated in Cohen et al., *Readings in Ancient Greek Philosophy*, 36–38:

> Come now, I will tell you—and bring away my story safely when you
>   have heard it—the only ways of inquiry there are for thinking:
> the one, that it is and that it is not possible for it not to be,
> is the path of Persuasion (for it attends upon Truth),
> the other, that it is not and that it is necessary for it not to be,
> this I point out to you to be a path completely unlearnable,
> for neither may you know that which is not (for it is not to be
>   accomplished)
> nor may you declare it. . . . For the same thing is for thinking and for
>   being.

6   Compare Simmel, *The Philosophy of Money*, 146: "One of the greatest advances made by mankind—the discovery of a new world out of the material of the old—is to establish a proportion between two quantities, not by direct comparison, but in terms of the fact that each of them relates to a third quantity and that these two relations are either equal or unequal."

7   Aristotle, *Metaphysics IV*, 1003a.

8   Benedict de Spinoza, *Ethics*, pt. 1, definition 3, in Curley, *A Spinoza Reader*, 85.

9   Heidegger, *What Is Called Thinking?* 223.

10 Aquinas, *Summa Contra Gentiles*, book 1, chaps. 21–22, 116–21.

11 Anselm was able to formulate the ontological argument for the existence of God because of his Neo-Platonic presuppositions. The mind has to consider "that than which nothing greater than can be conceived" as existing. To explain the possibility of the fool, he distinguished between two senses of "conceiving." "For in one sense a thing is thought when the word signifying it is thought; in another sense when the very object which the thing is is understood": Anselm, *Proslogion*, in Davies, *Anselm of Canterbury—The Major Works*, 88–89. These correspond to differing kinds of reason—one consisting of the manipulation of signs and ideas by the mind, including the use of propositions that signify what is thought to be the case; the other when the very object discloses itself to the understanding

through illumination. In the latter case, thought and existence are no longer independent; thought depends on existence. Here existence is no mere predicate added to a representation. Existence generates thought. This is hardly surprising, given that thought actually exists. For Immanuel Kant, by contrast, thought has no necessary relation to existence. To posit a triangle and to reject its three angles is self-contradictory, but there is no contradiction in rejecting the triangle together with its three angles: Kant, *Critique of Pure Reason*, 502. Anselm would no doubt reply that it is one thing to reject the existence of a posited triangle, but to reject the existence of "that than which nothing greater can be conceived" is merely foolish.

12   Kant, *Critique of Pure Reason*, 505 ("thalers" is used instead of "dollars" in the original).

13   Anselm develops his so-called ontological argument to demonstrate that God is "greater than that which can be conceived": Anselm, *Proslogion*, in Davies, *Anselm of Canterbury — The Major Works*, chap. 15.

14   Hence, the frequency of the motif that neoliberal economic orthodoxy is itself a religion: see, e.g., Nelson, *Economics as Religion*. This is not directly our concern here, however.

15   It is clear that most schemes for the creation of alternative currencies, such as local exchange trading schemes, do not address the source of the power of contemporary debt money with which they will have to compete. For a critical review of such schemes, see Hutchinson et al., *The Politics of Money*, chap. 9. It is notable that these authors, while heavily influenced by the Social Credit Movement and enthusiastic about a citizen's income, stop short of endorsing any particular reform.

SEVEN THE PRICE OF CREDIT

1   *Bibliotheca Sanctorum*, cited in Buchan, *Frozen Desire*, 64.

2   Quoted in Jackson, *The Oxford Book of Money*, 285.

3   Note the view of Charles Lamb in 1843: "The human species, according to the best theory I can form of it, is composed of two distinct races, *the men who borrow*, and *the men who lend*. . . . The infinite superiority of the former, which I choose to designate as the *great race*, is discernible in their figure, port, and a certain instinctive sovereignty. The latter are born degraded" (quoted in Jackson, *The Oxford Book of Money*, 214).

4   Hobbes, *Leviathan*, 174–75.

5   William Shakespeare, *The Merchant of Venice*, Act 3, Scene 2, lines 262–5.

6   Buchan, *Frozen Desire*, 90.

7   For the contrast between these as fundamental social orders, see Hénaff, *Le prix de la vérité*.

8   Shakespeare, *The Merchant of Venice*, Act 4, Scene 1, lines 184–93.

9   Quoted in Ingham, *The Nature of Money*, 126.

10 C. Muldrew, *The Economy of Obligation*, cited in ibid.

11 For the significance of public debt in the wealth of nations, see Ferguson, *The Cash Nexus*, chap. 4.

12 It is interesting to note that the Bank of England was predominantly a Whig corporation, and 43 percent of its initial directors were Protestant dissenters: see Carruthers, *City of Capital*, 139.

13 For the social forces involved in the transformation of credit into currency, see the luminous account of Ingham, *The Nature of Money*, 121–31.

14 It is notable that there were early attempts to cause a run on the Bank by rivals, such as goldsmiths in 1696 and the old East India Company in 1701, which failed. See Carruthers, *City of Capital*, 139.

15 See ibid., 9–10.

16 Dickson, *The Financial Revolution in England*, 9.

17 Qualifying Geoffrey Ingham, who merely lists state, rentiers, and taxpayers: Ingham, *The Nature of Money*, 131.

18 Ibid., 126.

19 John Locke distinguished between the commonwealth, "a society of men constituted only for the procuring, preserving and advancing of their own civil interests" (these being life, liberty, health, leisure, and possessions), and a church, "a voluntary society for the public worship of God" (this being in such a manner as they judge effective for the eventual salvation of their souls): John Locke, "Letter on Toleration," in Yolton, *The Locke Reader*, 245, 248.

20 The theological dimensions of the notion of kingship are explored in Kantorowicz, *The King's Two Bodies*.

21 Schmitt, *The Concept of the Political*, 33.

22 See Walter Benjamin, "Critique of Violence," in idem, *Selected Writings, Volume 1*, 236–52.

23 It is important to note here the historical correlation between sovereign states and the issuing of their own currencies, even in the recent break-up and unification of states: see Goodhart, "The Two Concepts of Money," in Ingham, *Concepts of Money*, 456.

24 "We keep most closely to the facts if we take as our test, that the money is accepted in payments made to the State's offices. Then all means by which a payment can be made to the State form part of the monetary system. On this basis it is not the issue, but the acceptation, as we call it, which is decisive. State acceptation delimits the monetary system": Georg Friedrich Knapp, quoted in Wray, *Understanding Modern Money*, 25.

25 Ingham, *The Nature of Money*, 126–31.

26 See Heinsohn and Steiger, "The Property Theory of Interest and Money," in Smithin, *What Is Money?* 91.

27 On the nature of political theology, see Philip Goodchild, "The Exceptional Po-
    litical Theology of Saint Paul," unpublished essay.
28 See Nietzsche, *Beyond Good and Evil*, 175.
29 Ibid., 134.

EIGHT A MODEST PROPOSAL

1 Note the comments of Joseph Addison in 1711: "A man who is furnished with
   arguments from the Mint will convince his antagonist much sooner than one
   who draws them from reason and philosophy. Gold is a wonderful clearer of the
   understanding: it dissipates every doubt and scruple in an instant, accommo-
   dates itself to the meanest of capacities, silences the loud and clamorous, and
   brings over the most obstinate and inflexible. Philip of Macedon was a man of
   most invincible reason this way. He refuted by it all the wisdom of Athens, con-
   founded their statesmen, struck their orators dumb, and at length argued them
   out of all their liberties" (quoted in Jackson, *The Oxford Book of Money*, 286).
2 Bernard Lietaer is enthusiastic about the unlimited technical possibilities: see
   Lietaer, *The Future of Money*.

BIBLIOGRAPHY

Agamben, Giorgio. *State of Exception*. Translated by Kevin Attell. Chicago: University of Chicago Press, 2005.

Aglietta, Michel, and André Orléan. *La monnaie entre violence et confiance*. Paris: Odile Jacob, 2002.

Altvater, Elmar. *The Future of the Market: An Essay on the Regulation of Money and Nature after the Collapse of "Actually Existing Socialism."* Translated by Patrick Camiller. London: Verso, 1993.

Amin, Samir. *Capitalism in the Age of Globalization: The Management of Contemporary Society*. London: Zed Books, 1997.

Aquinas, Thomas. *Summa Contra Gentiles*. Translated by Anton C. Pegis. Notre Dame, Ind.: University of Notre Dame Press, 1975.

Aristotle. *Metaphysics, Books* Gamma, Delta, *and* Epsilon. Translated by Christopher Kirwan. Oxford: Claredon Press, 1993.

——. *Politics*. Edited and Translated by Stephen Everson. Cambridge: Cambridge University Press, 1988.

Augustine. *City of God*. Translated by Henry Bettenson. London: Penguin Books, 2003.

Bandarage, Asoka. *Women, Population and Global Crisis: A Political-Economic Analysis*. London: Zed Books, 1997.

Baran, Paul A. *The Political Economy of Growth*. New York: Monthly Review Press, 1962.

Benjamin, Walter. *Selected Writings, Volume 1: 1913–1926*. Edited by Marcus Bullock and Michael W. Jennings. Cambridge, Mass.: Harvard University Press, 1996.

Benson, Bruce Ellis, and Norman Wirzba, eds. *The Phenomenology of Prayer*. New York: Fordham University Press, 2005.

Bergson, Henri. *An Introduction to Metaphysics*. Translated by T. E. Hulme. London: Macmillan, 1913.

Boff, Leonardo. *Ecology and Liberation.* Translated by John Cumming. Maryknoll, N.Y.: Orbis, 1995.

Bonefeld, Werner, and John Holloway, eds. *Global Capital, National State and the Politics of Money.* Basingstoke, U.K.: Macmillan, 1996.

Bourdieu, Pierre. *The Logic of Practice.* Translated by Richard Nice. Cambridge, U.K.: Polity Press, 1990.

Bradstock, Andrew, and Christopher Rowland, eds. *Radical Christian Writings: A Reader.* Oxford: Blackwell, 2002.

Braudel, Fernand. *The Wheels of Commerce,* Vol. 2, *Civilization and Capitalism, 15th–18th Century.* Berkeley: University of California Press, 1992.

Brenner, Robert. *The Boom and the Bubble: The U.S. in the World Economy.* London: Verso, 2002.

———. *Merchants and Revolution: Commercial Change, Political Conflict, and London's Overseas Traders, 1550–1653.* London: Verso, 2003.

Buchan, James. *Frozen Desire: An Inquiry into the Meaning of Money.* London: Picador, 1997.

Burbach, Roger, Orlando Nunez, and Boris Kagarlitsky. *Globalization and Its Discontents: The Rise of Postmodern Socialisms.* London: Pluto Press, 1997.

Campbell, Colin, ed. *The Essence of Oil and Gas Depletion: Collected Papers and Excerpts.* Brentwood, U.K.: Multi-Science, 2003.

Carrette, Jeremy, and Richard King. *Selling Spirituality: The Silent Takeover of Religion.* London: Routledge, 2005.

Carruthers, Bruce G. *City of Capital: Politics and Markets in the English Financial Revolution.* Princeton, N.J.: Princeton University Press, 1996.

Cavanagh, John, and Jerry Mander, eds. *Alternatives to Economic Globalization: A Better World Is Possible.* San Francisco: Berrett-Koehler, 2002.

Cencini, Alvaro. *Money, Income and Time: A Quantum-Theoretical Approach.* London: Pinter, 1988.

Chossudovsky, Michel. *The Globalization of Poverty: Impacts of World Bank and IMF Reforms.* Penang, Malaysia: Third World Network, 1997.

Cohen, Benjamin J. *The Geography of Money.* Ithaca, N.Y.: Cornell University Press, 1998.

Cohen, S. Marc, Patricia Curd, and C.D.C. Reeve, eds. *Readings in Ancient Greek Philosophy.* Indianapolis: Hackett, 1995.

Cox, John D. *Climate Crash: Abrupt Climate Change and What It Means for Our Future.* Washington, D.C.: Joseph Henry, 2005.

Crockett, Andrew. *Money: Theory, Policy and Institutions.* London: Thomas Nelson and Sons, 1973.

Cromwell, David. *Private Planet: Corporate Plunder and the Fight Back.* Charlbury, U.K.: Jon Carpenter, 2001.

Crossan, John Dominic. *The Historical Jesus: The Life of a Mediterranean Jewish Peasant.* San Francisco: Harper San Francisco, 1991.

Crossley, James G., and Christian Karner, eds. *Writing History, Constructing Religion.* Aldershot: Ashgate, 2005.

Curley, Edwin, ed. *A Spinoza Reader.* Princeton, N.J.: Princeton University Press, 1994.

Daly, Herman E. *Beyond Growth: The Economics of Sustainable Development.* Boston: Beacon Press, 1996.

———, ed. *Toward Steady-State Economics.* San Francisco: W. H. Freeman, 1973.

Daly, Herman E., and John Cobb. *For the Common Good: Redirecting the Economy towards Community, the Environment, and a Sustainable Future.* London: Green Print, 1990.

Davies, Brian, and Gill Evans, eds. *Anselm of Canterbury — The Major Works.* Oxford: Oxford University Press, 1998.

Davies, Glyn. *A History of Money from Ancient Times to the Present Day.* Cardiff: University of Wales Press, 2002.

Davis, Creston, John Milbank, and Slavoj Žižek, eds. *Theology and the Political: The New Debate.* Durham: Duke University Press, 2005.

de Brunhoff, Suzanne. *Marx on Money.* Translated by Maurice J. Goldbloom. New York: Urizen Books, 1976.

Deffeyes, Kenneth. *Hubbert's Peak: The Impending World Oil Shortage.* Princeton, N.J.: Princeton University Press, 2003.

De Landa, Manuel. *A Thousand Years of Non-Linear History.* New York: Zone Books, 1997.

Deleuze, Gilles. *Bergsonism.* Translated by Hugh Tomlinson and Barbara Habberjam. London: Athlone, 1991.

———. *Nietzsche and Philosophy.* Translated by Hugh Tomlinson. London: Athlone, 1983.

Deleuze, Gilles, and Félix Guattari. *Anti-Oedipus: Capitalism and Schizophrenia.* Translated by Robert Hurley, Mark Seem, and Helen R. Lane. London: Athlone, 1984.

———. *A Thousand Plateaus: Capitalism and Schizophrenia.* Translated by Brian Massumi. London: Athlone, 1988.

Derrida, Jacques. *Spectres of Marx: The State of the Debt, the Work of Mourning, and the New International.* Translated by Peggy Kamuf. London: Routledge, 1994.

de Soto, Hernando. *The Mystery of Capital: Why Capitalism Triumphs in the West and Fails Everywhere Else.* London: Black Swan, 2001.

de Vries, Hent, and Lawrence E. Sullivan, eds. *Political Theologies: Public Religions in a Post-Secular World.* New York: Fordham University Press, 2006.

Dickson, P.G.M. *The Financial Revolution in England: A Study in the Development of Public Credit 1688–1756.* London: Macmillan, 1967.

Doctrine Commission of the General Synod of the Church of England. *Being Human: A Christian Understanding of Personhood Illustrated with Respect to Money, Power, Sex and Time.* London: Church House Publishing, 2003.

Dodd, Nigel. *The Sociology of Money: Economics, Reason and Contemporary Society.* Cambridge, U.K.: Polity Press, 1994.

Douglas, C. H. *Economic Democracy* (1920), 5th edition. Epsom, U.K.: Bloomfield, 1974.

———. *The Monopoly of Credit* (1931), 4th edition. Sudbury, U.K.: Bloomfield, 1979.

Douglas, Mary. *Purity and Danger: An Analysis of Concept of Pollution and Taboo.* London: Routledge, 1991.

Douthwaite, Richard. *The Ecology of Money.* Totnes, U.K.: Green Books, 1999.

———. *The Growth Illusion: How Economic Growth Has Enriched the Few, Impoverished the Many, and Endangered the Planet.* Totnes, U.K.: Green Books, 1999.

———. *Short Circuit: Strengthening Local Economies for Security in an Unstable World.* Dublin: Lilliput, 1996.

Dowd, Douglas. *Capitalism and Its Economics: A Critical History.* London: Pluto Press, 2000.

———, ed. *Understanding Capitalism: Critical Analysis from Karl Marx to Amartya Sen.* London: Pluto Press, 2002.

Duchrow, Ulrich. *Alternatives to Global Capitalism.* Utrecht, Netherlands: International Books, 1995.

Duchrow, Ulrich, and Franz Hinkelammert. *Property for People, Not for Profit: Alternatives to the Tyranny of Global Capital.* London: Zed Books, 2004.

The Ecologist. *Whose Common Future? Reclaiming the Commons.* London: Earthscan, 1993.

Edwards, David. *The Compassionate Revolution: Radical Politics and Buddhism.* Totnes, U.K.: Green Books, 1998.

Ferguson, Niall. *The Cash Nexus: Money and Power in the Modern World, 1700–2000.* London: Penguin, 2001.

Fitzgerald, Timothy. *The Ideology of Religious Studies.* Oxford: Oxford University Press, 2000.

Foster, John Bellamy. *Marx's Ecology: Materialism and Nature.* New York: Monthly Review Press, 2000.

Gabriel, Jean. *The Dollar Hegemony: Dollar, Dollarization and Progress.* San Jose, Calif.: Writers Club, 2000.

Galbraith, John Kenneth. *Money: Whence It Came, Where It Went.* London: Deutsch, 1975.

Gay, Craig M. *Cash Values: The Value of Money, the Nature of Worth.* Sydney: University of New South Wales Press, 2003.

George, Henry. *Progress and Poverty* (1897). Edited by A. W. Madsen. New York: Robert Schalkenbach Foundation, 1998.

Goede, Marieke de. *Virtue, Fortune and Faith: A Genealogy of Finance.* Minneapolis: University of Minnesota Press, 2005.

Goldsmith, Edward. *The Way: An Ecological Worldview.* Revised edition. Athens: University of Georgia Press, 1998.

Goodchild, Philip. *Capitalism and Religion: The Price of Piety*. London: Routledge, 2002.

Gorringe, Timothy. *Fair Shares: Ethics and the Global Economy*. London: Thames and Hudson, 1999.

Gowan, Peter. *The Global Gamble: Washington's Faustian Bid for World Dominance*. London: Verso, 1999.

Goux, Jean-Joseph. *Symbolic Economies after Marx and Freud*. Translated by Jennifer Curtiss Gage. Ithaca, N.Y.: Cornell University Press, 1990.

Grau, Marion. *Of Divine Economy: Refinancing Redemption*. London: T. and T. Clark, 2004.

Gray, John. *False Dawn: The Delusions of Global Capitalism*. New York: New Press, 1998.

Greider, William. *One World, Ready or Not: The Manic Logic of Global Capitalism*. New York: Simon and Schuster, 1997.

Griswold, Charles L. *Adam Smith and the Virtues of the Enlightenment*. Cambridge: Cambridge University Press, 1999.

Hadley Centre. *Modelling Climate Change, 1860–2050*. London: Meteorological Office, 1995.

Hahnel, Robin. *The ABCs of Political Economy*. London: Pluto, 2002.

———. *Panic Rules: Everything You Need to Know about the Global Economy*. Cambridge, Mass.: South End Press, 1999.

Hardt, Michael, and Antonio Negri. *Empire*. Cambridge, Mass.: Harvard University Press, 2000.

Harvey, David. *Justice, Nature and the Geography of Difference*. Oxford: Blackwell, 1996.

———. *The Limits to Capital*. New edition. London: Verso, 1999.

———. *The New Imperialism*. Oxford: Oxford University Press, 2003.

Heidegger, Martin. *What Is Called Thinking?* Translated by Fred D. Wieck and J. Glenn Gray. New York: Harper and Row, 1968.

Heilbroner, Robert. *Twenty-First Century Capitalism*. London: UCL Press, 1993.

Heinberg, Richard. *The Party's Over: Oil, War and the Fate of Industrial Societies*. Forest Row, U.K.: Clairview, 2003.

———. *Powerdown: Options and Actions for a Post-Carbon World*. Forest Row, U.K.: Clairview, 2005.

Held, David, and Anthony McGrew, eds. *The Global Transformations Reader: An Introduction to the Globalization Debate*, Cambridge, U.K.: Polity Press, 2000.

Hénaff, Marcel. *Le prix de la vérité: Le don, l'argent, la philosophie*. Paris: Seuil, 2002.

Herman, Edward S., and Noam Chomsky. *Manufacturing Consent: The Political Economy of the Mass Media*. London: Vintage, 1994.

Hertz, Noreena. *The Silent Takeover: Global Capitalism and the Death of Democracy*. London: William Heinemann, 2001.

Hobbes, Thomas. *Leviathan* (1651). Edited by Richard Tuck. Cambridge: Cambridge University Press, 1996.

Horsley, Richard, ed. *Paul and Empire: Religion and Power in Roman Imperial Society.* Philadelphia: Trinity Press, 1997.

Horsley, Richard, and Asher Silberman. *The Message and the Kingdom: How Jesus and Paul Ignited a Revolution and Transformed the Ancient World.* Philadelphia: Fortress, 2002.

Huber, Joseph, and James Robertson. *Creating New Money: A Monetary Reform for the Information Age.* London: New Economics Foundation, 2000.

Hudson, Wayne. *The Reform of Utopia.* Aldershot, U.K.: Ashgate, 2003.

Hume, David. *A Treatise of Human Nature* (1739). Edited by A. L. Selby-Bigge. Oxford: Oxford University Press, 1978.

Hutchinson, Frances. *What Everybody Really Wants to Know about Money.* Charlbury, U.K.: Jon Carpenter, 1998.

Hutchinson, Frances, and Brian Burkitt. *The Political Economy of Social Credit and Guild Socialism.* London: Routledge, 1997.

Hutchinson, Frances, Mary Mellor, and Wendy Olsen. *The Politics of Money: Towards Sustainability and Economic Democracy.* London: Pluto Press, 2002.

Ingham, Geoffrey. *The Nature of Money: New Directions in Political Economy.* Cambridge, U.K.: Polity Press, 2002.

————, ed. *Concepts of Money: Interdisciplinary Perspectives from Economics, Sociology and Political Science.* Cheltenham, U.K.: Edward Elgar, 2005.

Intergovernmental Panel on Climate Change. *Fourth Assessment Report 2007.* Cambridge: Cambridge University Press, 2007–2008.

Jackson, Kevin, ed. *The Oxford Book of Money.* Oxford: Oxford University Press, 1996.

Jardine, Murra. *The Making and Unmaking of Technological Society: How Christianity Can Save Modernity from Itself.* Grand Rapids, Mich.: Brazos Press, 2004.

Jenkins, David. *Market Whys and Human Wherefores: Thinking Again about Markets, Politics and People.* London: Cassell, 2000.

Franz Kafka. *The Collected Short Stories of Franz Kafka.* Edited by Nahum N. Glatzer. London: Penguin, 1988.

Kant, Immanuel. *Critique of Pure Reason.* Translated by Norman Kemp Smith. Basingstoke, U.K.: Macmillan, 1929.

Kantorowicz, Ernst H. *The King's Two Bodies: A Study in Medieval Political Theology.* Princeton, N.J.: Princeton University Press, 1957.

Karatani, Kojìn. *Transcritique: On Kant and Marx.* Translated by Sabu Kohso. Cambridge, Mass.: MIT Press, 2003.

Kelly, Patrick Hyde, ed. *Locke on Money,* 2 vols. Oxford: Clarendon, 1991.

Keynes, John Maynard. *A Treatise on Money.* 2 vols. London: Macmillan, 1930.

Khor, Martin. *Rethinking Globalization: Critical Issues and Policy Choices.* London: Zed Books, 2001.

Kindleberger, Charles P. *Manias, Panics and Crashes: A History of Financial Crises.* 4th edition. New York: John Wiley, 2000.

King, Richard. *Orientalism and Religion: Postcolonial Theory, India and "the Mystic East."* London: Routledge, 1999.

Knitter, Paul, and Chandra Muzaffar, eds. *Subverting Greed: Religious Perspectives on the Global Economy.* Maryknoll, N.Y.: Orbis, 2002.

Kunstler, James Howard. *The Long Emergency: Surviving the Converging Catastrophes of the Twenty-First Century.* London: Atlantic Books, 2005.

Lacan, Jacques. *The Four Fundamental Concepts of Psychoanalysis.* Translated by Alan Sheridan. London: Penguin, 1979.

Landes, David S. *The Wealth and Poverty of Nations: Why Some are So Rich and Some So Poor.* London: Little, Brown, 1998.

Leggett, Jeremy. *Half Gone: Oil, Gas, Hot Air, and the Global Energy Crisis.* London: Portobello, 2005.

Le Goff, Jacques. *Your Money or Your Life: Economy and Religion in the Middle Ages.* Translated by Patricia Ranum. New York: Zone, 1990.

Levinson, Brett. *Market and Thought: Meditations on the Political and the Biopolitical.* New York: Fordham University Press, 2004.

Lewis, Mervyn K., and Paul D. Mizen. *Monetary Economics.* Oxford: Oxford University Press, 2000.

Leyshon, Andrew, and Nigel Thrift. *Money Space: Geographies of Monetary Transformation.* London: Routledge, 1997.

Lietaer, Bernard. *The Future of Money: Creating New Wealth, Work, and a Wiser World.* London: Century, 2001.

Locke, John. *An Essay Concerning Human Understanding* (1690). Edited by Peter H. Nidditch. Oxford: Clarendon, 1979.

———. *The Reasonableness of Christianity* (1695). Edited by I. T. Ramsey. London: Black, 1958.

———. *Two Treatises of Government* (1689). Edited by Peter Laslett. Cambridge: Cambridge University Press, 1988.

Lovelock, James. *The Revenge of Gaia: Earth's Climate in Crisis and the Fate of Humanity.* New York: Basic Books, 2006.

Loy, David. *The Great Awakening: A Buddhist Social Theory.* Boston: Wisdom, 2003.

———. *Lack and Transcendence: Problems of Death and Life in Psychotherapy, Existentialism and Buddhism.* Amherst, N.Y.: Humanity Books, 2000.

Madron, Roy, and John Jopling. *Gaian Democracies: Redefining Globalisation and People-Power.* Totnes, U.K.: Green Books, 2003.

Mander, Jerry, and Edward Goldsmith, eds. *The Case against the Global Economy and for a Turn toward the Local.* San Francisco: Sierra Club Books, 1996.

Manent, Pierre. *An Intellectual History of Liberalism.* Translated by Rebecca Balinski. Princeton, N.J.: Princeton University Press, 1994.

Marsden, Richard. *The Nature of Capital: Marx after Foucault*. London: Routledge, 1999.

Marx, Karl. *Capital*, vol. 1 (1867). London: Penguin, 1976.

———. *Capital*, vol. 3 (1894). Chicago: Charles Kerr, 1909.

———. *Grundrisse: Foundations for a Critique of Political Economy* (1941). Translated by Martin Nicolaus. Harmondsworth, U.K.: Penguin, 1973.

McBurney, Stuart. *Ecology into Economics Won't Go, or Life is Not a Concept*. Bideford, U.K.: Green Books, 1990.

McIntosh, Alastair. *Soil and Soul: People versus Corporate Power*. London: Aurum Books, 2001.

McKillop, Andrew, ed. *The Final Energy Crisis*. London: Pluto Press, 2005.

McLellan, David. *Marxism and Religion: A Description and Assessment of the Marxist Critique of Christianity*. Basingstoke, U.K.: Macmillan, 1987.

McMurtry, John. *The Cancer Stage of Global Capitalism*. London: Pluto Press, 1999.

———. *Value Wars: The Global Market versus the Life Economy*. London: Pluto Press, 2002.

Meadows, Donella H., Dennis L. Meadows, and Jørgen Randers. *Beyond the Limits: Global Collapse or a Sustainable Future*. London: Earthscan, 1992.

Merchant, Carolyn, ed. *Key Concepts in Critical Theory: Ecology*. Atlantic Highlands, N.J.: Humanities International, 1994.

Mies, Maria, and Vandana Shiva. *Ecofeminism*. London: Zed Books, 1993.

Mies, Maria, and Veronica Bennholdt-Thomsen. *The Subsistence Perspective: Beyond the Globalized Economy*. Translated by Marie Mies and Patrick Camiller. New York: Zed Books, 1999.

Mofid, Kamran. *Globalisation for the Common Good*. London: Shepheard-Walwyn, 2002.

Monbiot, George. *Captive State: The Corporate Takeover of Britain*. London: Macmillan, 2000.

More, Sir Thomas. *Utopia*. Translated by Paul Turner. Harmondsworth, U.K.: Penguin, 1965.

Myers, Milton L. *The Soul of Modern Economic Man: Ideas of Self-Interest; Thomas Hobbes to Adam Smith*. Chicago: University of Chicago Press, 1983.

Narayan, Deepa. *Voices of the Poor: Can Anyone Hear Us?* Oxford: World Bank Publications, 2000.

National Research Council. *Abrupt Climate Change: Inevitable Surprises*. Washington D.C.: National Academy Press, 2002.

Negri, Antonio. *Time for Revolution*. Translated by Matteo Mandarini. London: Continuum, 2003.

Nelson, Robert H. *Economics as Religion: From Samuelson to Chicago and Beyond*. University Park: Pennsylvania State University Press, 2001.

Nietzsche, Friedrich. *Beyond Good and Evil*. Translated by R. J. Hollingdale. Harmondsworth, U.K.: Penguin, 1973.

———. *Daybreak*. Translated by R. J. Hollingdale. Cambridge: Cambridge University Press, 1982.

Northcott, Michael. *The Environment and Christian Ethics*. Cambridge: Cambridge University Press, 1996.

———. *Life after Debt: Christianity and Global Justice*. London: Society for Promoting Christian Knowledge, 1999.

Nürnberger, Klaus. *Prosperity, Poverty and Pollution: Managing the Approaching Crisis*. London: Zed Books, 1999.

O'Donovan, Oliver. *The Desire of the Nations: Rediscovering the Roots of Political Theology*. Cambridge: Cambridge University Press, 1996.

———. *The Ways of Judgment*. Grand Rapids, Mich.: Eerdmans, 2005.

Ormerod, Paul. *The Death of Economics*. London: Faber, 1994.

Pierson, Christopher, ed. *The Marx Reader*. Oxford: Polity Press, 1997.

Plumwood, Val. *Feminism and the Mastery of Nature*. London: Routledge, 1993.

Polanyi, Karl. *The Great Transformation*. Boston: Beacon Press, 1944.

Poovey, Mary. *A History of the Modern Fact: Problems of Knowledge in the Science of Wealth and Society*. Chicago: University of Chicago Press, 1998.

Postone, Moishe. *Time, Labor and Social Domination: A Reinterpretation of Marx's Critical Theory*. Cambridge: Cambridge University Press, 1993.

Primavesi, Anne. *Sacred Gaia: Holistic Theology and Earth System Science*. London: Routledge, 2000.

Purcell Jr., Edward A. *The Crisis of Democratic Theory: Scientific Naturalism and the Problem of Value*. Lexington: University Press of Kentucky, 1973.

Rahnema, Majid, ed. *The Post-Development Reader*. London: Zed Books, 1997.

Ricardo, David. *On the Principles of Political Economy and Taxation* (1817). Edited by R. M. Hartwell. Harmondsworth, U.K.: Penguin, 1971.

Ritter, Lawrence S., William L. Silber, and Gregory F. Udell. *Principles of Money, Banking and Financial Markets*, 11th edition. Boston: Pearson, 2004.

Rowbotham, Michael. *The Grip of Death: A Study of Modern Money, Debt Slavery and Destructive Economics*. Charlbury, U.K.: Jon Carpenter, 1998.

Scott, Peter. *A Political Theology of Nature*. Cambridge: Cambridge University Press, 2003.

Schmitt, Carl. *The Concept of the Political* (1927). Translated by George Schwab. Chicago: University of Chicago Press, 1996.

———. *The Crisis of Parliamentary Democracy* (1923). Translated by Ellen Kennedy. Cambridge, Mass.: MIT Press, 1988.

———. *Political Theology: Four Chapters on the Concept of Sovereignty* (1922). Translated by George Schwab. Chicago: University of Chicago Press, 2005.

Schroeder, Jeanne L. *Triumph of Venus: The Erotics of the Market*. Berkeley: University of California Press, 2004.

Schumpeter, Joseph A. *Capitalism, Socialism and Democracy* (1943), 4th edition. London: Allen and Unwin, 1966.

————. *A History of Economic Analysis* (1954). Edited by Elizabeth Boody. London: Routledge, 1994.

Selby, Peter. *Grace and Mortgage: The Language of Faith and the Debt of the World.* London: Darton, Longman and Todd, 1997.

Sen, Amartya. *Development as Freedom.* Oxford: Oxford University Press, 1999.

Shakespeare, Rodney, and Peter Challen. *Seven Steps to Justice.* London: New European Publications, 2002.

Shell, Marc. *Money, Language and Thought: Literary and Philosophic Economies from the Medieval to the Modern Era.* Baltimore, Md.: John Hopkins University Press, 1982.

Simmel, Georg. *The Philosophy of Money* (1900), 2nd edition. Translated by Tom Bottomore and David Frisby. London: Routledge, 1990.

Simmons, Matthew. *Twilight in the Desert: The Coming Saudi Oil Shock and the World Economy.* New York: John Wiley, 2005.

Singer, Peter. *One World: The Ethics of Globalization.* New Haven, Conn.: Yale University Press, 2002.

Smith, Adam. *The Wealth of Nations* (1776). Edited by Andrew Skinner. Harmondsworth, U.K.: Penguin, 1970.

Smithin, John, ed. *What Is Money?* London: Routledge, 2000.

Soros, George. *The Crisis of Global Capitalism: Open Society Endangered.* London: Little, Brown, 1998.

Spaemann, Robert. *Happiness and Benevolence.* Translated by Jeremiah Alberg. Edinburgh: T. and T. Clark, 2000.

Spinoza, Benedict de. *The Chief Works of Benedict de Spinoza: A Theologico-Political Treatise and a Political Treatise.* Translated by E.H.M. Elwes. New York: Dover, 1951.

Spowers, Rory. *Rising Tide: A History of the Environmental Revolution and Visions for an Ecological Age.* Edinburgh: Canongate, 2002.

Stern, Nicholes. *Stern Review on the Economics of Climate Change.* 2006. www.hm-treasury.gov.uk.

Storkey, Alan. *Jesus and Politics: Confronting the Powers.* Grand Rapids, Mich.: Baker Academic, 2005.

Strahan, David. *The Last Oil Shock: A Survival Guide to the Imminent Extinction of Petroleum Man.* London: John Murray, 2007.

Tanner, Kathryn. *Economy of Grace.* Minneapolis: Fortress Press, 2005.

Tawney, R. H. *Religion and the Rise of Capitalism.* London: John Murray, 1936.

Taylor, Mark C. *Confidence Games: Money and Markets in a World without Redemption.* Chicago: University of Chicago Press, 2004.

Thoburn, Nicholas. *Deleuze, Marx and Politics.* London: Routledge, 2003.

United Nations Environment Programme. *Global Environmental Outlook 3.* London: Earthscan, 2002.

Veblen, Thorstein. *The Portable Veblen*. Edited by Max Lerner. New York: Viking Press, 1948.

———. *Theory of the Leisure Class* (1899), 2nd edition. New York: Macmillan, 1912.

Weber, Max. *The Protestant Ethic and the Spirit of Capitalism* (1905). Translated by Talcott Parsons. London: Routledge, 1992.

Wink, Walter. *Engaging the Powers: Discernment and Resistance in an Age of Domination*. Minneapolis: Fortress, 1992.

———. *Unmasking the Powers: The Invisible Forces that Determine Human Existence*. Philadelphia: Fortress, 1986.

Wood, Ellen Meiksins, and Neal Wood. *A Trumpet of Sedition: Political Theory and the Rise of Capitalism 1509–1688*. New York: New York University Press, 1997.

Wray, L. Randall, ed. *Understanding Modern Money*. Cheltenham, U.K.: Edward Elgar, 1998.

Yoder, John Howard. *The Politics of Jesus*, 2nd ed. Grand Rapids, Mich.: Eerdmans, 1972.

Yolton, John W., ed. *The Locke Reader*. Cambridge: Cambridge University Press, 1977.

Zelizer, Viviana A. *The Social Meaning of Money: Pin Money, Paychecks, Poor Relief, and Other Currencies*. Princeton, N.J.: Princeton University Press, 1997.

Žižek, Slavoj. *The Fragile Absolute, or Why Is the Christian Legacy Worth Fighting For?* London: Verso, 2000.

INDEX

PHILIP GOODCHILD is a professor of religion and philosophy in the Department of Theology and Religious Studies, University of Nottingham. He is the author of *Capitalism and Religion: The Price of Piety* (2002), *Deleuze and Guattari: An Introduction to the Politics of Desire* (1996) and *Gilles Deleuze and the Question of Philosophy* (1996), and editor of *Rethinking Philosophy of Religion: Approaches from Continental Philosophy* (2002). He is also a co-editor of Duke University Press's New Slant: Religion, Politics, Ontology series.

Library of Congress Cataloging-in-Publication Data

Goodchild, Philip, 1965–
Theology of money / Philip Goodchild.
p. cm. — (New slant : religion, politics, ontology)
Includes bibliographical references and index.
ISBN 978-0-8223-4438-4 (cloth : alk. paper)
ISBN 978-0-8223-4450-6 (pbk. : alk. paper)
1. Wealth — Religious aspects — Christianity.
2. Money — Religious aspects — Christianity.
I. Title. II. Series: New slant.
BR115.W4G66 2009
220.8′3324 — dc22
2009010100

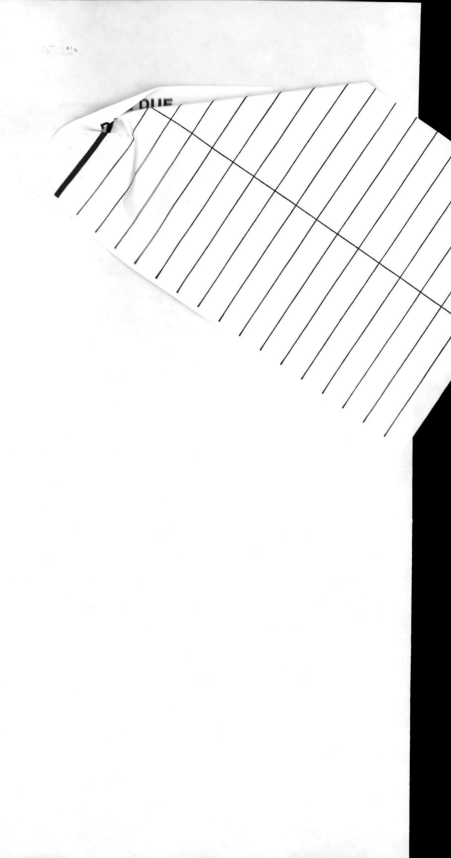